MEDIEVAL CLASSICS

GENERAL EDITORS
V. H. Galbraith and R. A. B. Mynors

CRONICA

JOCELINI DE BRAKELONDA

THE CHRONICLE

OF JOCELIN OF BRAKELOND

Cronica
Jocelini de Brakelonda

de rebus gestis

Samsonis

Abbatis Monasterii Sancti Edmundi

Thomas Nelson and Sons Ltd
London Edinburgh Paris Melbourne Toronto and New York

The Chronicle of Jocelin of Brakelond

concerning the acts of

Samson

Abbot of the Monastery of St. Edmund

Translated from the Latin with Introduction
Notes and Appendices by
H. E. Butler M.A.(OXON.) D.LITT.(LONDON)
formerly Professor of Latin, University of London

Thomas Nelson and Sons Ltd

London Edinburgh Paris Melbourne Toronto and New York

THOMAS NELSON AND SONS LTD
Parkside Works Edinburgh 9
3 Henrietta Street London WC2
312 Flinders Street Melbourne C1
91–93 Wellington Street West   Toronto 1

THOMAS NELSON AND SONS
385 Madison Avenue New York 17

SOCIÉTÉ FRANÇAISE D'EDITIONS NELSON
25 rue Henri Barbusse Paris V^e

———

First published in this series 1949

CONTENTS

ABBREVIATIONS

DB   Domesday Book

EHR   English Historical Review

FD   D. C. Douglas, *Feudal Documents from the Abbey of Bury St. Edmunds*, London (British Academy) 1932

L   M. D. Lobel, *The Borough of St. Edmunds*, Oxford 1935

Mem.   *Memorials of St. Edmund's Abbey*, Ed. by T. Arnold, Rolls Series, 3 vols. 1890–96

MRJ   M. R. James, *On the Abbey of St. Edmund at Bury* (Cambridge Antiquarian Society, Octavo Publications No. xxviii, 1895)

PM   F. Pollock and F. W. Maitland, *History of English Law*, 2 vols. (2nd edn), Cambridge 1898

RS   Rolls Series (Chronicles and Memorials of Great Britain and Ireland during the Middle Ages)

THE LIBERTY OF

Quidenham

Lakenheath •   • Wangford
Thetford •   • Brettenham

Elveden •   Euston •   Coney Weston   Hopton •
                                                    • Thelnetham
LACKFORD   Fakenham • Barningham   Hindercley •
                                Honington • Sapiston   Hepworth •
Mildenhall •   Bardwell • Stanton Wattisfield Rickingh
                    Icklingham •   Wordwell • Little Livermere Troston •
                            West Stowe   Livermere   Ixworth
    Herringswell •   Lackford •   Ingham • Ampton   Stowe Langtoft
                    Flempton •   Fornham   Pakenham   Hunston • Ashfield   Cotto
        Kentford •   Fornham All Saints   St. Genevieve   •
                        • Risby   Fornham   Great Barton
                    Westley •   St. Martin   Thurston •   Elmswell •
                THINGOE   BURY   Tostock •
        Little Saxham •   Bury   Rougham • Woolpit   Wetherden •
        Great Saxham •   Horningsheath •   Rushbrook •
                    Hargrave • Ickworth •   Nowton •   THEDWESTREY   Onehouse •
            Chevington •   Hawstead • Welnetham   STOW
                        Whepstead •   Bradfield •   Rattlesden •
                                Stanningfield Gedding • Felsham •
            Rede • Brockley •   Manton •
                                        Cockfield •   Brettenham
    Wickhambrook •   Hitcham   Wattisham •
        RISBRIDGE   Preston •
                                                Lavenham •   Chelsworth •
                        Glemsford •   Eleigh •   Milden •   Semer • Elmsett
            Clare •   Melford •   COSFORD Whatfield
                                BABERGH   Lindsey •
                                Groton •
                                                        Neyland •

viii

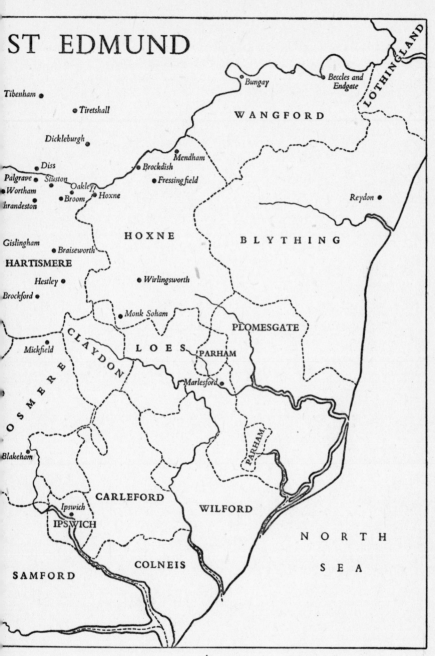

ST EDMUND

Tibenham

Tiretshall

Dickleburgh

Diss
Palgrave Stuston
Wortham Oakley
hrandeston Broom Hoxne

Gislingham Braiseworth
HARTISMERE
Hestley
Brockford

HOXNE

Mendham
Brockdish
Fressingfield

Bungay

Beccles and
Endgate

WANGFORD

LOTHINGLAND

Reydon

BLYTHING

Wirlingsworth

Mickfield

Monk Soham

CLAYDON

LOES

PARHAM

Marlesford

PLOMESGATE

OSMERE

Blakeham

CARLEFORD

Ipswich
IPSWICH

PARHAM

WILFORD

NORTH

SEA

COLNEIS

SAMFORD

INTRODUCTION

I

THE MANUSCRIPTS

THE only known complete text of the *Chronicle* of Jocelin of Brakelond is to be found in the *Liber Albus* of Bury St. Edmunds, a well-known collection of texts relating to the Abbey, now Harleian MS 1005 in the British Museum. Folios 121–63 (according to the numbers added in the familiar hand of a fifteenth-century Bury librarian ; in the Museum foliation they are 127–70) form a separate section, written in two columns of thirty-five lines in a good hand of the second half of the thirteenth century, with plain red capitals ; the hand gets progressively larger, but is probably the same throughout. This seems to be a very faithful copy, and may have been made from the author's autograph. Here and there a fifteenth-century hand has made corrections which must be accepted as obviously right, and the scribe makes a few minor slips (e.g. *crux* for *crus*, *sit* for *scit*), which have been silently put right in the printed editions. Otherwise in both text and spelling (but not punctuation) we follow the MS as closely as possible.

A slightly earlier copy was to be found in another MS now in the Museum, Cotton Vitellius D. XV, until its almost complete destruction in the fire at Ashburnham House in 1731 that damaged so many of Sir Robert Cotton's MSS. All that now survives is most of the inner columns of thirteen leaves, darkened and distorted but still mainly legible, and we can see that this was written perhaps about the middle of the thirteenth century in a very good but very small hand, also in two columns of thirty-five lines, and with plain red capitals to the paragraphs. A certain number of mistakes in the surviving fragments show that we are not confronted with the author's autograph, nor with the MS from which the Harleian was copied, but with an independent transcript, probably of about the same value.

By good fortune there are (as Arnold pointed out) two MSS in the Bodleian Library at Oxford, both from Bury Abbey, which contain excerpts from Jocelin. MS Bodley 297 (2468) is a fine twelfth-century chronicle, at the very end of which, on pp. 423–25, a hand of the thirteenth has copied two sections, *Miraculum de cipho sancti Ædmundi* (pp. 106–9 below) and *Qualiter abbas Samson vidit corpus Ædmundi* (pp. 111–16). The same two chapters, and also the account of the vision and conversion of Henry of Essex (pp. 68–71), are included in a compilation of St. Edmund's miracles in MS Bodley 240 (2469), a great collection of Saints' lives and other texts written at Bury in 1377. These two sets of excerpts, which although mainly overlapping are independent one of the other, enable us to correct two or three mistakes of the Harleian MS, which would otherwise have been quite beyond our control. It is fortunate that we are not further dependent on them, for the first excerpt in MS 297 has been tampered with to improve the Latin, and the compiler of MS 240 has felt himself at liberty to reduce and alter Jocelin's text, removing some of his detail and much of his personal raciness of style, in order to adapt his account of these miracles to form part of a composite work of general edification.

We also have a second copy of the passage on the Customs of the town of Bury on ff. 123–4 of the Harleian MS.

Jocelin's *Chronicle* was first printed in 1840 by John Gage Rokewode (formerly Gage) as volume 13 of the publications of the Camden Society. Rokewode made a few mistakes, most of which are listed, with a discussion of some difficult passages, in an article by the present editor in *Medium Aevum* X (1941), pp. 94–6. For its date, however, his was an excellent performance, and he laid a firm foundation for all work on Jocelin ever since.

The only other edition of the Latin is that of T. Arnold in the Rolls Series, *Memorials of St. Edmund's Abbey* I (1890), pp. 209–336, which is drawn from Rokewode with some corrections. There have also been three or four translations into English. R. A. B. MYNORS

II

JOCELIN OF BRAKELOND

Of Jocelin's life little is known. He derived his surname from the name of the street in Bury St. Edmunds, where presumably he lived before he entered the monastery in 1173 (see p. 1). At the time of Abbot Samson's election in 1182 he was the Prior's chaplain, and four months later he became chaplain to the new Abbot (p. 26). For six years he tells us (p. 36) he was with him night and day. At a later date he became guestmaster (*hospiciarius*), and still held that office when Herbert was elected Prior in 1200 (p. 128). Later he was appointed almoner (*elemosinarius ;* p. 68), as we learn from the story of Henry of Essex, interpolated by another writer, who had heard the story from Jocelin's own lips, and describes him as *uir religionis eximie, potens in sermone et opere*. He is probably identical with Jocelin the almoner who played an active part in the election of Samson's successor (see *Mem.* II, xi), despite the fact that the author of the *Electio Hugonis* describes him as *duplex et uarius*. In addition to the *Chronicle*, he also wrote an account, now lost, of the martyrdom of little St. Robert, a boy alleged to have been murdered by the Jews in Bury in 1181 (p. 16). Beyond these meagre facts we have no direct information concerning him.

But though we know so little of the details of his life, we

know the man himself most intimately. For he lives in the pages of his book—a shrewd observer of his fellows, humorous and wise, interested in every detail of the life not merely of Abbot Samson, but of the community in which the greater part of his life was spent. As a scholar he was inferior, no doubt, to the best of his contemporaries. He lacked their command of style, and was less influenced by the classical tradition. But he had received a good education, and used his somewhat homelier idiom to perfection ; and though he is far from being the greatest writer of his day, he is certainly the most lovable, while his theme is of absorbing interest. No-one has given us such an intensely vivid picture of the life of a great monastery ; it has a quality which is all its own. He has his faults no doubt ; his chronology is at times obscure and inaccurate, and his narrative has a tendency to ramble. He loses himself occasionally when the story he has to tell is complicated. Take, for example, the curious story concerning the living of Hopton (p. 61) ; as it stands it is barely intelligible, and we have to go to the Registrum Nigrum to find out what really happened. Again his description of the quarrels between Abbot Samson and the Bishop of Ely over their respective rights at Lakenheath and Glemsford (Appendices T and U) is, despite its liveliness, both careless and obscure.

But, despite these defects, his chronicle, besides being a delight to read, is a mine of information, not merely about the life of a great monastery, but also concerning the management and organisation of a vast feudal estate, and something more than that ; for within its ample limits the Abbot was not merely the most important tenant in chief, but in addition took the place of the King's Sheriff ; indeed it is not improbable that Jocelin and his Abbot would both have thought this an understatement.

Moreover, the town of Bury St. Edmunds belonged to the Abbey, and Jocelin throws much light on the growth of the town and its institutions during its tutelage, and further on the unusual importance of the Sacrist and the Cellarer in the administration of the town itself and its banlieue.

Jocelin is never dull even when his material is dry and technical ; he never strays far from the human side of his theme, and there his charm and skill are extraordinary. His character sketches and his description of the debates of the monks before the election of a successor to Abbot Hugh are lifelike in the extreme and full of humour. No less effective and vivid is his account of the fire in the Abbey church and the subsequent exhumation of St. Edmund, while his portrait of Samson, as he looked and as he lived, is unforgettable. There is nothing anywhere else quite like his chronicle, and its fame is well-deserved. When we reach its close we have only one regret—that it ends too soon. For, though Jocelin survived Samson, he breaks off eight years before the latter's death, nor is there any reason to think that he continued it.

III

THE SAINT AND HIS ABBEY

For the existence of Edmund, King of the East Saxons, and his death at the hands of the Danish invaders in 870, we have the evidence of Asser, his contemporary, and the Anglo-Saxon Chronicle. For the details of his life and death we have little information on which we can rely, as a mass of legend resting on no sure foundation soon gathered about him. None the less the first life of the Saint (see *Mem.* I), the *Passio Sancti Ædmundi*, by Abbo of Fleury, claims to be based on good oral tradition. The work is dedicated to St. Dunstan, whom Abbo visited three years before his death (in 988), ' You told us,' he writes in his preface, ' that you had heard this story in your youth

from the lips of an aged and decrepit man, who told it simply
and with full faith to King Athelstan, asserting with an oath
that he had been St. Edmund's armour-bearer on the very
day of his martyrdom.' The story stripped of its miraculous
details is as follows. Edmund came of the ancient stock of the
Old Saxons, and was a devout Christian from his earliest years.
A raiding host of Danes, led by Ingwar, invaded East Anglia,
and fought and captured the King. Ingwar offered him his
life if he would consent to rule as his vassal. The King refused
to submit to a heathen, was scourged, shot with arrows and
finally beheaded at a place Haegilisdun, now unidentifiable, but
generally assumed to be near Hoxne. The Danes left the body
where it fell, but hid the head in a thicket. Both were recovered
and miraculously united. His remains were buried at Hoxne,
and a chapel was built over them. There for a while they
reposed, until, at some date between 903 and 925, they were
removed to Bedricsworth, now Bury St. Edmunds, and reburied
in a church of wood. In 925 King Athelstan is said to have
founded a College of Seculars, consisting of two priests and four
deacons, to watch over the body of the Saint ; and to this
college at a later date Edmund, the brother of Athelstan, gave
lands in the neighbourhood of the town. There the Saint rested
undisturbed till the threat of Danish raids caused his removal
to London. A layman named Ailwin (or Egelwin) was
custodian of the Saint's tomb, over which he watched with
peculiar devotion. When it was known that the Danes under
Thurkill had landed at Ipswich in 1010, he took up the body
and carried it, not without adventures on the way, to London,
and placed it in the church of St. Gregory, which stood close
to the S.W. corner of St. Pauls ; there it remained in safety for
three years. At the end of that time he sought to remove his
precious charge. But the Saint had continued to work miracles
in his temporary residence, and the Bishop and citizens, re-
luctant to be deprived of so valuable an asset, resisted with

force. The Saint, however, was too much for them. When they sought to remove his coffin into St. Paul's hard by, they could not lift it. Ailwin, however, and three faithful followers found no difficulty and lifted the coffin as if it were of no weight at all, and thus the Saint returned in triumph to Bedricsworth.

IV

THE MONASTERY AND ITS ABBOTS

Under Canute the fame of St. Edmund grew, and the king himself held him in special veneration. In 1120 he ordered that the wooden church at Bedricsworth should be replaced by one of stone. Further, with his approval, and on the advice of Aelfwin, Bishop of Elmham, himself once a monk of Ely, the little college of seculars was abolished, and in its place was founded a monastery of Benedictines, drawn from the houses of St. Benet Hulme and Ely, Uvius, the Prior of Hulme, being chosen as its first Abbot. In 1028 Canute gave a charter to the Abbey, conferring upon it perpetual possession of its lands, absolute independence of episcopal control and sole jurisdiction over all such vills as it then owned or might own in days to come. These privileges were still further increased in 1044, when Edward the Confessor, a fervent votary of the Saint, visited the Abbey and gave it not only the rich manor of Mildenhall, but sole jurisdiction over eight and a half hundreds in Suffolk, a region whose bounds were virtually identical with those of the administrative district of West Suffolk today.

In that same year Uvius died and was succeeded by Leofstan. Herman, in his ' Miracles of St. Edmund ' (*Mem.* I, pp. 51ff.), praises his character, but alleges that, during the first years of his abbacy, St. Edmund did not get his due, until the remonstrances of a woman, cured of dumbness at his shrine, moved him to see if all was well with the Saint within his tomb.

To the delight of Ailwin, now a monk and nearly blind, the Saint was exhumed. He felt the body to discover whether it was in the same condition as when it was reinterred after its return from London. All was in order ; the crucifix which St. Aelphege, Archbishop of Canterbury, had once sought to secure for himself, still lay on the Saint's breast, and the body was redolent with the odour of sanctity. Then followed a strange and unedifying scene. The abbot, anxious to test the truth of the tradition that the Saint's head had been miraculously reunited to its body, himself laid hold of the head and bade a young monk, named Turstan, to grasp the feet. Leofstan pulled and drew both Saint and monk towards him. Herman states that, after this successful though unseemly experiment, the abbot's hands suffered from palsy until his death, while his sight and speech were also affected. The Saint was reinterred, after having been stripped of his clothing, stained with blood and pierced with many a wound, and reclad in new grave-clothes, such as are described by Jocelin, when Abbot Samson, in his turn, viewed the body.

In 1065 Leofstan died, and Baldwin, a French monk of St. Denys succeeded to the Abbacy. He owed his appointment to Edward the Confessor, whose friend and physician he had been. The monks accepted him and he proved one of the best and ablest of their abbots. Under his rule the town increased, and the possessions of the Abbey grew, while he was as acceptable to William the Conqueror as he had been to the Confessor. Two notable achievements adorn his abbacy : his vindication of the independence of the Abbey against the attempt of Arfast, Bishop of Thetford, to transfer his see to Bury, and his decision to build a great Abbey church in lieu of that erected in the reign of Canute. Arfast put forward his claim about 1070 ; Baldwin appealed to Rome, which he visited in 1071 ; he found favour with the Pope, Alexander II, and returned with a *priuilegium* forbidding from that time forth the establishment of any bishop-

ric at Bury—for it is at this time that the name of St. Edmund's
Bury begins to take the place of Bedricsworth—and despite the
persistance of Arfast, the quarrel was finally settled by the King
at Winchester in 1081. The great church, begun at the king's
command and with promise of his generous support, was ready
to receive the body of the Saint in 1094, the eastern portion
being complete up to the crossing ; and in 1095 on the 29th
April the translation of St. Edmund to his new resting-place was
celebrated with great pomp and enthusiasm. Two years later
Baldwin died full of years and honour, and was buried in the
middle of the choir which he had built.

The Abbey had to wait three years for a successor. At last,
in 1100, Robert, a young monk of St. Evroult, and bastard son
of Hugh Lupus, Earl of Chester, was thrust into the vacancy.
The appointment was not a success and was uncanonical.
Anselm appealed to Rome, and Herbert Losinga, Bishop of
Norwich, attempted to assert episcopal control over the Abbey
in 1101. He failed in his attempt, and in 1102 Anselm deposed
Robert. He was succeeded by Robert II, a monk of Westminster, who left behind him a happy memory both as a builder
and as an administrator. With the assistance of his Sacrist,
Godefrey, a man of huge stature and energy, he lengthened
the choir by a bay, built the four piers for the central tower,
and probably a portion of the tower itself, as well as completing
the Chapterhouse, the Infirmary, Refectory and Abbot's Hall,
and according to one account the Cloister as well. Further,
he divided the possessions of the Abbey between the Abbot and
the Convent, a policy which was ratified by a charter from the
King (FD, p. 69). It was destined to be of great value during
subsequent vacancies ; for on earlier occasions all the temporalities of the Abbey fell into the hands of the King, until a new
Abbot was elected, whereas from this time forth the possessions
of the Convent were immune. The dates of Robert's election
and death have been disputed. Arnold (*Mem.* I, Introd.)

holds that he was elected in 1102 and consecrated in 1107, dying a month later—a view which is strongly supported by contemporary evidence. Battely (Ant. S. Edm., pp. 54ff.) argues with much ingenuity and force that he was elected in 1107 shortly before his consecration and died about 1112. The charter of Henry I, mentioned above, though it cannot have been granted before 1109, has nothing in it to prove that Robert was still alive (see FD, p. 69).

The next Abbot was Albold, a monk of Bec (1114–19), of whose activities we hear little for good or ill. He was succeeded in 1121 by Anselm, Abbot of St. Saba in Rome, and nephew of St. Anselm. In 1136 he was chosen by a majority of the Canons to be Bishop of London. The minority appealed to Rome. Nevertheless Anselm was received as Bishop, and in 1138 was succeeded in the Abbacy by Ording. Thurstan, however, the Archbishop of York, wrote to the Pope that Anselm deserved rather to be deprived of his Abbacy than to be promoted to the See of London ; and eventually the election was quashed. Anselm returned to the Abbey. After some difficulty Ording was induced to resign in his favour, and Anselm became Abbot for the second time. He died in 1148, and Ording once more took his place. The little that we know of Anselm suggests that he was ambitious and liked to be in the public eye, and, as we have seen, the Archbishop of York thought ill of him as an Abbot. But he left his mark upon the Abbey. Aided by exceptional Sacrists, *uiri totius prudentiae*, Ralph and Hervey, he seems to have completed the nave of the Abbey church. Such at least is the inference to be drawn from the fact that the great western doors were made during his abbacy. But much was also done besides. Anselm founded the church of St. James, and built a tower, perhaps that which is known today as the Norman Tower, and is still one of the glories of Bury. It is a gateway tower, and may be identical with the *porta cimeterii* (see p. 37). We hear also of the building of the church of St. Mary, and of an edifice described as the Clocarium (i.e. the belfry). Whether this was a separate tower, or whether it indicates the completion of the great central tower of the Abbey cannot be determined.

Of Ording little is known save that he was a staunch defender of the rights of St. Edmund (see p. 11), and that he was a good administrator and economist. A disastrous fire broke out during his abbacy, destroying the Abbot's Hall, the Refectory, the Dormitory, the Infirmary and the Chapter-house, all of which were rebuilt by the Abbot's nephew, the Sacrist Helyas. The Abbey church escaped, and we hear nothing of any building in its connexion. But he adorned the ' great altar with a silver front, worth 100 marks, and set up a cross in the choir and statues of the Virgin and St. John, incomparably carved by Master Hugo.' Ording died Jan. 31, 1156.

He was succeeded by Hugh, Prior of Westminster, in 1157. Our knowledge of his character is mainly derived from Jocelin (pp. 1ff.). But it is worth while recording his efforts to secure all episcopal authority. On his election he had made his profession of canonical obedience to Theobald, Archbishop of Canterbury. But in 1172 he secured a bull from Alexander III, forbidding the Abbot of St. Edmunds to make profession to any Bishop or Archbishop, and ordering that such profession should be made to the Pope alone. And later, in 1175, he secured special exemption from any authority other than that of the Pope or his *legatus a latere*. The Archbishop of Canterbury was *legatus natus*, that is *ex officio*, but he was not normally *legatus a latere*. Further, in 1176, he secured exemption from the authority of Richard, Archbishop of Canterbury, who was actually *legatus a latere* (p. 5). In his later years his administration of the Abbey deteriorated, and no building of any great importance is reported during his tenure of office. That is not surprising since the Abbey church was all but finished. The great tower at the west end was all that was needed for its completion ; the finances of the Abbey were in bad condition, and the work had perhaps been postponed for that reason. Samson, his successor, who was then sub-sacrist had, however, by somewhat questionable methods, made preparations for its erection, and as soon as he became Abbot he carried out his design. He had already adorned the interior of the Church with a richly painted choir screen.

V

THE ABBEY CHURCH

The details of the growth of the Church have already been mentioned, but a brief description of its general appearance at the close of Samson's abbacy remains to be given. It was a vast Norman building at least 500 feet long. At the East end three apsidal chapels projected from the main building. At the West end stood Samson's great tower, flanked to north and south by octagonal structures, each containing two chapels, one above the other. The crossing was crowned by a large central tower. Within, the choir was surrounded by a screen on which Samson had caused ninety scenes from the Old Testament to be painted. Behind the High Altar stood the shrine of St. Edmund, a wooden structure supported on a base of marble. In shape it resembled a church ; it was made of wood, encrusted with plates of silver gilt, with a gold cresting on the top, while at its western end was a golden 'Majesty,' a relief representing Christ in glory. Four great candles stood round it, burning night and day. It was one of these which caused the fire described by Jocelin (p. 106). Pictures of the shrine are to be found in the delightful manuscript (Harl. 2278), containing Lydgate's Life of St. Edmund, set forth in English verse. Though they agree more or less as to the general design, they disagree widely as to its detail and its colouring, so that they cannot be trusted in matters of detail.

A few words may be said concerning the subsequent history of one of the largest of English churches. A great tower fell within a few days of Samson's death in 1210. Whether it was the Western or the Central tower is uncertain. Probably it was the latter. Such towers had a habit of collapsing in the Middle Ages. The Western tower fell in 1430, and in 1465 almost the whole church was consumed by fire. But once more the shrine of the Saint and the tomb of his faithful guardian Ailwin escaped destruction.

Of all this hardly anything remains today. The two big parish churches of St. James and St. Mary sufficed the needs of the townsfolk, and the Abbey church became superfluous after the dissolution of the monasteries. It was stripped of all that was of value, and was allowed to fall into decay. Only a portion of the West front remains embedded in private houses ; traces of the two octagonal chapels are still to be seen. The rest is level with the ground, only the bases of columns and scanty indications of the foundations of the walls being visible. The sites of the tombs of the Abbots, who were buried in the Chapterhouse, have been discovered, and the names of the Abbots have been placed above them. The crypt beneath the choir is believed to be intact but has not been explored. It is conceivable that the body of St. Edmund may have been placed there when his shrine was destroyed. The work of M. R. James, *On the Abbey of St. Edmund at Bury*, published in 1895, is still the only work of importance on the subject, and further exploration of the site is much to be desired.

The sole building connected with the Abbey that survives out of those which were standing in Samson's day is the fine Norman Tower, which is one of the two entrances to the huge enclosure which contained the monastery and its church. The other even finer gate which gave entry to the Abbot's court dates from the fourteenth century. Of the monastic buildings nothing remains save traces of their foundations. They together with the cloisters all lay on the North side of the church.

VI

THE LIBERTY OF ST. EDMUND

The whole of the administrative region now known as West Suffolk was once known as the Liberty of St. Edmund, having been granted to the Abbey by Edward the Confessor in 1044 (see Appendix, p. 148). The Abbot was a tenant in chief of the Crown and held a position at least equivalent to that of the King's Sheriff in other shires. All cases that would in other shires have gone to the County Court went to the Abbot's Court; indeed it is not clear that Abbot Samson did not still claim jurisdiction in cases which would elsewhere have come before the Justices in Eyre (pp. 161), though this was not the case in the 13th century. There were, however, a number of manors within the Liberty which belonged to others, such as the Bishop of Ely, the Archbishop of Canterbury, and the Earl of Clare. As a result disputes arose and the Abbot was not always successful in maintaining the rights of jurisdiction which he claimed. Similarly the Abbey of St. Edmund had possessions outside the limits of the Liberty, as for example, at Harlow in Essex. It may be noted that the hundred of Stowe in East Suffolk and the half-hundred of Harlow in Essex had been granted by Stephen to the Abbey, though these grants were apparently cancelled on the accession of Henry II (FD, p. clii). The Abbot was tenant-in-chief of the Crown and owed service of forty knights. The Liberty was, in fact, a great feudal estate consisting of eight and a half hundreds. These hundreds had at the time of Abbot Samson's accession been let out at farm, i.e. at rent ; the balance of fees and all other profits accruing from the business of the hundred which were left after payment of these rents remained in the hands of the bailliffs. One of Samson's first acts was to resume the hundreds into his own hands. The possessions of the Abbey were, from the time of Abbot Robert II (page xix), divided between the Abbot and the Convent. This did not impair the Abbot's supreme control over all these possessions, but it served an important purpose. For when the Abbacy was vacant the temporalities of the Abbot passed into the hands of the Crown until such time as a new Abbot was appointed ; and the interregnum was often very long (pp. xix sqq.) ; this was profitable to the Crown, but entailed heavy loss to the Abbey. The division of the Abbey's possessions between the Abbot and the Convent, a procedure adopted by other religious houses as well, ensured that only the temporalities of the Abbot should be affected on these occasions.

The town of Bury St. Edmunds in the hundred of Thingoe was a separate unit with an organisation of its own under the general control of the Sacrist. In all matters which were not immediately the concern of the abbey, it was administered by its two *prefecti* or *bailliui*, appointed by the Sacrist with the consent of the convent. They presided over the portman-moot, or town council, the name being derived from the A.S. ' port ' = town. This body appears as a court to have had the duties and powers of the hundred court and the court of the shire, since it was laid down in the charter granted to the town by Abbot Anselm that the burgesses should not attend shire court or hundred court, but only their own portman-moot. Above it stood the Abbot's court, the Abbot or his deputy at this period and for this special purpose taking the place of the justices in eyre (see L, p. 34).

Outside the walled town was the bannaleuca (the French *banlieue*), its outer boundary being marked by four crosses, and roughly corresponding with the town-boundary of today. This belt of land was likewise under the control of the Sacrist. But the Cellarer also played a not unimportant part in this connexion. He had certain tenements and special privileges within the walls and held his Court near the Eastgate in a messuage which, Jocelin tells us (p. 102), had been the 'dwelling-place of Bedric, once lord of this town.' He also controlled a large portion of the lands within the *bannaleuca*, and in the neighbourhood. The revenues and the food produced by these holdings served to help him in carrying out his primary duty, namely, the maintenance of the abbey and its inhabitants. His powers overlapped at times with those of the Sacrist, and there were frequent disputes between them. Under the vigilant administration of Samson his powers and privileges seem to have increased. The details are to be found on pp. 102 sqq. of the text. (For a full discussion see L, pp. 16–59.)

VII

THE INTERNAL ORGANISATION OF THE ABBEY

As the name Abbas implies, the Abbot was the father of the community. Theoretically his rule was absolute, but even in the smaller houses he delegated many of his duties. In the case of St. Edmunds, the Abbot, being also a great feudal baron with wide domains, had recourse to delegation on a very wide scale. He could of course intervene, and frequently did so. He was not bound to consult the convent, but such consultations were not infrequent.

Beneath him came the Prior, who was responsible for the discipline of the monks and the observance of the Rule. He had sub-priors to assist him as he might require. He was appointed by the Abbot after consultation with the convent; in the Abbot's absence he acted as his deputy.

After the Priors came the officials known as obedientiaries. The Cantor or Precentor had charge of the choral services in the church, and was also chief librarian and director of the studies of the cloister-monks (*claustrales*).

The Sacrist was in charge of the service of the Altar, the vestments, hangings and lighting of the church ; he was also sometimes, as at Bury, responsible for building operations and repairs. He had a sub-sacrist to assist him in the performance of these duties ; and in addition to all this he was, at Bury, in charge of the town. The revenues which were derived from this source were devoted to the service of the Abbey church.

The Cellarer was the general manager of the house, the purveyor of all necessities—food, fuel, transport and materials for repairs, and at Bury was in charge of lands in the neighbour-hood of the town, the produce of which whether in money or in kind went toward the maintenance of the convent.

After these important officials came the *camerarius* or Chamberlain, who was responsible for the clothes, their washing and repairs, bedding, baths, etc. The Master of the novices had charge of the novices and their training. The Infirmarer was in charge of the sick-house. The *hospitiarius* or Guestmaster looked after the guests of the Abbey. The Almoner (*elemo-sinarius*) visited and relieved the poor, and disposed of the broken meats ; while the *pitentiarius* or Pittancer managed the pittances or extra dishes provided on special occasions.

In addition to these there were many other minor obedienti-aries, such as the *magister almarii* or library clerk, and monks detailed for special duties within the wide boundaries of the Liberty of St. Edmunds.

The whole community met daily in the Chapterhouse immediately after Prime (which took place at 6 in summer and 6.45 in winter). The meeting began with a sermon or a reading from some edifying book, after which orders were issued for the day, work detailed, penances imposed and minor questions discussed, though the discussion of more important matters was far from being precluded, witness the debates on the procedure to be adopted for selecting a successor to Abbot Hugh (p. 16), the appointment of a new Prior (p. 126), and the problem posed by the grievances of Ralph, the janitor (pp. 117–18), which gave rise to such acrimony that the Prior tried to closure the meeting by singing the psalm ' Verba mea,' which regularly ended proceedings.

LATIN TEXT
and
ENGLISH TRANSLATION

CRONICA

JOCELINI DE BRAKELONDA

[*MS. Harl. 1005, Fol. 121*]

QUOD uidi et audiui scribere curaui, quedam mala inter-serens ad cautelam, quedam bona ad usum, que conti-gerunt in ecclesia Sancti Ædmundi in diebus nostris, ab anno quo Flandrenses [1] capti sunt extra uillam, quo habitum religionis suscepi, quo anno Hugo prior de-positus est et R. prior substitutus. Tunc temporis senuit Hugo abbas, et aliquantulum caligauerunt oculi [2] eius ; homo pius et benignus, monachus religiosus et bonus, set nec bonus nec prouidus in secularibus exerciciis : qui nimis confidebat suis et nimis eis credebat, de alieno pocius quam de proprio pendens consilio. Ordo quidem et religio feruebant in claustro, et ea que ad ordinem spectant ; set exteriora male tractabantur, dum quisque, seruiens sub domino simplice et iam senescente, fecit quod uoluit, non quod decuit. Dabantur uille [3] abbatis et omnes hundredi [4] ad firmam ; nemora destruebantur ; domus maneriorum minabantur ruinam ; omnia de die in diem in deteriorem statum uertebantur. Unicum erat refugium et consolacionis remedium abbati, de-narios appruntare, ut saltem sic honorem domus sue posset sustentare. Non erat terminus Pasce nec Sancti Michaelis octo annis ante obitum eius, quin centum libre uel ducente ad minus crescerent in debitum ; semper

---

[1] The Earl of Leicester, in rebellion against Henry II, landed with a strong force of Flemings at Walton in Suffolk, and was completely de-feated by the royal forces at Fornham St. Geneviève (October 16, 1173).

[2] Genesis xxvii. 1

[3] The vills of the Abbot as opposed to those of the convent. See p. xx.

[4] See p. xvii

1

THE CHRONICLE

OF JOCELIN OF BRAKELOND

I HAVE been at pains to set down the things that I have
seen and heard, which came to pass in the Church of
St. Edmund in our days, from the year in which the
Flemings were taken prisoner outside the town, that
being the year in which I assumed the religious habit,
and Prior Hugh was deposed and his office given to
Robert ; and I have included certain evil things for a
warning, and certain good as an example to others. At
that time Abbot Hugh was grown old and his eyes waxed
somewhat dim. Pious he was and kindly, a strict monk
and good, but in the business of this world neither good
nor wise. For he trusted those about him overmuch and
gave them too ready credence, relying always on the
wisdom of others rather than his own. Discipline and
religion and all things pertaining to the Rule were zeal-
ously observed within the cloister ; but outside all things
were badly handled, and every man did, not what he
ought, but what he would, since his lord was simple and
growing old. The townships of the Abbot and all the
hundreds were given out to farm ; the woods were
destroyed, the houses of the manors threatened to fall
in ruin, and day by day all things went from bad to
worse. The Abbot found but one remedy and one
consolation—to borrow money, that thus at least he
might be able to maintain the honour of his house. No
Easter nor Michaelmas came round during the eight
years before his death but that one or two hundred
pounds were added to his debt ; the bonds were con-

renouabantur carte, et usura que excreuit uertebatur
in katallum.[1] Descendebat hec infirmitas a capite in
menbra, a prelato in subiectos, unde contigit quod
quilibet obedientiarius [2] haberet sigillum proprium, et
debito se obligaret tam iudeis quam christianis pro
uoluntate sua. Sepe cappe serice et ampulle auree et
alia ornamenta ecclesie impignorabantur inconsulto
conuentu. Uidi cartam fieri Willelmo filio Isabel mille
librarum et xl, set nec causam nec originem sciui. Uidi
et aliam cartam fieri Isaac filio Raby Ioce cccc. librarum,
set nescio quare. Uidi et terciam cartam fieri Benedicto
iudeo de Norwico, octies c. librarum et quater uiginti;
et hec fuit origo et causa huius debiti. Destructa fuit
camera nostra, et recepit eam Willelmus sacrista[3] uolens
uel nolens, ut eam instauraret ; et occulte appruntauit
a Benedicto iudeo xl. marcas [4] ad usuram, et ei fecit
cartam signatam quodam sigillo [5] quod solebat pendere
ad feretrum sancti Ædmundi, unde gilde et fraterna-
ciones [6] solebant sigillari, quod postea set tarde fractum
est, iubente conuentu. Cum autem creuisset debitum
illud usque ad c. libras, uenit iudeus portans literas
domini regis [7] de debito sacriste ; et tunc demum patuit
quod latuit abbatem et conuentum. Iratus autem abbas
uoluit deponere sacristam, pretendens priuilegium [8]

---

[1] *katallum*, ' capital,' derived from *capitale*. It can also mean ' cattle '
and ' chattel.'

[2] See p. xxvii

[3] See p. 30. The meaning of *camera* is uncertain. Perhaps ' treasury '
or ' storehouse.'

[4] The silver mark is a monetary unit worth thirteen shillings and four
pence, never an actual coin. The gold mark was worth about six pounds.

[5] The seal was hung on the shrine to secure its safety ; it would be
sacrilege for any unauthorised person to touch it. The altar was also
sometimes used where we should use a safe.

[6] Bury shared with six other monastic boroughs the rare privilege of
gild merchant. There was also in existence at this time the craft gild of
bakers and two religious confraternities—the gilds of St. Edmund (FD 129),
and that of the Translation of St. Nicholas (L 72, 73).

tinually renewed, and the interest as it grew was turned into capital. This infirmity spread from the head to the members—from the superior to his subjects. And so it came about that each obedientiary had his own seal and bound himself in debt to Jews and Christians as he pleased. Often silken copes and flasks of gold and other ornaments of the church were placed in pawn without the knowledge of the Convent. I saw a bond given to William FitzIsabel for one thousand and forty pounds, and have never known the why or the wherefore. I saw another bond given to Isaac the son of Rabbi Joce for four hundred pounds, but I know not why ; and yet a third to Benedict the Jew of Norwich for eight hundred and fourscore ; and the cause of this last debt was as follows : our chamber was fallen in ruin, and the Sacrist, willy-nilly, undertook to restore it, and secretly borrowed forty marks at interest from Benedict the Jew and gave him a bond sealed with the seal that used to hang from the feretory of St. Edmund, and with which the instruments of the guilds and fraternities used to be sealed : it was broken up afterwards, at the bidding of the Convent, but all too late. Now when this debt had increased to one hundred pounds, the Jew came with letters from our lord the King concerning the Sacrist's debt, and at last that which had been hidden from the Abbot and the Convent was revealed. The Abbot was angry and would have deposed the Sacrist, alleging a privilege

---

[7] ' The Jews, wheresoever they be in the realm, are under the liege wardship and protection of the king . . . they and all they have are the king's, and should anyone detain them or their chattels, the king may demand them as his own ' (*Leges Edw. Conf.* cap. 25) ; see PM i pp. 468ff.

[8] No such document is known ; the Abbot's power was absolute, but it is possible that the Pope if consulted by the Abbot when he visited Rome may have reminded him of the fact.

domini pape, ut posset deponere Willelmum sacristam suum, quando uellet. Uenit autem aliquis ad abbatem, et, loquens pro sacrista, ita circumuenit abbatem, quod

F.121v passus est cartam fieri Benedicto iudeo / cccc. librarum, reddendarum in fine iiii^or annorum, scilicet pro c. libris que iam excreuerant in usuram, et aliis c. libris quas idem iudeus commodauit sacriste ad opus abbatis. Et sacrista suscepit omne debitum illud reddendum in pleno capitulo,[1] et facta est carta sigillo conuentus signata, abbate dissimulante et sigillum suum non apponente, tanquam illud debitum non pertineret ad illum. In fine uero quatuor annorum non erat unde illud debitum possit reddi ; et facta est nova carta octies c. librarum et quater uiginti librarum, reddendarum ad terminos statutos, annis singulis quater xx. librarum. Habuit et idem iudeus plures alias cartas de minoribus debitis, et aliquam cartam que erat xiiii. annorum, ita quod summa debiti illius iudei erat mille et cc. librarum, preter usuram que excreuerat. Ueniensque R. elemosinarius domini regis significauit domino abbati rumorem talem uenisse ad regem de tantis debitis. Et inito consilio cum priore et paucis aliis, ductus est elemosinarius in capitulum ; nobisque assidentibus et tacentibus, dixit abbas : ' Ecce elemosinarius regis, dominus et amicus noster et uester, qui, ductus amore Dei et sancti Ædmundi, nobis ostendit dominum regem quiddam sinistrum audisse de nobis et uobis, et res ecclesie male tractari interius et exterius. Et ideo uolo et precipio in ui obedientie, ut dicatis et cognoscatis palam qualiter res se habeant.' Surgens ergo prior et loquens, quasi unus pro omnibus, dixit ecclesiam in bono statu esse, et ordinem bene et relligiose obseruari interius, et exteriora bene et discrete

---

[1] See p. xxvii

granted him by the Lord Pope, enabling him to depose William his Sacrist when he would. But someone came to the Abbot and speaking on the Sacrist's behalf, so deluded the Abbot that he allowed a bond to be given to Benedict the Jew for four hundred pounds, to be paid at the end of four years, to wit, for the hundred pounds already accumulated at interest and another hundred pounds which the said Jew had lent the Sacrist on the Abbot's behalf. And the Sacrist undertook in full chapter to repay the whole debt, and a bond was given sealed with the Convent's seal : for the Abbot dissembled and would not set his seal to the bond, as though the debt was no concern of his. But at the end of four years there was not the wherewithal to pay the debt, and a new bond was made for eight hundred and fourscore pounds, to be paid off at stated times at the rate of fourscore pounds a year. The same Jew also held a number of bonds for smaller debts and one that was of fourteen years' standing, so that the total debt due to him amounted to twelve hundred pounds not counting the accumulated interest. And R. the almoner of our lord the King came and made it known to the Abbot that a rumour had reached the King concerning these great debts. So after the Abbot had taken counsel with the prior and a few others, the Almoner was brought into the Chapter ; and, while we sat by in silence, the Abbot said : ' Here is the King's Almoner, my lord and friend and yours also, who led by his love of God and of St. Edmund, has told us that our lord the King has heard something untoward concerning us, and that the affairs of our Church are ill-managed both within and without. Wherefore it is my will, and I charge you on your obedience that you should say and openly acknowledge how matters stand.' The Prior therefore arose, and

tractari, debito tamen aliquantulo obligatos nos esse sicut
ceteros uicinos nostros, nec esse aliquod debitum quod
nos grauaret. Audiens hoc, elemosinarius dixit se ualde
letum esse ex hoc quod audierat testimonium conuentus,
id est, prioris sic loquentis. Hec eadem uerba respondit
prior alia uice, et magister Galfridus de Constantino,
loquentes et excusantes abbatem, quando Ricardus [1]
archiepiscopus iure legacie uenit in capitulum nostrum,
antequam talem exempcionem haberemus sicut nunc
habemus. Ego uero tunc temporis nouicius data oportunitate magistrum meum super hiis conueni, qui me
docebat ordinem et cuius custodie deputatus fui, scilicet
magistrum Sampsonem, postea abbatem. ' Quid est,'
inquam, ' quod audio? Ut quid taces qui talia uides
et audis, tu qui claustralis [2] es nec obedientias cupis, et
Deum times magis quam hominem?' At ille respondens
ait : 'Filii mi, puer nouiter [3] conbustus timet ignem ;
ita est de me et pluribus aliis. Hugo prior nouiter depositus est de prioratu suo et in exilium missus ; Dionisius
et H. et R. de Hingham de exilio nuper domum redierunt.
Ego similiter incarceratus fui, et postea apud Acram
missus, quia locuti sumus pro communi bono ecclesie
F.122 nostre contra/uoluntatem abbatis. Hec est hora tene-

[1] See p. xxi
[2] See p. xxvii
[3] The incidents to which Samson refers seem to be (1) his first attempt
to secure for the Convent the *pensio* due to it from the Church of Woolpit
in 1161, as a result of which he was imprisoned and sent into exile at the
Cluniac monastery of Castle Acre. (2) It is not impossible that he may have
got into like trouble in 1173 or 1174 when the Church of Woolpit was
again given in frankalmoin, and the *pensio* lost for a second time. What
happened to him then we do not know ; but he says that he suffered many
other countless ills on account of the Church of Woolpit. See. pp. 48,
49, and Appendix I. Roger of Hingham, mentioned as having only recently
been released from exile, had accompanied him to Rome on the first
occasion. H. is presumably Hugo his brother. Nothing is known of the
causes for the punishment of Prior Hugh or Dionysius. The latter may be
D. the Cellarer (p. 6) or the individual mentioned on p. 16.

speaking as it were on behalf of us all, he said that the
Church was in good state, and that the Rule was well
and religiously observed within our house, while without our affairs were well and wisely handled, though
none the less we had incurred some small amount of debt,
like others of our neighbours ; but that there was no
debt of sufficient magnitude to be a burden to us. Hearing this the Almoner replied that he was very glad to
have heard the testimony of the Convent—that is to say,
the Prior speaking as he did. The Prior said the same
thing on another occasion, and with him Master Geoffrey
de Constantine, both of them speaking and excusing the
Abbot, when Archbishop Richard came to our Chapter
in virtue of his office as legate, before we possessed such
exemption as we now enjoy. But at that time I was a
novice and, when the opportunity offered, I spoke concerning these matters with my master, who used to teach
me the Rule and to whose care I had been assigned—to
wit, Master Samson, who was afterwards Abbot, ' What
is this,' I said, ' that I hear ? Why are you silent,
who see and hear such things as these, you who are a
cloister monk and have no desire for office and fear
God more than you fear man ? ' But he made answer
and said, ' My son, a child newly burned dreads the
fire ; thus it is with me and many others. Hugh the
Prior has of late been deposed from his priorship and
sent into exile. Denys and Hugh and Roger of Hingham
have but lately returned from exile. I like them was imprisoned and afterwards sent to Acre, because we had
spoken on behalf of the common good of our Church
against the will of the Abbot. This is the hour of
darkness ; this is the hour in which flatterers prevail and
are believed ; their power is made strong and we can

brarum [1] ; hec est hora qua adulatores dominantur et eis creditur : confortata est potentia eorum, nec [2] possumus ad eam.[3] Dissimulanda sunt ista pro tempore ; uideat Dominus et iudicet.' [4]

Uenit rumor ad abbatem H. quod R. archiepiscopus Cantuariensis uellet uenire ad scrutinium faciendum in ecclesia nostra, auctoritate legatie sue ; et, accepto consilio, misit abbas Romam et impetrauit exempcionem a potestate predicti legati. Redeunte nuntio ad nos de Roma, non erat unde solui poterat quod ipse promiserat [5] domino pape et cardinalibus, nisi ex circumstantiis crux que erat super magnum altare, et Mariola et Iohannes,[6] quas ymagines Stigandus archiepiscopus magno pondere auri et argenti ornauerat et sancto Ædmundo dederat. Dixerunt etiam quidam ex nostris qui abbatem familiarius diligebant, quod ipsum feretrum sancti Ædmundi deberet excrustari propter talem libertatem, non aduertentes magnum periculum posse nasci de tali libertate ; quod, si forte fuerit aliquis abbas noster qui res ecclesie uoluerit dilapidare et conuentum suum male tractare, non erit persona cui conuentus possit conqueri de iniuriis abbatis, qui nec episcopum nec archiepiscopum nec legatum timebit, et impunitas ausum prebebit delinquendi.

In diebus illis celerarius, sicut ceteri officiales, appruntauit denarios a Iurneto iudeo, inconsulto conuentu, super cartam supradicto sigillo signatam. Cum autem excreuit debitum usque ad sexaginta libras, summonitus est conuentus ad soluendum debitum celerarii. Depositus

---

[1] Luke xxii. 53
[2] The MS reads *ne* for *nec*
[3] Ps. cxxxviii. 6 (Vulg.), cxxxix. 6 (A.V.)
[4] Exod. v. 21
[5] The literature of the time, both prose and verse, is full of complaints against the corruption of the Papal curia.

do nothing against it.   We must for a time shut our eyes
to these things.   Let the Lord behold and judge.'

A rumour reached Abbot Hugh that Richard, Archbishop of Canterbury, desired to come to us and hold
a scrutiny in our Church, by virtue of his authority as
legate ; and after taking counsel the Abbot sent to Rome
and obtained exemption from the power of the said
legate.   When our messenger returned from Rome, we
had not the wherewithal to pay the sums that he had
promised the Lord Pope and the cardinals, except, under
the circumstances, the cross that was above the High
Altar and the little image of the Virgin and that of St.
John, which images Stigand the Archbishop had adorned
with a great weight of gold and silver, and had given to
St. Edmund.   Some of our brethren who were close
friends of the Abbot went so far as to say that even the
feretory of St. Edmund ought to be stripped of its plating
to pay for such a liberty as this, not noting the great peril
that might arise from such a liberty.   For if there should
arise some Abbot of ours who desired to dilapidate the
property of our Church and to treat his Convent ill,
there will be no man to whom the Convent will be able
to complain of the wrongs done by the Abbot, who will
fear neither Bishop or Archbishop or Legate, and his
impunity will make him all the bolder to do wrong.

In those days the Cellarer, like the rest of our officials,
without the knowledge of the Convent borrowed money
from Jurnet the Jew on a bond sealed with the afore-
mentioned seal.   But when the debt grew to no less than
sixty pounds, the Convent was summoned to pay the

---

[6] These statues were placed on the great beam behind the High Altar
in 1198 (p. 108), so that it may be assumed that the proposal to sell them
to pay off debts incurred at Rome was not carried into effect.   They are
not to be confused with the statues of the Virgin and St. John made during
the abbacy of Anselm.

est celerarius, licet allegaret grauamen suum, dicens quod susceperat tribus annis hospites omnes in domo hospitum ad preceptum abbatis, siue abbas fuerit presens siue absens, quos debeat suscipere abbas secundum consuetudinem abbatie. Substitutus est magister Dionisius, qui per prouidenciam suam et cautelam minorauit debitum lx. librarum usque ad xxx. libras ; de quo debito [1] reddidimus xxx^{ta} marcas, quas Benedictus de Blakeham dedit conuentui pro maneriis Neutone et Wepstede tenendis ; sed carta iudei usque hodie remansit apud iudeum, in qua continentur xxvi. libre de katallo et de debito celerarii.

Tercio die postquam magister Dionisius fuit celerarius, ducti sunt tres milites cum armigeris suis usque in domum hospitum, ut ibi reficerentur, abbate domi existente et in [2] talamo suo residente. Quod cum audisset magnanimus ille Eacides,[3] nolens pendere in bailiua sua, sicut ceteri, surrexit et accepit claues cellarii, et ducens secum milites illos usque in aulam abbatis, ueniensque ad abbatem, dixit : ‘ Domine, bene nouistis quod consuetudo abbatie
F.112v est, ut milites et laici recipiantur in curia uestra, / si abbas domi fuerit ; nec uolo nec possum recipere hospites [4] qui ad uos pertinent. Alioquin, accipite claues cellarii uestri, et alium constituere celerarium pro beneplacito uestro.’ Audiens hoc abbas, uolens uel nolens recepit illos milites, et semper postea milites et laicos recepit secundum antiquam consuetudinem ; et adhuc recipiuntur, abbate domi existente.

Uolens aliquando abbas magistrum Sampsonem con-

[1] The statement is ambiguous, as *debito* may refer to the original debt of £60 or to the reduced debt of £30, but the fact that at a considerably later date £26 was still owing suggests that the thirty marks (£20) were employed on the reduction of the £60.

[2] *talamo* (Greek θάλαμος) strictly means ‘ room,’ but is perhaps used in the wider sense of ‘ lodgings ’

[3] *Aeacides.* Achilles, grandson of Aeacus (Statius, *Achilleis* I. 1)

[4] See p. 39

Cellarer's debt. The Cellarer was deposed, although he alleged in his defence that a heavy burden was placed upon him, saying that during the last three years he had by order of the Abbot entertained in the guest-house, whether the Abbot was present or absent, all those guests who ought, according to the custom of the Abbey, to be entertained by the Abbot. Master Denys was made Cellarer in his place, and by his forethought and caution reduced the debt from sixty to thirty pounds—of which debt we paid thirty marks, that Benedict of Blakenham gave the Convent for his tenancy of the manors of Nowton and Whepstead. But the Jew's bond has to this day remained in the possession of the Jew, and in it twenty-six pounds are set down as the capital sum owed by the Cellarer.

On the third day after Master Denys was made Cellarer, three knights with their squires were brought to the guest-house to be entertained there, though the Abbot was at home and residing in his lodgings. But when that high-souled son of Aeacus heard this, since he did not wish to be slack in his office like the rest, he rose up with the keys of his cellary and, taking the knights with him to the Abbot's hall, he came to the Abbot and said, ' My lord, you know well that the custom of the Abbey is that knights and laymen should be received in your court, if the Abbot is at home. I neither can nor will accept guests who belong to you. Else take the keys of your cellary and appoint another Cellarer according to your good pleasure.' And when the Abbot heard this, willy-nilly he received those knights, and ever afterwards received knights and laymen according to the ancient custom ; and they are still so received when the Abbot is at home.

The Abbot once desiring to win Master Samson to be

ciliare sibi in gratiam, subsacristam eum constituit ; qui
sepius accusatus, sepius de officio in officium est trans-
latus ; quandoque factus est magister hospitum, quandoque pitentiarius, quandoque tercius prior, et iterum
subsacrista ; et multi ei aduersabantur qui postea ei
adulabantur. Ille uero aliter agens quam ceteri officiales,
nunquam ad adulandum flecti potuit ; unde dicebat
abbas suis familiaribus, se nunquam uidisse talem
hominem, quem non posset conuerti [1] ad suam uoluntatem, preter Sampsonem subsacristam.

Uenit abbati in mentem, anno uicesimo tercio abbatie
sue, adire sanctum Thomam orandi gratia ; arreptoque
in itinere, in crastino natiuitatis sancte Marie [2] prope
Rouecestriam miserabiliter cecidit, ita quod patella tibie
de proprio loco exiuit et resedit in poblete. Occurrerunt
medici, et eum multis modis cruciabant, set non sanabant.
Reportatus est ad nos in feretro equitario, et deuote susceptus, sicut decuit. Quid multa? conputruit crus [3] eius,
et ascendit dolor usque ad cor, et ex dolore arripuit
eum febris terciana, et in quarta accessione expirauit, et
animam reddidit Deo in crastino sancti Bricii. [4] Antequam mortuus esset, distracta fuerunt omnia a seruientibus suis, ita quod nichil omnino in domibus abbatis
remanserat, nisi tripodes et mense que asportari non
poterant. Uix abbati remanserant coopertorium suum
et due stragule que ueteres erant et fracte, quas aliquis
apposuerat qui integras abstulerat. Non erat aliquid ad
precium unius denarii quod possit distribui pauperibus pro
anima eius. Sacrista dicit non pertinere ad eum ut hoc
faceret, dicens se expensas abbati et familie sue inuenisse

---

[1] Either *quem conuerti* is a slip for *qui conuerti* or *quem conuertere*, or we
have here the late Latin use of *potest* as an impersonal verb.
[2] 9th September 1180
[3] The MS reads *crux*
[4] 14th November 1180

friends with him appointed him sub-sacrist. He was often accused and transferred from office to office. At one time he was made guest-master, at another pittancer, at another third prior and then again sub-sacrist. And many were his adversaries then, who afterwards used to flatter him. But he, unlike the rest of our officials, could never be bent to flattery ; wherefore the Abbot used to say to his close friends that he had never seen a man whom he could not bend to his will, save only Samson the sub-sacrist.

In the twenty-third year of his abbacy it came into Abbot Hugh's mind to go to the shrine of St. Thomas to pray ; and on his way thither upon the day after the Nativity of the Virgin he had a grievous fall near Rochester, so that his knee-cap was put out and lodged in the ham of his leg. Physicians hastened to him and tortured him in many ways, but healed him not ; and he was carried back to us in a horse litter and devoutly received as was his due. To cut a long story short, his leg mortified and the pain ascended even to his heart, and by reason of the pain a tertian fever laid hold on him, in the fourth fit of which he died and gave up his soul to God on the morrow of the day of St. Brice. Before he died, everything was pillaged by his servants so that nothing was left in his house but three-legged stools and tables which they were unable to carry off. The Abbot himself was scarce left with his coverlet and two old torn blankets which someone had placed over him after removing those that were whole. There was nothing worth a single penny that could be distributed to the poor for the benefit of his soul. The Sacrist said that it was no business of his, asserting that he had found all expenses for the Abbot and his household for a whole month. For the tenants of the townships refused to give

per mensem integrum ; quia nec firmarii, qui uillas tenebant, uolebant aliquid dare ante tempus constitutum, nec
creditores uolebant aliquid comodare, uidentes eum
infirmum usque ad mortem. Quinquaginta tamen
solidos inuenit firmarius de Palegraua ad distribuendum
pauperibus, hac ratione, quia firmam de Palgraua
intrauit illa die. Set illi quinquaginta solidi erant postea
redditi iterum bailiuis [1] regis, firmam integram exigentibus ad opus regis.

Sepulto abbate, decretum est in capitulo, ut aliquis
nunciaret Ranulfo de Glanuill, iusticiario Anglie, mortem
abbatis. Magister Sampson et Magister R. Ruffus,
F.123 monachi nostri,/cito transfretauerunt, nunciantes hoc
idem domino regi, et impetrauerunt literas, ut res et
redditus conuentus, qui separati sunt a rebus et redditibus abbatis, essent integre in manu prioris et conuentus,
et reliqua pars abbatie esset in manu regis. Data est
custodia [2] abbacie Roberto de Cokefeld et R. de Flam-
uille senescallo, qui statim omnes famulos abbatis et
parentes eius, quibus abbas aliquid donauerat postquam
infirmus fuerat, uel qui aliquid de rebus abbatis abstu-
lerant, posuerunt per uadium et plegios,[3] et eciam
capellanum abbatis, monachum nostrum, quem prior
plegiauit ; et intrantes uestiarium nostrum omnia ornamenta ecclesie in cirographo subscribi fecerunt.

Uacante abbatia, prior [4] super omnia studuit ad

---

[1] During the vacancy the temporalities of the Abbot reverted to the
Crown, and the sum was therefore claimed by the king's bailiffs. See p. 41,
where it is stated that Richard had to pay up, the church belonging to the
Abbot, and not to the Convent, whose temporalities were immune. See
pp. 41, 63, 81.
[2] The rent-roll of the Abbot from Michaelmas 1180 to Michaelmas
1181 was £326, 12s. 4d., of which the bailiffs paid £21 to cover his expenses during the last six weeks before his death, and £25 for the keep of
the Archbishop of Trondjem in Norway, then an exile and the Abbot's
guest. See p. 15.

anything before the appointed time and his creditors
would lend him nothing, when they saw that he was sick
even unto death. None the less the tenant of Palgrave
found fifty shillings for distribution to the poor, since he
entered on his tenancy of Palgrave on that day. But
those fifty shillings were later given back to the King's
bailiffs who demanded the whole rent on behalf of the
King.

When Abbot Hugh had been buried, it was resolved
in the Chapter that a messenger should announce his
death to Ranulph de Glanvill, Justiciar of England.
Master Samson and Master R. Ruff, monks of our house,
crossed the sea and bore this news to our lord the King :
and from him they secured letters to the effect that the
property and revenues of the Convent, which were
separated from those of the Abbot, should be wholly in
the hands of the Prior and the Convent, while the rest
of the Abbey should be in the hands of the King. The
custody of the Abbey was given to Robert de Cockfield
and Robert de Flamville, our Steward, who straightway
placed under gage and pledge all the servants and
kinsfolk of the Abbot, to whom he had given anything
before he fell sick or who had taken anything from his
property ; and they did this even to the Abbot's chaplain, one of our monks, for whom the Prior stood security :
and entering our vestry they caused an inventory to be
made of all the ornaments of the church.

While the abbacy was vacant, the Prior was above

---

³ ' Under gage and pledges.' *Uadium* is the term used for security in
the form of property or money ; *plegius* is a person who stands security for
another.
⁴ The Prior acts as head of the Convent *ex officio* during the vacancy.
See Index under Robert.

pacem conseruandam in conuentu, et ad honorem
ecclesie conseruandum in hospitibus suscipiendis, neminem uolens turbare, neminem ad iracundiam prouocare,
ut omnes et omnia in pace posset conseruare ; dissimulans tamen quedam corrigenda de obedientiariis
nostris, et maxime de sacrista, tanquam non curaret quid
ipse ageret de sacristia, qui, tempore quo abbatia uacauit,
nec debitum aliquod adquietauit nec aliquid edificauit ;
set oblationes et obuentiones stulte distrahebantur. Unde
prior, qui capud conuentus erat, pluribus uidebatur
uituperandus et remissus dicebatur. Et hoc memorabant
fratres nostri inter se, quando peruentum fuit ad faciendam electionem abbatis.

Celerarius noster omnes hospites, cuiuscumque condicionis essent, suscepit ad expensas conuentus.

Willelmus sacrista ex sua parte dabat et expendebat ;
homo benignus, dans danda et non danda, oculos
omnium excecans muneribus.[1]

Sampson subsacrista, magister super operarios, nichil
fractum, nichil rimatum, nichil fissum, nichil inemen-
datum reliquit pro posse suo ; unde conuentum et
maxime claustrales sibi conciliauit in gratiam. In diebus
illis chorus [2] noster fuit erectus, Samsone procurante,
historias picture ordinante, et uersus elegiacos dictante.
Attractum fecit magnum de lapidibus et sabulo ad
magnam turrim [3] ecclesie construendam. Et interrogatus unde denarios haberet ad hoc faciendum, respondit
quosdam burgenses dedisse ei occulte pecuniam ad turrim
edificandam et perficiendam. Dicebant tamen quidam
fratres nostri, quod Warinus monachus noster, custos

---

[1] Deut. xvi. 19

[2] Not the choir but the choir-screen. The ‘elegiac couplets’ are
probably the lines preserved in MS. Arundel, xxx, College of Arms, although
these are in fact leonine hexameters. See MRJ pp. 131 and 202.

[3] Samson completed the first storey, and during his abbacy it was
completed by the sacrist Hugo. See MRJ p. 120.

all things zealous for the maintenance of peace in the
Convent and the preservation of the honour of our
Church in the entertainment of guests, desiring neither
to disturb anyone or provoke any to anger, so that he
might keep all men and all things in peace. Yet none
the less he shut his eyes to certain things that deserved
correction in the conduct of our obedientiaries, above all
of the Sacrist who, during the vacancy, as though he did
not care what he did with the sacristy, paid not a single
debt nor built anything at all, but oblations and chance
incomings were foolishly squandered. Wherefore the
Prior who was the head of the Convent was thought
blameworthy and called remiss. And our brethren
spoke of this among themselves, when the time came
for the election of an Abbot.

Our Cellarer received all guests of whatever rank at
the expense of the Convent. William the Sacrist gave
and spent as he pleased, a kindly man, giving away both
that which should be given and that which should not,
and ' blinding the eyes of all with gifts.' Samson the
sub-sacrist, being master over the workmen, left nothing
broken or cracked or split or unrepaired to the best of
his power : wherefore he won the favour of the Convent
and above all of the cloister monks. In those days our
choir-screen was built under the direction of Samson,
who arranged the painted stories from the Bible and
composed elegiac verses for each. He had a great
quantity of stone and sand hauled for the building of the
great tower of the church. And when he was asked
whence he got the money to do this, he replied that certain of the burgesses had secretly given it to him for the
building and completion of the tower. Yet certain of
our brethren said that Warin, one of our monks and
guardian of the feretory, and Samson the sub-sacrist had

feretri, et Samson subsacrista communi consilio surri-
puerunt, quasi furtiue, porcionem aliquam de oblatio-
nibus feretri, ut eam in usus necessarios ecclesie, et
nominatim ad edificacionem turris, expenderent ; hac
F.123v ratione/ducti, quia uidebant quod oblaciones in usus
extraordinarios expendebantur ab aliis, qui, ut uerius
dicam, eas furabantur. Et ut tam felicis furti sui suspi-
cionem tollerent prenominati duo uiri, truncum [1] quendam fecerunt, concauum et perforatum in medio uel in
summo, et obseratum sera ferrea ; et erigi fecerunt in
magna ecclesia, iuxta hostium extra chorum in communi
transitu uulgi, ut ibi ponerent homines elemosinam suam
ad edificacionem turris.

Willelmus uero sacrista socium suum Sampsonem
suspectum habuit, et multi alii qui partem eiusdem
Willelmi fouebant, tam christiani quam iudei. Iudei,
inquam, quibus sacrista pater et patronus dicebatur ;
de cuius protectione gaudebant, et liberum ingressum
et egressum habebant, et passim ibant per monasterium,
uagantes per altaria et circa feretrum, dum missarum
celebrarentur sollemnia ; et denarii eorum in thesauro
nostro sub custodia sacriste reponebantur, et, quod
absurdius est, uxores eorum cum pueris suis in pitanceria
nostra tempore werre [2] hospitabantur.

Accepto itaque consilio qualiter irruerent in Samsonem inimici uel aduersarii eius, conuenerunt Robertum
de Cokefeld et socium eius,[3] qui custodes erant abbacie,
et induxerunt eos ad hoc quod illi prohibuerant ex parte
regis, ne aliquis aliquod opus uel aliquod edificium
faceret, quamdiu abbacia uacaret ; sed pocius denarii
ex oblacionibus colligerentur et conseruarentur ad

---

[1] Cp. the French *tronc*=offertory box. Here the epithet *concauum*
implies that it was actually hollowed out of a tree trunk.
[2] Presumably the rebellion of 1173-74
[3] Robert de Flamville

taken counsel together and had appropriated a certain
portion of the oblations at the feretory as it were by
stealth, that they might spend it for the necessary purposes of the church, and more especially for the building
of the tower, being led thereto because they saw that the
oblations were being spent on extraordinary purposes by
others, who (to put the matter more truly) stole them.
And that they might remove from themselves all suspicion of so felicitous a theft, these two men made a
hollow trunk with a hole in the middle on the top, and
fastened with an iron bar, and caused it to be set up in
the great church near the door outside the choir, where
the common folk pass to and fro, so that they might
place their alms therein for the building of the tower.

But William the Sacrist regarded Samson, his asso-
ciate, with suspicion, as did many others, both Christians
and Jews, who took William's side : the Jews, I say, for
the Sacrist was called their father and their patron ;
they rejoiced in his protection, had free entrance and
exit, and went everywhere through the monastery,
wandering by the altars and about the feretory, while
masses were being sung, and their money was kept in
our treasury under the Sacrist's custody—and more
unseemly still, in the days of the war their wives and
children took refuge in our pittancery.

So after taking counsel how his enemies or adversaries
might fall upon Samson, they spoke to Robert de Cockfield and his colleague, who had the Abbey in their
custody, and induced them on behalf of the King to
forbid anyone to carry out any work or building, so long
as the abbacy was vacant, and to give orders instead that
the money received from oblations should be collected and

faciendam solucionem alicuius debiti. Et sic illusus est
Samson, et recessit ab eo fortitudo eius [1] ; nec de cetero
aliquid operari potuit, sicut uoluit. Potuerunt quidem
aduersarii eius rem differre, set non auferre ; quia
resumptis uiribus suis, et subuersis duobus columpnis,[2]
id est, remotis duobus custodibus abbacie quibus aliorum
malitia innitebatur, dedit ei Dominus processu temporis
potestatem perficiendi uotum suum ut predictam turrim
edificaret, et pro desiderio suo consummaret. Et factum
est ac si ei diuinitus diceretur : ' Euge, serue bone et
fidelis, quia super pauca fuisti fidelis, super multa, &c.' [3]

Uacante abbatia, sepe, sicut decuit, rogauimus
Dominum et sanctum martirem Ædmundum, ut nobis
et ecclesie nostre congruum darent pastorem, singulis
ebdomadibus ter cantantes vii. psalmos penitenciales [4]
prostrati in choro, post exitum in [5] capitulo : et erant
aliqui, quibus si constaret quis futurus esset abbas, non
ita deuote orassent. De eligendo abbate, si rex nobis
liberam concederet electionem, diuersi diuersis modis
loquebantur, quidam publice, quidam occulte ; et
' quot homines tot sententie.' [6] Dixit quidam de
quodam : ' Ille, ille frater, bonus monachus est, pro-
babilis persona ; multum scit de ordine et consuetudinibus ecclesie: licet non sit tam perfectus philosophus /
F.124 sicut quidam alii, bene potest esse abbas. Abbas Ordingus homo illiteratus fuit, et tamen fuit bonus abbas et
sapienter domum istam rexit : legitur etiam in fabulis,

[1] Judges xvi. 17, 19
[2] Judges xvi. 29, 30
[3] Matt. xxv. 21
[4] Ps. vi ; xxxii ; xxxviii ; li ; cii ; cxxx ; cxliii
[5] *in* should perhaps be *de*, as on p. 24
[6] Terence, *Phormio*, II. iv. 14. (The MS reads *scientie*)

kept, to enable them to pay off some portion of their
debt. And thus Samson was outwitted and ' his strength
went from him,' nor could he for the rest of the time
carry out any work as he desired. His adversaries were
able to postpone his work, but they could not take it
from him ; for when he had recovered his strength and
those two pillars were removed, that is to say the two
guardians by whom his enemies' malice was supported,
the Lord in the fullness of time gave him power to
accomplish his design of building the tower and complete it according to his desire, as though it were said
to him from on high, ' Well done, thou good and faithful
servant : thou hast been faithful over a few things, I
will make thee ruler over many things.'

While the abbacy was vacant, we often besought
God and his holy martyr, St. Edmund, as was meet and
right, to give us a fitting shepherd for our Church, thrice
every week prostrating ourselves in the choir after leaving
the chapter house, and singing the seven penitential
psalms ; and some there were who, if they had known
who was to be our Abbot, would not have prayed so
devoutly. As to the choice of an Abbot, should the King
grant us a free election, divers persons spoke in divers
manners, some in public, some in private, and every
man had his own opinion. And one said of another,
' That brother is a good monk, a person worthy of
approval : he knows much concerning the Rule and
the customs of the Church ; though he be not so perfect
a philosopher as certain others he might well fill the
office of Abbot. Abbot Ording was an illiterate man,
and yet he was a good Abbot and ruled this house wisely ;

melius fuit ranis [1] eligere truncum in regem, super quem
confidere possent, quam serpentem, qui uenenose sibi-
laret, et post sibillum subiectas deuoraret.' Respondit
alter : ' Quomodo potest hoc fieri ? quomodo potest
facere sermonem in capitulo, uel ad populum diebus
festiuis, homo qui literas non nouit ? quomodo habebit
scientiam ligandi et soluendi,[2] qui scripturas non intelligit?
cum sit ars artium, scientia scientiarum, regimen animarum. Absit ut statua muta erigatur in ecclesia sancti
Ædmundi, ubi multi literati uiri et industrii esse di-
noscuntur.'

Item dixit alius de alio : ' Ille frater uir literatus est,
eloquens et prouidus, rigidus in ordine ; multum dilexit
conuentum, et multa mala pertulit pro bonis ecclesie :
dignus est ut fiat abbas.' Respondit alter : ' A bonis
clericis libera nos, Domine : ut a baratoribus [3] de
Norfolchia nos conseruare digneris, te rogamus, audi
nos.' Item dixit quidam de quodam : ' Ille frater
bonus husebondus est : quod probatur ex warda sua,
et ex obedienciis quas bene seruauit, et edificiis et
emendacionibus quas fecit. Multum potest laborare et
domum defendere, et est aliquantulum clericus, quamuis
nimie litere non faciant eum insanire [4] : ille dignus est
abbatia.' Respondit alter : ' Nolit Deus ut homo, qui non
potest legere, nec cantare, nec diuina officia celebrare,
homo inprobus et iniustus, et excoriator pauperum
hominum, fiat abbas.' Item dixit aliquis de aliquo : ' Ille
frater homo benignus est, affabilis et amabilis, pacificus

---

[1] See Æsop ; Phaedrus, I, 2, etc.
[2] Cp. Matt. xvi. 19. An important part of the *regimen animarum* or
ars artium, as it is styled by St Gregory.
[3] *barator* is a word used of dishonest lawyers, cheats, etc., and more
especially those who make illicit profits out of their office ; they have a
special place reserved for them by Dante in his *Inferno* (xxi, xxii). Here
there may be an allusion to Norfolk love of lawsuits. Samson was born
at Tottington in Norfolk and spoke the Norfolk dialect (see p. 40).
[4] Acts xxvi. 24

moreover, we read in the Fables that it proved better for
the frogs to choose a log for their king, in whom they
could trust, than a serpent who hissed venomously and
after hissing devoured his subjects.' To this another made
answer, ' How may that be ? How can he, a man who
has no knowledge of letters, preach a sermon in Chapter,
or on feast days to the people ? How shall he who does
not understand the Scriptures, have knowledge how to
bind and how to loose ? seeing that " the rule of souls is
the art of arts and the science of sciences." God forbid
that a dumb image should be set up in the Church of St.
Edmund, where it is known that there are many men of
learning and of industry.' Again another said of yet
another, ' That brother is literate, eloquent and prudent,
strict in his observance of the Rule ; he has greatly loved
the Convent, and has endured many ills for the possessions of the Church ; he is worthy to be made Abbot.'
And another replied, ' From all good clerks, O Lord
deliver us ; that it may please Thee to preserve us from
all Norfolk barrators, we beseech Thee to hear us.'
Again one said of a certain brother, ' That brother is
a good manager, as is proved by the performance of his
tasks and by the offices that he has filled so well, and
the buildings and repairs that he has made. He knows
how to work hard and to defend our house, and he is
something of a clerk, though " much learning maketh
him not mad." He is worthy to be Abbot.' The other
made answer, ' God forbid that a man who cannot read or
sing or celebrate the holy offices, a wicked man and unjust,
a flayer of the poor—God forbid that such an one should
be made Abbot ! ' Again a certain brother said of someone, ' that brother is a kindly man, affable and amiable,
peaceful and composed, bountiful and generous, a
literate man and eloquent, a very proper man in aspect

et conpositus, largus et liberalis, uir literatus et eloquens,
et satis idonea persona in uultu et in gestu, et a multis
dilectus intus et extra ; et talis homo ad magnum
honorem ecclesie posset fieri abbas, si Deus uellet.'
Respondit alter : ' Non honor esset set onus [1] de homine
qui nimis delicatus est in cibo et potu ; qui uirtutem
reputat multum dormire ; qui multum scit expendere et
parum adquirere ; qui stertit quando ceteri uigilant ;
qui semper uult esse in habundantia, nec curat de debitis
que crescunt de die in diem, nec de expensis unde adquie-
tari possint ; solicitudinem et laborem odio habens,
nichil curans, dummodo unus dies uadat et alter ueniat :
homo adulatores et mendaces diligens et fouens : homo
alius in uerbo et alius in opere. A tali prelato defendat
nos Dominus.' Item dixit quidam de socio suo : ' Ille
uir fere sapientior est omnibus nobis, et in secularibus
et in / ecclesiasticis ; uir magni consilii, rigidus in ordine,
literatus et eloquens et personalis stature : talis prelatus
decet ecclesiam nostram.' Respondit alter : ' Uerum
est, si esset rate et probate opinionis. Fama eius laborat,
que forte mentitur forte non mentitur ; et licet ille homo
sapiens sit, humilis in capitulo, deuotus in psalmis,
rigidus in claustro, dum claustralis est, ex consuetudine
tamen habet quod, si preest in obedientia aliqua, nimis
indignans est, monachos paruipendens, seculares homines
familiarius diligens, et, si iratus fuerit, uix aliquid uerbum
uult alicui fratri respondere, nec etiam interroganti.'
Audiui scilicet alium fratrem reprobatum a quibusdam,
quia impeditioris lingue fuerat ; de quo dicebatur quod
habebat pastum uel draschium in ore suo, cum loqui
deberet. Et ego quidem, tunc temporis iuuenis, sapiebam

F.124v

---

[1] This play upon words first appears in Ovid, *Heroides*, ix. 31, *Non
honor est sed onus.*

and bearing, who is loved by many both within and
without.   And such a man, God willing, might be made
Abbot to the great honour of the Church.'   The other
made answer, ' Nay ; it would be an onus rather than
an honour to have such a man ; for he is over nice about
his food and drink, thinks it a virtue to sleep long, knows
how to spend much and gain little, snores when others
keep vigil, would always be in the midst of abundance
and gives no thought to the debts that grow from day to
day, nor to the expenditure, how it may be met ; hating
all toil and anxiety and caring for naught, provided that
one day go and another come,—a man that loves and
cherishes flatterers and liars, and himself says one thing
and does another.   From such a ruler may the Lord
defend us ! '   Again one said of his comrade, ' That man
is wiser almost than any of us, both in the things of the
world and the things of the Church : a man of great
wisdom, strict in observance of the Rule, literate and
eloquent and personable in bearing.   Such a ruler
would beseem our Church.'   Another replied, ' True, if
only he were of sound and approved repute.   But his
reputation is deemed unsound, perhaps truly, perhaps
falsely.   And though he be a wise man, humble in
Chapter, devout in the singing of Psalms, and strict in
the cloister, while he is in cloister, yet, if he chances to
hold any office, he is apt to be disdainful, scorning monks
and loving men of the world more than he should ; and
if he should happen to be angry, he will not say a word
in answer to any of the brethren, not even if he be asked
a question.'   And in truth I heard another brother condemned by certain persons, because he had an impedi-
ment in his speech, wherefore it was said of him that he
had draff or paste in his mouth, when he was called upon
to speak.   And I indeed, being a young man, ' understood

ut iuuenis, loquebar ut iuuenis,[1] et dixi quod non con-
sentirem alicui ut fieret abbas, nisi sciret aliquid de
dialetica, et sciret discernere uerum a falso. Item dixit
quidam, qui sibi uidebatur sapiens : ' Stultum et
idiotam pastorem tribuat nobis omnipotens Dominus, ut
necesse sit ei se adiuuare de nobis.' Audiui scilicet
quendam uirum, industrium, et literatum, et nobilitate
generis splendidum, reprobatum esse a quibusdam
prioribus [2] nostris hac causa, quia nouicius erat. Nouicii
dicebant de prioribus suis, quod senes ualitudinarii erant
et ad abbatiam regendam minus idonei. Et ita multi
multa loquebantur, et unusquisque habundat in suo
sensu.[3] Uidi Samsonem subsacristam assidentem quondam[4] huiusmodi conuenticulis tempore minucionis,[5] quo
tempore claustrales solent alternatim secreta cordis
reuelare et adinuicem conferre, uidi eum assidentem et
subridentem et tacentem, et singulorum uerba notantem,
et aliqua ex prescriptis sentenciis in fine xx. annorum
memorantem. Quo audiente, solebam respondere ita
iudicantibus, dicens, quod, si debemus expectare ad
eligendum abbatem donec inueniamus aliquem qui sine
omni reprehensione et macula fuerit, nunquam talem
inueniemus, quia nemo sine crimine uiuit, et nichil omni
parte beatum.[6] Quodam tempore non potui cohibere
spiritum meum quin precipitarem sententiam meam,
putans me loqui fidis auribus, et dixi quendam indignum
abbatia, qui me multum dilexerat prius et multa bona
contulerat ; et alium dignum dixi, et nominaui aliquem,

---

[1] Cp. 1 Cor. xiii. 11
[2] *prioribus*, here virtually = ' seniors,' ' persons of importance.'
[3] Rom. xiv. 5
[4] The MS has *qm* ; previous editors give *quoniam*, which is meaningless.
Quondam seems a certain emendation.
[5] ' Blood-letting ' performed at stated intervals as a medical precaution.
The monks had three days off work on these occasions ; *licencia minucionis*

as a child and spoke as a child,' and I said that I would
not agree to any man being made Abbot, unless he knew
something of dialectic and could distinguish between
false argument and true. Again another, who thought
himself wise, said, ' May God Almighty give us for our
shepherd one who is a fool and ignorant, so that he will
have to ask us to help him ! ' And I heard indeed that
a certain man who was industrious and literate and of
noble birth, was condemned by certain of our seniors
because he was a novice, while the novices said of the
seniors that they were decrepit old men, unfit to rule the
Abbey. And so, many men said many things, and each
of them ' was fully persuaded in his own mind.' I once
saw Samson the sub-sacrist sitting by at gatherings of this
kind at the time of blood-letting, when the cloister monks
are wont to reveal the secrets of their hearts, each to
each, and to confer with one another—I saw him sitting
by and smiling, without a word, and noting the words
of each ; and I heard him repeat some of the aforesaid
opinions after twenty years had passed. And as he
listened, I used to reply to those who passed judgment
after this fashion, saying that if we had to wait to elect an
Abbot until we found someone who was free of all blame
and without spot, we should never find such an one, since
no one lives wholly without censure, and ' naught is in
all things blest.' On one occasion I could not contain
my spirit, but blurted out what I thought, thinking that
I spoke to faithful ears, and I said that a certain brother
was unworthy to be Abbot, though he had loved me and

---

was sometimes sought as a means of getting a rest or even a holiday. See
David Knowles, *The Monastic Order in England, 943–1216* (Cambridge 1940),
p. 455.
  [6] Horace, *Odes*, II. xvi. 27

quem minus diligebam. Loquebar secundum conscientiam meam, considerans pocius communem utilitatem
ecclesie quam meam promocionem, et uerum dixi ;
quod sequentia probauerunt. Et ecce unus ex filiis
Belial dictum meum reuelauit benefactori meo et amico ;
ob quam causam, usque ad hodiernum diem nunquam
postea nec prece nec precio [1] potui recuperare gratiam
eius ad plenum. Quod dixi, dixi,[2]

> et semel emissum uolat irreuocabile uerbum.[3]

Unum restat, quod caueam mihi de cetero, et, si
F.125 tamdiu / uixero ut uideam abbatiam uacare, uidebo quid,
cui, et quando loquar de tali materia, ne uel Deum
offendam mentiendo uel hominem importune loquendo.
Consilium meum tamen erit, si tamen durauero, ut
aliquem eligamus non multum bonum monachum, non
multum sapientem clericum, nec nimis idiotam nec
nimis dissolutum ; ne si nimis sapiat, de se et de proprio
sensu nimis confidat et alios uilipendat ; uel si nimis
brutescat, in opprobrium aliis fiat. Scio quis dixerit :
' medio tutissimus ibis [4] ; ' et illud, ' medium tenuere
beati.' Uel forte, sanius consilium erit omnino tacere,
ut dicam in corde meo : ' Qui potest capere, capiat.' [5]

Uacante abbatia perhendinauit Augustinus [6] archi-
piscopus Norweie apud nos in domibus abbatis, habens
per preceptum regis singulis diebus x. solidos de denariis
abbatie ; qui multum ualuit nobis ad habendam liberam
electionem nostram, testimonium perhibens de bono, et

---

[1] The play upon words is as old as the days of Cicero ; cp. *Auct. ad
Herenn.* III. 3, 4.
[2] John xix. 22
[3] Horace, *Epistles*, I. xviii. 71
[4] Ovid, *Metamorphoses*, II. 137
[5] Matt. xix. 12
[6] Augustinus (Eystein), Archbishop of Trondhjem, having refused to
crown Sverrir, who had deposed Magnus King of Norway, was driven

conferred many benefits upon me ; and said I thought
another worthy to be made Abbot, and named a man
whom I loved less.   And behold ! one of the sons of
Belial revealed what I had said to my benefactor and
friend : for which cause to this very day I have never
either by prayer or gift been able to recover his favour to
the full.   What I have said I have said, and

> The word once spoken flieth past recall.

One thing remains, that for the future I should be on
my guard and, if I live long enough to see the abbacy
vacant once again, I shall take care what I say on the
matter, and to whom and when I say it, lest I should
offend God by lying or man by speaking out of season.
It will, however, if I last till then, be my counsel that
we should choose one who is not too good a monk or too
good a clerk, nor yet too ignorant or too weak, lest, if he
know too much, he should be too confident in himself
and his opinions and disdain others, or, if he be too stupid,
should be a reproach to the rest of us.   I know who said
' The middle way is safest,' and ' How blest are they who
hold the middle path.'   Or perhaps it will be wiser to
say nothing at all, so that I may say in my heart, ' He
that is able to receive, let him receive it.'

While the abbacy was vacant, Augustine, Archbishop
of Norway, stayed with us in the Abbot's lodgings, receiving ten shillings daily from the Abbot's money, by
order of the King.   And he was of great help to us in
securing a free election, bearing witness to our merits
and declaring publicly in the King's presence what he

---

into exile, came to England and stayed at the Abbey of St. Edmund from
August 9, 1181, to February 16, 1182.   The accounts of the *bailliui* show
that they paid £94, 10s. for his expenses during that time.

publice protestans coram rege quod uiderat et audierat. Eodem tempore fuit sanctus puer Robertus [1] martirizatus, et in ecclesia nostra sepultus, et fiebant prodigia et signa multa in plebe, sicut alibi scripsimus.

Post mortem Hugonis abbatis, peracto anno cum tribus mensibus, precepit dominus rex per literas suas, ut prior noster et duodecim de conuentu, in quorum ore uniuersitatis concordaret sententia, apparerent die statuto coram eo, ad eligendum abbatem. In crastino post suscepcionem literarum, conuenimus in capitulo de tanto tractaturi negocio. In primis lecte sunt litere domini regis in conuentu ; postea rogauimus et honerauimus priorem in periculo anime sue, ut xii. secundum conscientiam suam nominaret secum ducendos, de quorum uita et moribus constaret eos a recto nolle deuiare. Qui petitis annuens, dictante Spiritu Sancto, sex ex una parte chori et sex ex altera [2] nominauit, et sine contradiccione nobis satisfecit. A dextro choro fuerunt Galfridus de Fordham, Benedictus, magister Dionisius, magister Samson subsacrista, Hugo tercius prior, et magister Hermerus, tunc temporis nouicius [3] : a sinistro, Willelmus sacrista, Andreas, Petrus de Broc, Rogerus celerarius, magister Ambrosius, magister Walterus medicus. Unus autem dixit : ' Quid fiet si isti tredecim non possunt coram rege concordare in abbate eligendo ? ' Respondit quidam quia ' hoc erit nobis

---

[1] Cp. the stories of Little St. William of Norwich (1137) and Little St. Hugh of Lincoln (1255) ; also the grotesque story of another ritual murder told by Richard of Devizes. Jocelin's work on the martyrdom of Little St. Robert has not survived. The date is recorded as June 10, 1181, by John of Taxster (*Florence of Worcester*, ed. Thorpe, ii. 155).

[2] I am indebted to the kindness of Dr. David Knowles for the following note, ' The monks proceed in and out of the choir two by two in strict order of seniority from reception as a novice—they also stand in choir from end to end in order of seniority. The two sides of the choir are thus

had seen and heard of us. At this same time the holy
boy Robert suffered martyrdom and was buried in our
church, and many signs and wonders were performed
among the common folk, as I have set down elsewhere.

After the death of Abbot Hugh, when a year and three
months were gone, our lord the King sent letters to us, .
commanding that our Prior and twelve of the Convent,
unanimously chosen by our whole body, should appear
before him on an appointed day to elect an Abbot. On
the day after we had received these letters we assembled
in the chapterhouse to deal with the matter. First of all
the King's letters were read before the Convent : after
this we asked the Prior and charged him on the peril of
his soul to nominate according to his conscience the
twelve whom he should take with him, men whose life
and character made it clear that they would refuse to
stray from the right way. And he, granting our petition
and inspired by the Holy Spirit, chose six from one side
of the choir and six from the other, and satisfied us, not
a voice being raised against his choice. From the right
side there were Geoffrey of Fordham, Benedict, Master
Denys, Master Samson the sub-sacrist, Hugh the third
prior, and Master Hermer, at that time a novice : from
the left William the Sacrist, Andrew, Peter of Brook,
Roger the Cellarer, Master Ambrose, and Master Walter
the physician. But one of us said, ' What will happen,
if those thirteen, when they come before the King, are

---

the only ready cross-section of the whole community. The Abbot's stall
was always on the right-hand side farthest from the altar ; the Prior's
corresponded on the other side.'

³ Jocelin seems to use *nouicius* at times of young professed monks, not
unprofessed novices. Novices form a group in Chapter to which novices
in the strict sense were not admitted. And here we have a novice chosen
as one of the electors. See Knowles, *op. cit.*, p. 423.

et ecclesie nostre in opprobrium sempiternum.' [1] Uoluerunt ideo plures ut electio fieret domi [2] antequam
ceteri recederent, ut per hanc prouidentiam non fieret
dissensio coram rege ; set illud nobis uidebatur stultum
et dissonum facere sine regis assensu, quia nondum constabat nobis posse impetrare a domino rege ut liberam
F.125v electionem haberemus.   Samson subsacrista / in spiritu
loquens : [3] ' Fiat,' inquid, ' media uia, ut hinc et inde
periculum euitetur.   Eligantur quatuor confessores de
conuentu et duo ex senioribus prioribus [4] de conuentu
bone opinionis, qui, uisis sacrosanctis,[5] tactis ewangeliis,
inter se eligant tres uiros de conuentu, ad hoc magis
idoneos iuxta regulam sancti Benedicti, et eorum nomina
in scriptum redigant, et scriptum sub sigillo includant,
et sic inclusum committatur nobis ituris ad curiam ; et
cum uenerimus coram rege, et constiterit nobis de libera
electione habenda, tunc demum frangatur sigillum, et
sic certi erimus qui tres nominandi erunt coram rege
[et constiterit nobis].[6] Si dominus rex noluerit concedere
nobis unum de nostris, reportetur sigillum integrum et
sex iuratoribus tradatur, ita quod secretum illorum
imperpetuum celetur in periculum animarum suarum.'
Huic consilio omnes adquieuimus, et nominati sunt
quatuor confessores ; scilicet Eustachius, Gilbertus de
Alued, Hugo tercius prior, Antonius, et alii duo senes,
Turstanus et Rualdus.   Quo facto, exiuimus cantantes,

---

[1] Jer. xxiii. 40
[2] See Appendix A
[3] 1 Cor. xxi. 3
[4] *senioribus* and *prioribus* are almost synonymous. The first lays stress
on their age, the second on their authority and influence.
[5] The holy mysteries of the Mass which they have seen celebrated
before taking their oath upon the Gospels.
[6] The words *et constiterit nobis* are repeated here in the MS, the scribe's
eye having strayed from *coram rege* to *coram rege* just above.

unable to agree in their choice of an Abbot ? ' And one
made answer, ' This will be an everlasting reproach to
us and to our Church.' Therefore a number of us were
for electing an Abbot at home before the others departed,
in order that by thus taking forethought there might be
no disagreement in the presence of the King. But it
seemed to us to be foolish and unseemly to do this without the King's assent, since we did not yet know whether
we should be able to secure a free election from our lord
the King. Samson the sub-sacrist, speaking in the spirit,
said, ' Let us take a middle course that we may avoid
peril on this side and on that. Let four confessors be
chosen from the Convent and two from among the elder of
our seniors, who are of good repute ; and let them when
they have looked upon the holy mysteries and laid their
hands upon the Gospels, choose three men from the
Convent whom they think best fitted for the office
according to the Rule of St. Benedict ; and let them
set down the names in writing and enclose what they
have written under seal ; and thus enclosed let it be con-
signed to those of us who are to go to the Court. And
when we are come into the King's presence and have
been assured of a free election, then at last let the seal
be broken, and thus we shall ascertain who are the three
whom we are to nominate before the King. If our lord
the King refuse to grant us one of our own house, the
seal shall be carried back unbroken and handed to the
six that have been sworn, so that their secret shall, on
peril of their souls, be hidden for ever. ' To this counsel
we all gave our assent : and four confessors were nominated, to wit Eustace, Gilbert of Elveden, Hugh the third
prior and Antony, and two others, Turstan and Ruald,
both of them old men. This done, we went out singing
' Verba mea,' and the aforesaid six remained behind,

'Uerba mea,'[1] et remanserunt predicti sex habentes
regulam sancti Benedicti pre manibus, et negocium sicut
prefinitum fuerat impleuerunt. Dum illi sex hoc tracta-
bant, nos de diuersis eligendis diuersa putabamus,
habentes tamen omnes quasi pro certo Samsonem esse
unum ex tribus, attendentes labores eius et pericula
mortis uersus Romam pro bonis ecclesie nostre, et qualiter
tractus et compeditus et incarceratus erat ab H. abbate,[2]
loquens pro communi utilitate; qui nec sic flecti potuit
ad adulandum, licet cogi potuit ad tacendum. Facta
autem mora, uocatus conuentus rediit in capitulum. Et
dixerunt senes se fecisse secundum quod preceptum eis
fuerat. Tunc prior quesiuit, quid fuerit si dominus rex
nollet aliquem ex illis tribus in scriptis recipere : et
responsum est, quod quemcunque uellet dominus rex
suscipere, susciperetur, dum modo esset processus[3]
ecclesie nostre. Adiectum est etiam quod, si illi tredecim
fratres uiderent aliquid in illo scripto quod emendari
deberet, secundum Deum de communi assensu uel consilio emendarent. Samson subsacrista sedens ad pedes
prioris dixit ecclesie expedire 'si omnes iuraremus in
uerbo ueritatis, ut super quemcumque sors electionis
caderet conuentum rationabiliter tractaret, nec capitales
obedienciales mutaret sine assensu conuentus, nec sacristam grauaret, nec aliquem monacaret sine uoluntate
conuentus ; ' et hoc ipsum concessimus, omnes dextras
erigentes in signum concessionis. Prouisum est quod, si
dominus rex uellet aliquem extraneum abbatem facere,

---

[1] The opening words of Ps. v, which was sung at the end of meetings
of the Chapter. Cp. p. 118, where the Prior closures a hot debate by singing
the psalm.
[2] See p. 48
[3] *Processus* is a noun

having the Rule of St. Benedict ready to hand ; and
thus they carried out the business according to their
instructions. While these six were thus busied, we held
divers opinions concerning those that should be chosen,
but every one of us was almost certain that Samson
would be one of the three, when we considered his labours
and the perils of death that he had faced when he
journeyed to Rome to defend the possessions of our
Church, and how he was haled away and fettered and
imprisoned by Abbot Hugh because he spoke out for the
common good, refusing to be bent to flattery, though he
might be forced to hold his tongue. But after some delay,
the Convent returned to the chapterhouse ; and the
seniors said that they had done as they were bidden.
Then the Prior asked what should be done if the King
refused to accept anyone of the three names that they
had written ; and he got the answer that we should
accept anyone whom our lord the King was ready to
accept, provided that he were a son of our Church. And
to this also was added that if these thirteen brethren saw
anything in that writing that needed correction, they
should alter it according to God's will, by the common
assent or counsel of them all. Samson the sub-sacrist,
who sat at the Prior's feet, said, ' It is expedient for the
sake of our Church that we should all swear upon the
word of truth that, on whomsoever the choice should
chance to fall, he should treat the Convent reasonably
and refrain from changing obedientiaries without the
consent of the Convent, or burdening the Sacrist or
admitting any man as a monk without the good-will of
the Convent.' And this we all of us granted, raising our
hands in token of assent. It was provided that if our
lord the King should desire to make Abbot one who was

non reciperetur a tredecim nisi per consilium fratrum domi remanencium.

In crastino ergo iter arripuerunt illi tredecim uersus curiam. Postremus omnium fuit Samson prouisor expensarum, quia subsacrista erat, circa collum scrinium portans, quo litere conuentus continebantur, quasi omnium minister solus, et, sine armigero, froggum suum F.126 in/ulnis baiulans, curiam exiuit, socios sequens a longe. In itinere uersus curiam conuenientibus fratribus in unum, dixit Samson bonum esse ut iurarent omnes, ut quicunque fieret abbas, redderet ecclesias de dominiis conuentus in usum hospitalitatis ; quod omnes concesserunt preter priorem, qui dixit : ' Satis iurauimus ; tantum potestis grauare abbatem, quod ego non curabo abbatiam.' Et hac occasione non iurauerunt ; et hoc bene actum est, quia si hoc esset iuratum, non esset obseruatum. Eodem die quo tredecim recesserunt, sedentibus nobis in claustro, dixit Willelmus de Hastinga unus ex fratribus nostris : ' Scio quod habemus abbatem unum de nostris ; ' et interrogatus quomodo hoc sciret, respondit, se uidisse in sompnis prophetam albis indutum stantem pre foribus monasterii, et se quesisse in nomine Domini utrum haberemus abbatem aliquem de nostris. Et respondit propheta : ' Habebitis unum de uestris, set seuiet inter uos ut lupus.' Cuius somnii significatio secuta in parte, quia futurus abbas studuit magis timeri quam amari, sicut plures dicebant. Assedit et alius

not of our Church, he should not be accepted by the
thirteen save with the counsel of the brethren who remained at home.

On the morrow therefore those thirteen set out upon
their journey to the Court. Last of them all went Samson, who had charge of their expenses, because he was
sub-sacristan. Hung about his neck he carried a case
containing the letters of the Convent, as though he were
the sole servant of them all ; and without any to squire
him, he went forth on his way to the Court, carrying his
frock tucked up on his arms and following his comrades
afar off. On the way to the Court, as the brethren talked
together, Samson said that it would be well that all of
them should swear that whosoever were made Abbot, he
should give back the Churches of the Convent's domain to
provide for the entertainment of guests, to which all gave
their assent save only the Prior who said, ' We have sworn
enough : you may put such a burden on the Abbot that
I for one should not care to have the abbacy.' And so on
this occasion they took no oath ; and it was well done,
because, if the oath had been sworn, it would not have
been kept. On the same day that the thirteen departed
from us, William of Hastings, one of our brethren, said
as we sat in the cloister, ' I know that we have one of
our own folk as Abbot.' And when he was asked how
he knew this, he said that he had seen in a vision, as
he slept, a prophet clad in white raiment standing before
the gate of the monastery, and that he had asked him
in the name of the Lord whether we should have one of
ourselves for Abbot. And the prophet replied, ' You
shall have one of your own, but he shall raven among
you like a wolf.' And the purport of the dream
was fulfilled in part, since he that was to be Abbot was
zealous to be feared rather than to be loved, as many

frater, Ædmundus nomine, asserens quod Samson futurus
esset abbas, et narrans uisionem quam proxima nocte
uiderat. Dixit se uidisse in sompnis R. celerarium et H.
tercium priorem stantes ante altare, et Sampsonem in
medio, eminentem ab humeris supra, pallio circum-
datum longo et talari, ligato in humeris eius, et stantem
quasi pugillem ad duellum faciendum. Et surrexit
sanctus Eadmundus de feretro, sicut ei sompnianti uisum
fuerat, et quasi languidus pedes et tibias nudas exposuit,
et accedente quodam et uolente operire pedes sancti,
dixit sanctus : ' Noli accedere. Ecce ! ille uelabit mihi
pedes,' protendens digitum uersus Samsonem. Hec est
interpretatio sompnii [1] :—Per hoc quod pugil uidebatur,
significatur quod futurus abbas semper in labore existens,[2]
quandoque mouens controuersiam contra archiepiscopum
Cantuariensem [3] de placitis corone, quandoque contra
milites Sancti Eadmundi pro scutagiis integre reddendis,[4]
quandoque cum burgensibus pro purpresturis in foro,[5]
quandoque cum sochemannis [6] pro sectis hundredorum ;
quasi pugil uolens pugnando superare aduersarios, ut iura
et libertates ecclesie sue posset reuocare. Uelauit autem
pedes sancti martiris, quando turres ecclesie a centum
annis inceptas perfecte consummauit.[7] Huiusmodi somp-
nia sompniabant fratres nostri, que statim diuulgabantur
primo per claustrum, postea per curiam, ita quod ante
uesperam publice dicebatur in plebe, ille et ille et ille
electi sunt, et unus eorum erit abbas.

Prior autem et xii. cum eo post labores et dilaciones

---

[1] Genesis xl. 12
[2] Grammar requires *existeret . . . mouens* or *existens . . . moueret*
[3] See pp. 50ff.
[4] See pp. 65ff.
[5] See p. 77
[6] No instance is given of any conflict with his sokemen
[7] By building the great Western tower

of us said.   And another brother was sitting with us, Edmund by name, who asserted that Samson would be Abbot, and told us of a vision that he had seen the night before.   He said that he had seen Roger the Cellarer and Hugh the third prior standing before the altar, and between them was Samson, towering above them from the shoulders upwards and wearing a long cloak that flowed down to his heels and was bound about his shoulders, and he stood with raised fists ready for a fight.   And St. Edmund arose from the feretory, as it seemed to him in his dreams and, as though some sickness was upon him, bared his feet and legs, and when someone drew near and would have covered his feet, the saint said, ' Draw not near ;   behold that man shall veil my feet ; ' and he pointed with his finger toward Samson.   Now this is the interpretation of the dream.   Inasmuch as he seemed like a fighter, it was foretold that the Abbot to be should live in toil, now contending with the Archbishop of Canterbury concerning the pleas of the crown, now against the knights of St. Edmund concerning the payment of full scutage, now with the burgesses over encroachments in the market, now with the sokemen over the suits of the hundreds, wishing like a fighter to overcome his adversaries in battle, that he might reclaim the rights and liberties of his Church.   As for the feet of the holy Martyr he veiled them, when he completed the towers of the church that were begun a hundred years before.   Such were the dreams our brothers dreamed, which were forthwith bruited abroad, first through the cloister and next through the court, so that before evening it was said openly among the common people, ' He and he and he have been chosen, and one of them will be Abbot.'

But the Prior and the twelve with him, after much

multas tandem steterunt coram rege apud Waltham,[1]
manerium Wintoniensis episcopi, secunda dominica
quadragesime. Quos dominus rex benigne suscepit, et
asserens se uelle secundum Deum agere et ad honorem
ecclesie nostre, precepit fratribus per internuntios, scilicet,
Ricardum episcopum Wintoniensem et G. cancellarium,
F.126v postea archiepiscopum Eboracensem / ut nominarent tres
de conuentu nostro. Prior uero et fratres se diuertentes,
quasi inde collocuturi, extraxerunt sigillum et fregerunt
et inuenerunt hec nomina sub tali ordine scripta,—
Samson subsacrista, R. celerarius, Hugo tercius prior.
Erubuerunt inde fratres qui maioris dignitatis erant.
Mirabantur etiam omnes eundem Hugonem esse elec-
torem et electum. Quia tamen rem mutare non poterant,
ordinem nominum de communi consilio mutauerunt,
pronuntiando primum H. quia tercius prior erat ;
secundo R. celerarium ; tercio Samsonem, facientes
uerbo tenus nouissimum primum et primum nouissimum.
Rex uero, primo querens an nati essent in sua terra, et
in cuius dominio, dixit se non nosse eos, mandans ut
cum illis tribus alios tres nominarent de conuentu. Quo
concesso, dixit W. sacrista : ' Prior noster debet nominari, quia capud nostrum est : ' quod cito concessum
est. Dixit prior : ' W. sacrista bonus uir est.' Similiter
dictum est de Dionisio, et concessum est. Quibus
nominatis coram rege sine omni mora, mirabatur rex,
dicens : ' Cito fecerunt isti. Deus est cum eis.' Postea
mandauit rex ut propter honorem regni sui nominarent
tres personas de aliis domibus. Quo audito, timebant
fratres suspicantes dolum. Tandem consilium inierunt

---

[1] Bishop's Waltham in Hampshire, February 21, 1182

toil and delay, at length stood before the King at
Waltham, a manor of the Bishop of Winchester, on
the second Sunday in Lent. Our lord the King received
them kindly and, declaring that he wished to act according to God's will and for the honour of the Church, he
commanded the brethren by the mouth of his intermediaries, Richard Bishop of Winchester and Geoffrey
the Chancellor, afterwards Archbishop of York, that
they should nominate three of our Convent. Whereupon the Prior and the brethren went aside, as though
to speak on this matter, and drew out the seal and broke
it, and found the names in the following order : Samson
the sub-sacrist, Roger the Cellarer and Hugh the third
prior. Whereat the brothers who were of higher rank
blushed. Moreover, all marvelled that the same Hugh
was both elector and elect. But since they could not
change the facts, by common consent they changed the
order, putting Hugh first, because he was third prior,
Roger the Cellarer second, and Samson third, making,
on the face of it, the first last and the last first. But the
King, after first enquiring whether those nominated
were born in his realm and within whose domain, said
that he did not know them and ordered that three others
of the Convent should be nominated as well as those
three. This being agreed, William the Sacrist said,
' Our Prior should be nominated because he is our
head.' This was readily allowed. Then said the Prior,
' William the Sacrist is a good man.' The same was
said of Denys, and it was allowed. These being nominated
without delay before the King, he marvelled saying,
' They have done this quickly ; God is with them.'
Afterwards the King demanded that for the honour of
his realm they should nominate three more from other
houses. Hearing this the brethren were afraid, suspecting

ut nominarent tres, set sub condicione, scilicet, ut nullum
reciperent nisi per consilium conuentus qui domi fuit.
Et nominauerunt tres, magistrum Nicholaum de Waringe-
ford, postea ad horam abbatem de Malmesberi ; et
Bertrandum priorem Sancte Fidis, postea abbatem de
Certeseia ; et dominum H. de Sancto Neoto, monachum
de Becco, uirum admodum religiosum et in temporalibus
et spiritualibus admodum circumspectum. Quo facto,
mandauit rex, gratias agens, ut tres remouerentur de
nouem, et statim remoti sunt alieni tres, scilicet prior
Sancte Fidei, postea Certeseiensis abbas, et Nicholaus
monachus Sancti Albani, postea abbas Malberiensis, et
prior Sancti Neoti. Willelmus sacrista sponte cessit ;
remoti sunt duo ex quinque per preceptum regis ; et
postea unus ex tribus, et remanserunt tantum duo,
scilicet, prior et Samson. Tunc tandem uocati sunt ad
consilium fratrum prenominati internuntii domini regis.
Et loquens Dionisius, unus pro omnibus, cepit commen-
dare personas prioris et Samsonis, dicens utrumque
eorum literatum, utrumque bonum, utrumque laudabilis
uite et integre opinionis, set semper in angulo sui sermonis
Samsonem pretulit, multiplicans uerba in laudem eius,
dicens eum esse uirum rigidum in conuersacione, seuerum
in corrigendis excessibus, et aptum ad labores, et in
secularibus curis prudentem, et in diuersis officiis pro-
batum. Respondit Wintoniensis : ' Bene intelligimus
quod uultis dicere ; ex uerbis uestris coniicimus quod
prior uester uobis uidetur aliquantulum remissus, et
illum qui Samson dicitur uultis habere.' Respondit
Dionisius : ' Uterque bonus est, set melliorem uellemus

guile. At length they agreed to name three, but on this condition that they should accept none of them without the counsel of those of the Convent who remained at home. And they nominated three : Master Nicholas of Wallingford, later and at the present time Abbot of Malmesbury, Bertrand, Prior of St. Faith, afterwards Abbot of Chertsey, and the Lord H. of St. Neots, a monk of Bec, a man of great religion and very circumspect both in matters temporal and spiritual. This done, the King thanked them and gave orders that three out of the nine should be struck off the list, whereupon the three aliens were at once removed, to wit, the Prior of St. Faith afterwards Abbot of Chertsey, Nicholas, monk of St. Albans, afterwards Abbot of Malmesbury, and the Prior of St. Neots. William the Sacrist withdrew of his own free will : two of the remaining five were struck off by order of the King, and then one of the three remaining, two only being left, namely the Prior and Samson. Finally the intermediaries of our lord the King whom I have mentioned above, were called in to take counsel with the brethren. And Denys, speaking for us all, began to commend the persons of the Prior and Samson, saying that both were literate, both good, both of praiseworthy life and of unblemished reputation ; but always in the corner of his speech thrusting Samson forward, multiplying the words he uttered in his praise and saying that he was a man strict in his behaviour, stern in chastising transgressions, a hard worker, prudent in wordly business, and proved in divers offices. The Bishop of Winchester replied, ' We understand clearly what you mean ; from your words we gather that your Prior seems to you to be somewhat slack and that you desire him whom you call Samson.' Denys replied, ' Both of them are good, but we should like, God willing, to have

habere si Deus uellet.' Cui episcopus : ' Duorum
bonorum magis bonum eligendum est : dicite aperte,
uultis habere Samsonem ? ' Et responsum est precise
a pluribus et a maiori parte, ' Uolumus Samsonem,'/
F.127 nullo reclamante, quibusdam tamen tacentibus ex industria, nec hunc nec illum offendere uolentibus.
Nominato Samsone coram domino rege, et habito breui
consilio cum suis, uocati sunt omnes, et dixit rex : ' Uos
presentastis mihi Samsonem : non noui eum : si pre-
sentaretis mihi priorem uestrum, illum reciperem quem
uidi et agnoui ; set modo faciam quod uultis. Cauete
uobis ; per ueros oculos Dei, si male feceritis, ego me
capiam ad uos.' Et interrogauit priorem si assentiret
et hoc uellet ; qui respondit se hoc uelle, et Samsonem
multo maiore dignum honore. Electus ergo, ad pedes
regis procidens et deosculans, festinanter surrexit et
festinanter ad altare tetendit, cantando : ' Miserere mei
Deus,' [1] cum fratribus, erecto capite, uultu non mutato.
Quod cum rex uidisset, dixit astantibus : ' Per oculos
Dei, iste electus uidetur sibi dignus abbatie custodiende.'
Huius electionis rumor cum ad conuentum perueniret,
omnes claustrales uel fere omnes, et quosdam obedienciales, set paucos, letificauit : ' Bene,' multi dicebant,
' quia bene est.' Alii dicebant quod ' non ; immo,
omnes seducti sumus.' Electus, antequam rediret ad
nos, benedictionem [2] suam accepit a domino Wintoniensi,
qui in eadem hora mitram capiti abbatis imponens et
anulum digito, ait : ' Hec est dignitas [3] abbatum sancti
Eadmundi : diu est ex quo sciui hoc.' Abbas itaque

---

[1] Ps. li (Vulgate Ps. l)
[2] At Merewell in the Isle of Wight, 28th February. The Bishop of
Winchester was assisted by the Bishop of Waterford (see *Mem.* II. 5 ;
III. 7).
[3] The right to the mitre and the ring

the better.' The Bishop made answer, ' Of two good
men you must choose the better. Tell me openly, do
you wish to have Samson ? ' And a number, making a
majority, answered clearly, ' We want Samson,' not
a voice being raised against them, though some of set
purpose said nothing, because they wished to offend
neither the one or the other. Samson then having been
nominated in the presence of the King, and the latter
having taken brief counsel with his advisers, all the rest
were summoned, and the King said, ' You have presented
Samson to me : I do not know him. If you had presented your Prior, I should have accepted him ; for I
have seen him and know him. But, as it is, I will do
what you desire. But have a care ; for by the very eyes
of God, if you do ill, I will be at you ! ' He then asked
the Prior, if he agreed to this and desired it. The Prior
answered that he did desire it and that Samson was
much more worthy of honour. The elect therefore fell
at the King's feet and kissed them, then rose in haste,
and in haste went to the altar with the brethren, singing
' Miserere mei, Deus,' his head held high and his
countenance unchanged. And when the King saw this,
he said to those who stood by, ' By God's eyes, this
elect thinks himself worthy to be the guardian of his
Abbey.' When the news of this election reached the
Convent, it gladdened all the cloister monks, or nearly
all, and certain of the obedientiaries, but only a few.
' It is well,' said many, ' because it is well.' Others said,
' Nay, in truth we have all been deceived.' The elect,
before he returned to us, received his benediction from
the Lord Bishop of Winchester, who at the same time
placed the mitre on his head and the ring upon his
finger, saying, ' This is the dignity of the Abbots of St.
Edmund : it is long since I knew this.' The Abbot

tres monachos secum retinens, alios domum premisit,
nuncians aduentum suum Dominica Palmarum,[1] quibusdam commendans curam ad prouidenda necessaria in
die festi sui. Redeunti multitudo nouorum parentum
occurrit, uolentium ei seruire ; qui omnibus respondit,
se esse contentum seruientibus prioris, nec alios posse
retinere, donec inde consuluisset conuentum suum.
Unum tamen militem retinuit eloquentem et iuris
peritum, non tantum consideracione proximitatis, set
ratione utilitatis, causis quidem secularibus assuetum ;
quem suscepit in nouitate sua quasi coadiutorem in
mundanis controuersiis, quia nouus abbas erat, et rudis
in talibus, sicut ipsemet protestatus est : quia nunquam
ante susceptam abbatiam loco interfuit ubi datum esset
uadium et plegium.[2] Cum debito honore et etiam
processione receptus est a conuentu suo, Dominica
Palmarum.

Susceptus est autem dominus abbas hoc modo :
proxima nocte iacuerat apud Chenteford, et accepta
temporis oportunitate, iuimus contra eum sollempniter,
post exitum de capitulo, usque ad portam cimiterii,
sonantibus campanis in choro et extra. Ipse uero
multitudine hominum constipatus, uidens conuentum,
descendit de equo extra limen porte, et faciens se
discalciari, intra portam nudipes susceptus est, priore
et sacrista hinc et inde ducentibus eum. Nos uero
cantauimus responsoria,[3] ' Benedictus Dominus,' de
F.127v Trinitate :   et post, ' Martiri / adhuc,' [4] de sancto

[1] 21st March
[2] *i.e.*, he had no experience of a secular court
[3] The words of this response at Matins on the feast of the Holy Trinity
run as follows : Resp. *Benedictus Dominus Deus Israel : qui facit mirabilia
solus. Et benedictum nomen Eius in eternum.* V. *Replebitur maiestate Eius omnis
terra : fiat, fiat.*
[4] See Appendix B

then, keeping three monks with him, sent all the rest home in advance, announcing that he would come to them on Palm Sunday, and charging some of them with the duty of providing all that was necessary for his feast. On his return journey a multitude of new kinsmen went to meet him, desiring to be taken into his service. But to all of them he made answer that he was content with the Prior's servants, and could not keep any others until he had consulted the Convent on the matter. But one knight he kept with him, an eloquent man and skilled in the law, not so much on account of his kinship, but for his usefulness, since he was accustomed to secular business. So being new in office he took him to be his helper in worldly disputes ; for he had but now received the abbacy and was unused to such matters, as he himself protested, since before he became Abbot he was never in any place where gage and pledge were given. He was received by the Convent on Palm Sunday with all due honour and a procession as well.

Now the manner in which the Lord Abbot was received was thus. On the night before, he lay at Kentford, and we, taking advantage of the opportunity, as soon as we had left the chapterhouse, went out in solemn state to meet him at the gate of the cemetery, while the bells both within the choir and without all rang together. But he, surrounded as he was by a multitude of men, as soon as he saw the Convent, dismounted from his horse outside the threshold of the gate, and after causing his sandals to be taken off, was received barefoot within the gate, the Prior and the Sacrist walking on either side. We on our part sang the responses ' Benedictus Dominus ' from the office for Trinity Sunday and ' Martyri adhuc ' from the office for the Feast of St. Edmund, and led the Abbot right

Eadmundo : ducentes abbatem usque ad magnum
altare. Quibus peractis, siluerunt et organa et campane,
et dicta oratione a priore,[1] ' Omnipotens sempiterne
Deus, miserere huic,' &c. super abbatem prostratum,
et facta oblacione ab abbate, et deosculato feretro, rediit
in chorum, et ibi recepit eum Samson cantor per manum,
et duxit usque ad sedem abbatis ad occidentalem partem,
ubi, eo stante, in directum incepit cantor : ' Te Deum
laudamus ; ' quod dum decantabatur, deosculatur a
priore et a toto conuentu per ordinem. Quibus expletis,
iuit abbas in capitulum, sequente conuentu et multis
aliis. Dicto autem ' Benedicite,'[2] in primis gratias egit
conuentui quod eum, ut aiebat, minimum eorum, non
suis meritis, set sola Dei uoluntate, in dominum et
pastorem elegerunt. Rogansque breuiter ut orarent pro
eo, conuertit sermonem ad clericos et milites, rogans, ut
eum consulerent ad sollicitudinem commissi regiminis.
Et respondens Wimerus uicecomes pro omnibus, dixit :
' Et nos parati sumus uobis consistere in consilio et auxilio omnibus modis, sicut caro domino quem Dominus
uocauit ad honorem suum et ad honorem sancti martiris
Eadmundi.' Et deinde extracte sunt carte regis, et lecte
in audientia de donacione abbatie. Facta autem oratione ab ipso abbate, ut ei Deus consuleret secundum
gratiam suam, et responso ' amen ' ab omnibus, iuit
conuentus ad primam missam. Abbas uero adhuc
nudipes iuit in talamum suum, diem festiuum agens
cum plus quam mille comedentibus, in gaudio
magno.

---

[1] The prayer runs : *Omnipotens sempiterne Deus, miserere famulo tuo et
dirige eum secundum tuam clementiam in uiam salutis eterne ut te donante tibi placita
cupiat et tota uirtute perficiat per Dominum*, etc. (Muratori, *Lit. Romana uetus*,
Venice 1748, II. col. 194)
[2] The greeting of the Abbot to his monks and of the monks to their
Abbot

up to the High Altar. This done, the organs and the bells were silent, and the Prior said the prayer ' Omnipotens sempiterne Deus miserere huic, etc.' over the Abbot lying prostrate. Then the Abbot made an oblation and kissed the feretory, after which he returned into the choir, and there Samson the Precentor took him by the hand and led him to the Abbot's seat at the west end of the choir, where (the Abbot still standing) the Precentor forthwith began to chant the ' Te deum laudamus ' ; and while this was being sung the Abbot was kissed by the Prior and by the whole Convent in order. These things being accomplished, the Abbot went into the chapterhouse followed by the Convent and many others. And after we had said ' Benedicite,' he first gave thanks to the Convent, because they had, not according to his deserts but by the will of God, chosen him, the least of them all (as he said), to be their lord and shepherd ; and after briefly asking them to pray for him, he turned to address the clerks and knights, asking them to advise him for the performance of the anxious duties of the governance committed to his care. And Wimer the Sheriff speaking for them all made answer saying, ' Aye, and we are ready to stand by you and give you counsel and to aid you in every way, as being our beloved lord, whom God has called for His own honour and for the honour of Edmund the holy Martyr.' Then the charters of the King concerning the donation of the abbacy were produced and read for all to hear. And after the Abbot had said a prayer beseeching God to care for him according to His grace, and all present had answered ' Amen,' the Convent went to the first Mass. Then the Abbot, still barefoot, went to his lodgings, where he held his feast amid great rejoicing, more than a thousand dining with him.

Quando hec fiebant, eram capellanus prioris, et infra
quatuor menses capellanus abbatis factus, plurima notans
et memorie commendans. In crastino ergo festi sui,
conuocauit priorem et alios quosdam paucos, quasi
consilium ab aliis querens : ipse enim sciebat quid esset
facturus.[1] Dixit nouum sigillum esse faciendum, et cum
mitra esse pingendum, licet predecessores sui tale non
haberent : sigillo autem prioris nostri hucusque usus
fuerat, singulis literis in fine subscribens, quod proprium
sigillum non habuit, unde et sigillo prioris oportuit uti
ad tempus. Postea disponens domui sue, diuersos
famulos diuersis officiis deputauit, dicens se precogitasse
uiginti sex equos in curia sua habendos ; et ad plus
asserens, 'puerum prius repere, postea firmius stare et
ire :' hoc super omnia famulis precipiens, ut cauerent
ne in nouitate sua possit infamari auaricia cibi uel potus,
set hospitalitatem domus solicite procurarent. In hiis
et in omnibus rebus agendis et constituendis de Dei
auxilio et proprio sensu plenius confidens, inglorium
duxit de alieno pendere consilio, tanquam ipse sibi
F.128 sufficeret. Mi / rabantur monachi, indignabantur milites ;
dampnantes eum arrogantia, et quodammodo infamantes
eum apud curiam regis, et dicentes quia nollet operari
secundum consilium suorum liberorum hominum. Ipse
magnates abbacie, tam laicos quam literatos, sine quorum
consilio et auxilio abbatia uidebatur non posse regi,
omnes a priuato suo elongauit consilio ; et hac occasione
Ranulfus de Glanuill, iusticiarius Anglie, primo eum
suspectum habebat, et minus propicius ei erat quam
deceret, donec ei certis indiciis constaret abbatem tam

---

[1] John vi. 6

When these things were done, I was the Prior's chaplain, and within four months I was made chaplain to the Abbot, and noted many things and stored them in my memory. On the morrow of his feast, then, he summoned the Prior and a few others as though to receive their counsel ; for ' he himself knew what he would do.' He said that a new seal must be made and that he should be represented with a mitre, though his predecessors had no such thing on their seals. Up to this time he used the Prior's seal, adding at the end of each letter that he had no seal of his own, wherefore he had to use the Prior's for the time being. Afterwards he made arrangements for his own house, and appointed divers servants to divers offices, saying that he had already determined to keep twenty-six horses in his court, and further declaring that a child must crawl before he can stand and walk securely. And he instructed his servants that they should above all see to it that, while he was new in office, no reproach should be brought against him of niggardliness in respect of food or drink, and that they should be at pains to provide fittingly for the hospitality of his house. And since in this and in all else that he did he had a firm trust in the help of God and in his own good sense, he thought it discreditable to lean upon the counsel of another, considering that he was sufficient unto himself. The monks marvelled, the knights were angry, condemning his arrogance and speaking evil of him at the King's court, and saying that he refused to follow the advice of his free men. He himself banished from his private counsels all the great men of the Abbey, both lay and literate, without whose advice and help it seemed that the Abbey could not be governed. Wherefore Ranulph de Glanvill, the Justiciar

in interioribus quam exterioribus negociis prouide et prudenter agere.

Facta summonicione generali, conueniunt omnes barones et milites et liberi homines ut facerent homagium quarto die Pasce : et ecce ! Thomas de Hastinga, cum magna multitudine militum, ducens Henricum nepotem suum nondum militem, clamans senescaldiam cum consuetudinibus suis, sicut carta eius loquitur. Quibus abbas statim respondit : ' Henrico non nego ius suum, nec negare uolo. Si sciret in propria persona mihi seruire, concederem ei et decem hominibus et octo equis necessaria in mea curia, sicut carta eius loquitur : si presentetis mihi senescaldum, uicarium eius, qui sciat et possit senescaldiam regere, recipiam eum in tali statu, sicut predecessor meus eum habuit die qua fuit uiuus et mortuus, scilicet cum iiij^{or} equis et pertinenciis. Quod si nolueritis, pono loquelam coram rege uel coram capitali iusticia.' Quo dicto, cepit res dilacionem : postea presentatus est ei quidam senescaldus simplex et idiota, Gilbertus nomine, quem antequam suscepisset, dixit familiaribus suis : ' Si defectus fuerit de iustitia regis servanda per insciciam senescaldi, ipse erit in misericordia regis et non ego, quia senescaldiam uendicat sibi iure hereditario : et ideo ad presens malo istum recipere, quam alium magis argutum ad me decipiendum. Ego mihi ero senescaldus cum auxilio Dei.'

Post homagia suscepta, petiuit abbas auxilium a militibus,[1] qui promiserunt ab unoquoque xx. solidos ; sed in

---

[1] The Abbot held his barony of the King by service of 40 knights, but had twelve other knights' fees owing no service to the King (see Appendix O). But the custom had grown up that all 52 knights should take a share in contributing the money demanded as scutage or castleward. They now proposed to do the same in respect of the aid demanded by the Abbot. His revenge is recorded on p. 65. A list is to be found of his knights' fees on p. 120. It will be noticed that there the total amounts to 52¾. But here Jocelin confines himself to round numbers.

of England, was at first suspicious of him and less well disposed toward him than was seemly, until clear evidence showed him that the Abbot acted with foresight and prudence in all his business whether within or without his house.

A general summons having been issued, all the barons and knights and free men came to do homage to him on the fourth day of Easter. And lo and behold, Thomas de Hastings came with a great multitude of knights, bringing with him Henry his nephew, who was not yet a knight, and claiming the stewardship on his behalf together with all the customs as stated in his charter. To this the Abbot at once made answer, ' Henry's rights I neither deny, nor wish to deny them. If he was able to serve me in person, I would give him all that is needful for the maintenance of ten men and eight horses in my court, as is stated in his charter. If you should present to me as his substitute, a steward who knows how to perform the duties of stewardship, I would accept him on the same terms as my predecessor granted to his steward on the day whereon he, the Abbot, was alive and dead, to wit, four horses and their appurtenances. But if you will not agree thereto, I place my plea before the King or his Chief Justice.' This said, the matter was postponed. Afterwards there was presented to him a simple and ignorant steward, Gilbert by name ; but before he accepted him, he said to his friends, ' If there is any default in the King's justice through the ignorance of the steward, it is he not I that will be accountable to the King, since he claims the stewardship by hereditary right : and therefore I prefer to accept him for the time being rather than take one who may be more skilled to deceive me. God helping, I will be my own steward.'

instanti inierunt consilium, et retraxerunt duodecim libras de duodecim militibus, dicentes, quod illi xii. debent
adiuuare alios xl. et ad wardas faciendas et ad scutagia,[1]
similiter et ad auxilium abbatis. Quod cum abbas audisset, iratus est, et dixit familiaribus suis, quod, si posset
uiuere, redderet eis uicem pro uice et grauamen pro grauamine. Post hec, per unumquodque manerium abbatie
fecit abbas inquiri annuos census liberorum hominum,[2]
et nomina rusticorum, et eorum tenementa, et singulorum
seruicia, et in scriptum omnia redigi. Aulas autem
ueteres et domos confractas, per quas milui et cornices
uolabant, reformauit ; capellas nouas edificauit, et /
F.128v talamos et solia pluribus locis, ubi nunquam fuerunt
edificia, nisi horrea solummodo. Plures etiam parcos
fecit, quos bestiis repleuit, uenatorem cum canibus
habens ; et, superueniente aliquo hospite magni nominis,
sedebat cum monachis suis in aliquo saltu nemoris, et
uidebat aliquando canes currere ; set de uenacione
nunquam uidi eum gustare. Plura etiam assartauit et
in agriculturam reduxit, in omnibus utilitati abbatie
prospiciens : set utinam super maneriis conuentus com-
mendandis consimili studio uigilaret. Maneria tamen
nostra de Bradefeld et Rutham recepit ad tempus in
manu sua, implens defectus firmarum per expensam xl.
librarum, que postea resignauit nobis, audito quod murmur erat in conuentu ex hoc quod maneria nostra tenuit
in manu sua. Eisdem etiam maneriis et omnibus aliis

---

[1] The term ' scutage ' is first found in a writ of Henry I ; see F. M.
Stenton, *English Feudalism*, Chap. 5. The document is printed in EHR
xxxvi (W. A. Morris) ; there it applies only to ecclesiastical tenants ; later
references to lay tenants become frequent. For the position of ecclesiastical
tenants at the close of twelfth century see Appendix Q.

[2] See Appendix C

After he had received homage, the Abbot demanded an aid from his knights, who promised him twenty shillings each ; but they had no sooner done so than they took counsel together and withdrew twelve pounds in respect of twelve knights, saying that those twelve ought to help the other forty in respect of castleward and scutages and likewise of aids to the Abbot. When the Abbot heard this, he was angry and said to his friends that, if he lived, he would render them like for like, and trouble for trouble. After this the Abbot caused an inquiry to be made as to the annual rents due from the free men in each manor and as to the names of the peasants and their holdings and the services due from each ; and he had them all set down in writing. But he restored old halls and ruinous houses, through which kites and crows were flying ; he built new chapels and lodgings and chambers in many places, where there had never before been buildings save only barns. He also made a number of parks which he filled with beasts, and kept a huntsman and hounds ; and when any distinguished guest came to him, he would sit at times with his monks in some woodland glade and watch the hounds run ; but I never saw him taste venison. He also cleared many lands and brought them back into cultivation, but would that he had shown like zeal and vigilance in his bestowal of the manors of the Convent. None the less he took our manors of Bradfield and Rougham into his own hands for the time being, making good the deficit in the rent by the expenditure of forty pounds ; these manors he afterwards returned to us, having heard that there were murmurs in the Convent because he kept our manors in his own hands. Also to rule these same manors and all others, he appointed both monks and laymen who were wiser than their

regendis, tam monachos quam laicos sapientiores prioribus custodibus constituit, qui et nobis et terris nostris
consultius prouiderent. Octo etiam hundredos in manu
sua, et post mortem Roberti [1] de Cokefeld recepit hundredum de Cosford, quos omnes seruientibus suis de mensa
sua custodiendos tradidit; que maioris questionis erant ad
se referens, et que minoris per alios terminans, et singula
ad suum commodum retorquens. Facta, eo iubente,
descriptio generalis [2] per hundredos de letis [3] et sectis,[4]
de hidagiis [5] et fodercorn,[6] de gallinis [7] reddendis, et aliis
consuetudinibus [8] et redditibus et exitibus, qui in magna
parte semper celati fuerant per firmarios, et omnia
redegit in scriptum, ita quod, infra iiii[or] annos ab elec-
cione sua, non erat qui posset eum decipere de redditibus
abbatie ad ualentiam unius denarii, cum de abbatia
custodienda nullum scriptum a predecessoribus suis recepisset, nisi sedulam paruam, qua continebantur nomina
militum Sancti Eadmundi et nomina maneriorum, et que
firma quam firmam sequi deberet. Hunc autem librum
uocauit Kalendarium suum, quo etiam inscribebantur
singula debita que adquietauerat ; quem librum fere
cotidie inspexit, tanquam ibi consideraret uultum probitatis sue in speculo.

Prima die qua tenuit capitulum, confirmauit nobis
nouo sigillo suo lx. solidos de Suthreia,[9] quos predecessores

---

[1] See pp. 8, 10, 51
[2] This Kalendarium is in Cambridge University Library (Add. MS.
6006). See Gage, *Hist. of Suffolk*, ' Hundred of Thingoe'; Douglas, FD
xxvi and clxiff, and *Social Structure of E. Anglia*, pp. 193ff.
[3] See Appendix D
[4] This section of the Kalendar deals with suits mostly to the Hundred
Court, but in some cases to the Aula or Manorial Court. The suits owed
by each vill are given. Then follows a statement of the number of carucates
in the hundred.
[5] Next follows a list of hidage and other dues in the vills of the nine
leets. Hidage is the money due to the Abbot per hide of land. The rate
works out approximately at a penny an acre.
[6] This given in the next section of the Kalendar under the head of
avena, fodder for the Abbot's horses

former wardens, that they might make more prudent provision for ourselves and our lands.   He kept eight hundreds in his own hands, and after the death of Robert de Cockfield he recovered the hundred of Cosford—all of which hundreds he handed over to the custody of his sergeants who ate at his own board, keeping the more important questions for himself and settling those of lesser importance through the agency of others, and turning everything to his own profit.   At his bidding a general inventory was made, in each hundred, of leets and suits, hidages and corn-dues, payments of hens, and other customs, revenues and expenses, which had hitherto been largely concealed by the tenants : and he had all these things set down in writing, so that within four years from his election there was not one who could deceive him concerning the revenues of the Abbey to a single pennyworth, and this although he had not received anything in writing from his predecessors concerning the administration of the Abbey, save for one small sheet containing the names of the knights of St. Edmund, the names of the manors and the rent due from each tenancy. Now this book, in which were also recorded the debts which he had paid off, he called his Kalendar, and consulted it almost every day, as though he could see therein the image of his own efficiency as in a mirror.

On the first day on which he held a Chapter, he confirmed to us with his new seal sixty shillings from Southrey, which his predecessors had unjustly taken for themselves, having received it in the first instance from

---

[7] No special section is given to this item.   But payment of one or more hens occurs from time to time.

[8] Such as *warpeni*, an old payment due once to the crown, but now to the abbey.   See FD p. cxxiv.

[9] See Appendix E

sui iniuste receperant primo ab Eadmundo, aureo
monacho dicto, ut posset tenere eandem uillam ad
firmam omnibus diebus uite sue. Et proposuit edictum
ut nullus de cetero ornamenta ecclesie inuadiaret sine
assensu conuentus, sicut solebat fieri, nec aliqua carta
sigillaretur sigillo conuentus nisi in capitulo coram
conuentu ; et fecit Hugonem subsacristam, statuens ut
Willelmus sacrista nichil omnino ageret de sacristia, nec
in receptis nec in expensis, nisi per assensum eius. Post
hec, set non eodem die, antiquos custodes oblacionum
transtulit ad alia officia. Postremo ipsum W. deposuit ;
unde quidam diligentes Willelmum dicebant : ' Ecce
abbas ! ecce lupus de quo sompniatum est ! ecce qualiter
seuit : ' et uoluerunt facere quidam conspiracionem
contra abbatem. Quod cum abbati reuelatum esset,
F.129 uolens / nec omnino tacere nec conuentum turbare,
intrauit capitulum in crastino, extrahens sacculum
plenum cartis cancellatis adhuc sigillis pendentibus,
scilicet, predecessoris sui, et partim prioris, partim
sacriste, partim camerarii, et aliorum officialium, quarum
summa erat trium millium librarum et lii., et una marca
de pura sorte,[1] preter usuram que excreuerat, cuius
magnitudo nunquam sciri poterat : de quibus omnibus
pacem fecerat infra annum post eleccionem suam, et
infra xii. annos omnia adquietauit. ' Ecce,' inquit,
' sapientia sacriste uestri Willelmi ! Ecce tot carte
sigillo eius signate, cum quibus impignorauerat cappas
sericas, dalmaticas,[2] turribula argenti, et textus aureos,[3]

---

[1] *Sors* is the classical equivalent for *katallum* in the sense of ' capital.'
[2] Permission was obtained from Alexander III, and again from Urban
for the use of the vestments known as dalmatics. See the *Pinchbeck Register*
(ed. by Lord Francis Hervey, 1925), ff.3b and 11b.
[3] The exact meaning is uncertain. It may mean ' Gospels written in
gold,' or ' Gospels richly illuminated in gold.'

Edmund, styled ' the golden monk,' that he might hold
the said township all the days of his life.   And he issued
an edict that henceforth no man should pledge any of
the ornaments of the church without the consent of the
Convent, as was commonly done, and that no charter
should be sealed with the seal of the Convent save in
Chapter in the presence of the Convent.   And he made
Hugh sub-sacrist, giving orders that William the Sacrist
should do nothing in the sacristy in respect either of
revenues or expenses, save with his assent.   After this,
but not on the same day, he transferred the former
guardians of the oblations to other offices.   And last of
all he deposed William himself ; whereat some who
loved William said, ' Behold the Abbot ! Behold the
wolf of the dream !   Behold how he ravens ! ' and some
wished to make a conspiracy against the Abbot.   But
this being revealed to the Abbot, since he did not wish
to keep wholly silent on the matter nor yet to disquiet
the Convent, he entered the Chapter on the morrow,
drawing forth a bag full of cancelled bonds, with
their seals still hanging from them, to wit, bonds given
some by his predecessor, some by the Prior, some by the
Sacrist, and some by the Chamberlain and other officials
—the total amounting to three thousand and fifty-two
pounds and one mark, all of capital alone apart from
the accumulated interest, the amount of which could
never be determined.   For all these bonds he had come
to terms within a year of his election, and within twelve
years he had paid them all.   ' Behold,' he said, ' the
wisdom of your Sacrist William ! Behold all these bonds
sealed with his seal, in which he has pledged silken
copes, dalmatics, silver thuribles and Gospels bound in

sine conuentu, que omnia adquietaui et uobis reconsig-
naui : ' et multa alia adiecit, ostendens quare deposuerat
W. ; precipuam tamen causam subticuit, nolens eum
scandalizare. Et cum substituisset Samsonem cantorem,
nobis omnibus placentem et omni exceptione maiorem,
in pace facta sunt omnia. Abbas uero domos sacriste
in cimiterio funditus precepit erui, tanquam non essent
digne stare super terram, propter frequentes bibaciones
et quedam tacenda, que nolens et dolens uiderat quando
fuit subsacrista ; et ita omnia complanari fecit, quod
infra annum, ubi steterat nobile edificium, uidimus fabas
pullulare, et ubi iacuerant dolia uini, urticas habundare.

Post clausum Pasche [1] iuit abbas per singula maneria
sua et nostra, et per illa que confirmauimus in feudum
firmariis, poscens ab omnibus et a singulis auxilium et
recognicionem [2] secundum consuetudinem regni ; cotidie
seculari scientia proficiens, et ad exteriora negocia dis-
cenda et promouenda animum conuertens. Cum autem
uenisset apud Werketunam, et nocte dormisset, uenit ei
uox, dicens : ' Samson, surge uelociter,' [3] et iterum,
' Surge, nimis moraris ; ' et surgens stupefactus, circumquaque respexit, et uidit lumen in domo necessaria,
candelam scilicet, paratam cadere super stramen, quam
Reinerus monachus ibi per incuriam reliquerat. Quam
cum abbas extinxisset, pergens per domum percepit
ostium, quod unicum erat, ita obseratum quod aperiri
non potuit nisi per clauem, et fenestras strictas, ita quod,

---

[1] The close of Easter is the next Monday after Easter week, known
as Hock Monday.

[2] *auxilium* is a general term, *recognicio* a more technical term for customary dues paid to the lord, in this case the Abbot, on his succession. The
two words are to be taken together. Cp. the account of *auxilia et recog-
niciones*, collected in the first year of John of Northwold (Abbot, 1371),
contained in *Pinchbeck Register*, f.201b.

[3] Acts xii. 7

gold, without leave of the Convent ; and all these things I have redeemed and restored to you.' And he added much else to show why he had deposed William ; but the chief cause he did not mention, not wishing to make a scandal of him. And when he had appointed Samson the Precentor in his place, a man who pleased all of us and was beyond all blame, all was peace again. But the Abbot caused the houses of the Sacristan in the cemetery to be razed to the ground, as being unworthy to stand upon the earth, on account of the frequent wine-bibbing and other things of which it is best to say nothing, which willy-nilly he had witnessed when he was sub-sacrist ; and so he ordered all to be levelled to the ground, so that within a year, in the place where a fine building had stood, we saw beans sprouting, and nettles in abundance where once had lain jars of wine.

After the close of Easter the Abbot visited all his manors and ours, and those too which we had confirmed in fee to tenants, demanding from each and all an aid and recognition, according to the custom of the realm ; and he grew daily in worldly knowledge and turned his mind to study and forward the external business of the Abbey. Now when he was come to Warkton and had fallen asleep at night, a voice came to him, saying, ' Samson, arise quickly ! ' and again, ' Arise, thou tarriest over-long,' and rising in amazement, he looked round about and saw a light in the place of easement —a candle which Reiner the monk had left there out of carelessness, and which was on the point of falling on the straw. And after the Abbot had put out the light, he went through the house and saw that the outer door, the only one in the house, was so firmly barred that it could not be opened save with a key, and that the windows were shut so fast that, if the fire had grown, he

si ignis excreuisset, ipse et omnes sui qui in solio illo
dormierant extincti essent ; quia non erat locus ubi exire
uel quo effugere possent. Quocunque ibat abbas, tunc
temporis, occurrebant tam iudei quam christiani exi-
gentes debita, turbantes et anxiantes eum, ita quod
sompnum amittebat, pallidus et macilentus effectus, et
dicens, quod ' nunquam cor meum quietum erit, donec
finem debiti mei sciero.' Ueniente festo sancti Michaelis,
omnia maneria sua in manu sua recepit cum paruis
admodum implementis et paucis instauramentis ; Waltero de Hatfeld condonauit xix. libras de firmis preteritis,
ut libere reciperet iiii^{or} maneria que abbas H. ei con-
firmauerat tenenda, scilicet Haregrauam et Saxham et
Cheuentonam et Stapelford : Herlauam autem distulit
F.129v abbas recipere hac / occasione. Cum forte transitum
faceremus in redeundo de Lundonia per forestam,
domino abbate audiente, quesiui a uetula transeunte
cuius hoc nemus esset, et de qua uilla, et quis dominus,
uel quis custos ? et respondit, quia nemus erat abbatis
Sancti Eadmundi, de uilla de Herlaua, et quod Ærnaldus[1]
dictus esset custos eius. De quo cum quererem, qualiter
se haberet uersus homines uille, respondit, quia demon
uiuus fuerat, inimicus Dei et excoriator rusticorum ; set
timet modo nouum abbatem Sancti Eadmundi, quem
sapientem et cautelem credit esse, et ideo tractat homines
pacifice. Quo audito, factus est abbas hillaris, et manerium recipere distulit ad tempus.

Ex insperato uenit tunc temporis rumor de morte
uxoris Herlewini de Rung, que cartam ad tenendam
eandem uillam in uita sua habebat ; et dixit abbas :

---

[1] Lands at Harlow were granted by Abbot Hugh to Arnaldus the son
of William. See FD p. 138.

and all his folk who had gone to sleep in that chamber
would have perished ; for there was no exit or way of
escape.   Wheresoever the Abbot went at that time,
both Jews and Christians came to meet him, demanding payment of the debts that were owing to them, dis-
quieting him and filling him with anxiety, so that he
lost his sleep, becoming pale and thin, and saying, ' My
soul shall never find rest till I know the end of my debts.'
When Michaelmas came round, he took all his manors
into his own hand, with but very few implements or
stock.   Walter of Hatfield was forgiven nineteen pounds
of rent for which he was in arrear, that so the Abbot
might get back the four manors which Abbot Hugh had
given him to hold, namely Hargrave, Saxham, Chevington, and Stapleford.   But the Abbot put off the resumption of Harlow for the following reason : it chanced
that on our returning from London we were journeying
through a forest, and in the Abbot's hearing I asked an
old woman, who was passing by, to whom the land
belonged and to what township, and who was the lord
or who held it.   And she replied that the wood belonged
to the Abbot of St. Edmund and to the township of
Harlow, and that a certain Ernald held it.   But when
I asked concerning him, how he bore himself towards
the men of the township, she replied that he was a devil
incarnate, an enemy of God and a flayer of the country
folk.   ' But,' she said, ' he fears the new Abbot of St.
Edmund ; for he thinks him wise and wary, and therefore he treats men peacefully.'   And when he heard this
the Abbot was merry and put off the resumption of the
manor for a time.

At that time there came unexpected news of the
death of the wife of Herlewin of Runcton, who had a
charter granting her the tenancy of that township for

'Heri dedissem lx. marcas ad liberandum illud manerium; modo liberauit illud Dominus.' Cumque sine omni dilacione illuc uenisset et recepisset uillam in manu sua, et incrastino isset Tilleneiam, menbrum illius manerii, uenit quidam miles offerens xxx. marcas, ut posset tenere illam carrucatam terre cum pertinentiis per antiquum seruicium, scilicet iiii. libras; quod noluit abbas, et habuit inde illo anno xxv. libras, secundo anno xx. libras. Hec et consimilia fecerunt eum omnia tenere in manu sua; scilicet quod alibi legitur: 'Omnia Cesar erat.'[1] Ille uero non segniter agens, horrea et bouerias edificare cepit in primis; ad wainandas[2] terras super omnia excolendas sollicitus, et ad boscos custodiendos uigilans, super quibus dandis uel minuendis ipse seipsum profitebatur auarum. Unum solum manerium de Torp[3] carta sua confirmauit cuidam Anglico natione, glebe ascripto,[4] de cuius fidelitate plenius confidebat quia bonus agricola erat, et quia nesciebat loqui Gallice.

Nondum transierant vii. menses post electionem suam, et ecce offerebantur ei litere domini pape constituentes eum iudicem[5] de causis cognoscendis, ad que exequenda rudis fuit et inexercitatus, licet liberalibus artibus et scripturis diuinis imbutus esset, utpote uir literatus, in scholis nutritus et rector scolarum,[6] in sua prouincia[7] notus et approbatus. Uocauit proinde duos

---

[1] Lucan III, 108

[2] *Wainare* means 'to cultivate with profit'; it is the same word as 'gain.'

[3] *Torp* cannot be identified. Thorpe Ixworth in the hands of the Blunts from DB on, and Thorpe Morieux, held by the house of Morieux may be ruled out. Thorpe near Pakenham (see FD p. clxviii *n.*) is a possibility as are Morningthorpe, Thorpe Abbots, and another Thorpe, all three in Norfolk.

[4] See Appendix F

[5] 'Judge delegate' appointed by Lucius III.

[6] He had been admitted to the school of William of Diss, when he was a poor clerk and had later studied in Paris, after which he became a schoolmaster. See p. 44.

her life time : and the Abbot said, ' Yesterday I would
have given sixty marks to free that manor ; but now
the Lord hath freed it.' And having come thither without delay and taken the township into his own hands,
he went on the morrow to Tilney, a part of that manor ;
and there a knight came to him offering him thirty
marks if he might hold that carucate of land with its
appurtenances, on terms of the ancient service, to wit,
four pounds : but the Abbot refused him, and that
year he got twenty-five pounds and the next year twenty
from that land. This happening and the like made him
hold everything in his own hand, even as we read elsewhere that ' Caesar was everything.' But he was no
sluggard, and began before all else to build barns and
byres : and he was more especially eager to cultivate his
lands with profit, and was also vigilant in looking after
his woods, concerning the granting or diminishing of
which he confessed himself most avaricious. One sole
manor, that of Thorp, he confirmed by charter to a
certain Englishman, an adscript to the soil, in whose
faithfulness he had all the greater confidence, because
he was a good farmer and could speak no French.

Seven months had not passed since his election,
when lo and behold ! letters of the Lord Pope were
brought to him, offering to appoint him judge delegate
for the hearing of causes, a task of which he had neither
knowledge nor experience, though he was learned in
the liberal arts and in the Holy Scriptures, being a
literate man, brought up in the schools and once a schoolmaster, well known and approved in his country. He

---

⁷ This should strictly mean Norfolk, but may well be used here in the
wider sense of E. Anglia. By 1159 he had come to Bury, and was probably a schoolmaster there, when the monks sent him on his adventurous
journey to Rome. See p. 48. He did not make his profession as a monk
till 1165 or 1166.

clericos legis peritos, et sibi associauit, quorum consilio
utebatur in ecclesiasticis negociis, decretis et decretalibus[1]
epistolis operam prebens, cum hora dabatur ; ita quod
infra breue tempus, tum librorum inspectione, tum
causarum exercitio, iudex discretus haberetur, secundum
formam iuris in iure procedens : unde quidam ait,
' Maledicta sit curia istius abbatis, ubi nec aurum nec
argentum mihi prodest ad confundendum aduersarium
meum ! ' Processu temporis, in causis secularibus
aliquantulum excercitatus, naturali ratione ductus, tam
subtilis ingenii erat quod omnes mirabantur, et ab
Osberto [2] filio Heruei subuicecomite dicebatur : ' Iste
abbas disputator est ; si procedit sicut incipit, nos omnes
excecabit quotquot sumus.' Abbas uero in huiusmodi /

causis approbatus, factus est iusticiarius errans,[3] set ab
errore et deuio se custodiens. Uerum ' summa petit
liuor.' [4] Cum homines sui conquererentur ei in curia
Sancti Ædmundi, quia nolebat precipitare sententiam
nec credere omni spiritui,[5] set ordine iudiciario procedere,
sciens quod merita causarum parcium assercione pan-
duntur, dicebatur quod nolebat facere iusticiam alicui
conquerenti, nisi interuentu pecunie date uel promisse ;
et quia erat ei aspectus accutus et penetrans, et frons
Catonis, raro blandiens, dicebatur magis declinare animum seueritati quam benignitati ; et, in misericordiis
accipiendis pro aliqua forisfactura, dicebatur iudicium
superexaltare misericordie [6] quia, sicut uisum fuit pluribus,

---

[1] *Decreta* refers to the corpus of Canon Law made by Gratian (1138–42),
Decretals are subsequent papal pronouncements
[2] One of the King's justices at Westminster in 1196
[3] A justice in eyre. Here the less common term ' justice errant ' has
been used in the translation to preserve the play upon words.
[4] Ovid, *Remedia Amoris* 369
[5] John iv. 1
[6] A jesting allusion to James ii. 13, *superexaltat misericordia iudicium*,
' Mercy exalteth itself over judgement.' Samson is said to reverse the
process, owing to his love of fines (*misericordiis*).

forthwith called to him two clerks skilled in the law and associated them with himself, making use of their counsel in ecclesiastical business, and studying the decrees and decretal letters, whenever he had time, so that within a short time by reading of books and practice in causes he came to be regarded as a wise judge, proceeding in court according to the form of law. Wherefore one said, ' A curse upon the court of this Abbot, where neither gold or silver may help me for the confounding of my adversary ! ' In process of time when he had acquired some practice in secular cases, being guided by his native power of reasoning, he showed himself so subtle of understanding, that all marvelled, and the Undersheriff Osbert FitzHervey said of him, ' This Abbot is a fine disputer : if he goes on as he has begun, he will blind us all, every one.' And having approved himself in causes of this kind, he was made a justice errant, though he erred not, but was careful not to wander from the right way. But ' Envy assails earth's highest ! ' When his men complained to him in the court of St. Edmund, because he would not give judgment hastily nor ' believe every spirit,' but proceeded in the order prescribed by law, knowing that the merits of causes are revealed by the statements of the parties, it was said that he was unwilling to do justice to any complainant, unless money were first given or promised ; and because his glance was sharp and penetrating, and his brow worthy of Cato and rarely relaxed into a smile, he was said to be more inclined to severity than kindness. And when he took amercements for any offence, he was said to exalt justice above mercy, because, as it seemed to many, when it was a matter of getting money, he rarely remitted what he might justly receive. As his wisdom grew, so also did his prudence in managing his property and increasing it,

cum peruentum erat ad denarios capiendos raro re-
mittebat quod iuste accipi potuit. Sicut profecit sapientia, ita et prouidentia in rebus custodiendis et
augendis et in expensis honorifice faciendis ; set et hic
multi detractores oblactauerunt, dicentes, quia accepit
de sacristia quod uoluit, propriis parcens denariis, per-
mittens bladum suum iacere usque ad tempus care
uendicionis, et iacens ad maneria sua aliter quam predecessores sui, onerans celerarium hospitibus ab abbate
pocius suscipiendis, per quod abbas posset dici sapiens
et instauratus et prouidus in fine anni ; conuentus uero
et obedienciales inscii et inprouidi haberentur. Ad has
detractiones solebam respondere, quod si de sacristia
aliquid accipit, ad utilitatem ecclesie illud conuertit ;
et hoc nullus inuidus negare potuit. Et ut uerum fatear,
multo maiora et plura bona fuerunt patrata ex oblacionibus sacristie, infra xv. annos post electionem suam,
quam quadraginta annis ante. Aliis obieccionibus,
quod abbas iacebat ad maneria sua, respondere solebam
et excusabam dicens, quia abbas magis est letus et
hilaris alibi quam domi ; et hoc utique uerum fuit, uel
propter conquerencium multitudinem qui occurrebant,
uel propter rumorum relatores, unde sepius contigit quod,
propter exibicionem rigidi uultus sui, ab hospitibus suis
multum perdidit fauoris et gratie, licet eis in cibo et
potu satisfecerit. Ego uero hoc attendens, nacta oportunitate, astans ei a secretis dixi : ' Duo sunt que
multum miror de uobis ; ' et cum quesisset que duo :
' Unum est, quod adhuc in tali statu fouetis sententiam
Meludinensium [1] dicentium ex falso nichil sequi, et
cetera friuola.' Quibus cum ipse respondisset quod

---

[1] A reference to the famous school of dialectic at Melun founded by
Abelard

and in all honourable expenditure. But in this also his
detractors used to bring charges against him, saying that
he took from the sacristy whatever he wanted, sparing
his own money, allowing his corn to lie until the time
came when it sold dear, and in lodging at his manors
as his predecessors had never done, thereby burdening
the Cellarer with guests who ought rather to have been
entertained by the Abbot, so that at the end of the year
he might be called a wise Abbot, well-stocked and full
of forethought, while the Convent and obedientiaries
were deemed both ignorant and improvident. To these
detractions I used to reply that, if he took anything from
the sacristy, he employed it for the profit of the church ;
and this no jealous critic could deny. And to confess the
truth, much greater and more frequent good was done
with the oblations of the sacristy during the fifteen years
after his election than in the forty years before. To
other objections, that the Abbot lay at his manors, I was
wont to answer and excuse him, saying that the Abbot
was happier and more cheerful elsewhere than at home ;
and this was very true, either because of the multitude
of persons who came to lay their complaints before him,
or on account of tale-bearers ; whence it often happened
that, because he showed them a stern face, he lost much
favour and gratitude with his guests, although he satisfied
them in respect of their food and drink. Now I, noting
this, once when I found the opportunity, for I was standing by him, being then his secretary, said to him, ' There
are two things about you whereat I marvel much.' And
when he asked, ' What two ? ' I made answer, ' One is
that, being in such a position as you now hold, you still
cherish the maxim of the men of Melun who say that
from false premises no conclusion can be drawn, and
such trifles as these.' And when he had answered this as

uoluit, adieci ego : ' Aliud nimirum est quod domi non exibetis uultum propicium sicut alibi, nec inter fratres [1] qui uos diligunt et dilexerunt et in dominum sibi eligerunt, set raro estis inter eos, nec tunc congaudetis eis, sicut dicunt.' Quibus auditis, uultum mutauit, et demisso capite respondit : ' Stultus es et stulte loqueris. F.130v Scire deberes quod Salomon ait : ' Filie tibi / sunt multe : uultum propicium ne ostendas eis.' [2] Ego uero tacui, de cetero ponens custodiam ori meo. Alia tamen uice dixi : ' Domine, audiui te in hac nocte post matutinas uigilantem et ualde suspirantem contra morem solitum.' Qui respondit : ' Non est mirum ; particeps es bonorum meorum in cibo et potu, et equitaturis, et similibus, set parum cogitas de procuracione domus et familie, de uariis et arduis negociis cure pastoralis, que me sollicitant, que animum meum gementem et anxium faciunt.' Quibus respondi, eleuatis manibus ad celum : ' Talem anxietatem [3] mihi omnipotens et misericors Dominus.' Audiui abbatem dicentem, quod si fuisset in eo statu quo fuit antequam monacharetur, et habuisset v. uel sex marcas redditus cum quibus sustentari possit in scolis, nunquam fieret monachus nec abbas. Alia uice dixit cum iuramento, quod, si presciuisset que et quanta esset sollicitudo abbatie custodiende, libentius uoluisset fieri magister almarii [4] et custos librorum, quam abbas et dominus. Illam utique obedienciam dixit pre omnibus aliis se semper desiderasse. Et quis talia crederet ? Uix ego ; nec etiam ego, nisi quia,

---

[1] Rokewode's suggestion that *manetis* has fallen out after *fratres* is wrong. the words go with *exhibetis uultum* ; *domi* (' your own house ') being contrasted with *inter fratres*.

[2] Ecclus. vii. 26

[3] *auferat* or *tollat* must be supplied here

[4] Another form of *armarii*, the aumbry or book-cupboard. The *cantor* was in charge of the Library, but was assisted by an obedientiary who acted as library clerk. See p. xxvii.

pleased him, I proceeded, ' The other is that at home you do not show as kind a face as elsewhere, not even among the brethren who love you still and loved you of old and chose you to be their lord, but you are rarely among them, nor do you rejoice with them, as they say.' When he heard this he changed countenance and hung his head and thus made answer, ' You are a fool and speak like a fool. You should know what Solomon says, " Thou hast many daughters. Show not thy face cheerful towards them." ' At that I was silent, and thenceforth set a guard upon my tongue. Yet on another occasion I said, ' My lord, last night I heard you after matins lying awake and sighing deeply, as is not your common custom.' And he replied, ' No wonder that I sigh ; you share my food and drink, my horses, and the like ; but you little think of the ordering of my house and household, or concerning the many troubles of my pastoral care, that vex me and cause my spirit to groan and to be filled with anxiety.' To which I made answer, raising my hands to heaven, ' Almighty God, grant that such anxiety may never be mine ! ' I heard the Abbot say that, if he had been in that state of life in which he was before he became a monk, and had had five or six marks of income wherewith he might have maintained himself in the schools, he would never have become monk or Abbot. On another occasion he said with an oath, that if he had sooner known what and how great the cares of his abbacy would be, he had sooner have been the master of the aumbrey and custodian of the books, than Abbot and lord ; for he said that of all offices this was the one which he had ever most desired. Who would believe it ? I found it hard ; nor indeed would I have believed it, had I not, by living with him six years, night and day, come to know the merits of his life and the

cum eo vi. annis existens [1] die ac nocte, uite scilicet meritum et sapientie doctrinam plenius agnoscerem. Narrauit aliquando, quod, cum esset puer ix. annorum, somniauit se stare pre foribus cimiterii ecclesie Sancti Eadmundi, et diabolum expansis ulnis uelle eum capere ; set sanctus Eadmundus, prope astans, recepit eum in brachiis suis ; cumque clamaret somniando, ' Sancte Ædmunde, adiuua me,' quem nunquam prius audierat nominari, expergefactus est. Mater uero eius de tanto et tali clamore obstupuit, que, audito somnio, duxit eum ad sanctum Eadmundum orationis gratia ; cumque uenissent ad portam cimiterii, dixit, ' Mater mea, ecce locus ! ecce eadem porta, quam in somnis uidi, quando diabolus uolebat me accipere : ' et cognouit locum, ut aiebat, ac si prius eum carnalibus oculis uidisset. Abbas ipse exposuit somnium, significans per diabolum uoluptatem huius seculi que eum uolebat allicere, set sanctus Eadmundus eum amplexatus est, quando eum monachum ecclesie sue fieri uoluit.

Quodam tempore cum nuntiatum esset ei quod quidam de conuentu murmurassent de quodam facto eius, dixit mihi assidenti : ' Deus, Deus,' inquit ille, ' multum expedit mihi memorare somnium illud quod somniatum est de me antequam fierem abbas, scilicet quod seuirem ut lupus. Certe hoc est quod super omnia mundana timeo, ne conuentus meus aliquid faciat, unde me seuire oporteat ; set ita est, cum dicunt uel agunt aliquid contra uoluntatem meam ; recolo illud somnium, et licet seuiam in animo meo, occulte fremens et frendens, uim mihi facio ne seuiam uerbo uel opere, et

strangulat inclusus dolor et cor estuat intus.[2]

---

[1] In 1144. See below.
[2] Ovid, *Tristia*, v. i. 63

depths of his wisdom in all their fullness. He told me once that when he was a boy nine years old, he dreamed that he was standing before the cemetery gates of the church of St. Edmund, and that the devil sought to catch him with outstretched arms ; but St. Edmund stood by and received him in his arms ; and when he cried out in his dream, ' St. Edmund, help me ! ' though he had never so much as heard his name, he suddenly awoke. But his mother was amazed at the loudness and the nature of his cry and, when she had heard his dream, she took him to St. Edmund's that he might pray there, and when they came to the cemetery gate, he said, ' Mother, behold the place, the selfsame gate which I saw in my dream, when the devil wished to catch me ! ' And he said that he recognised the place as clearly as if he had seen it with his fleshly eyes. The Abbot himself expounded his dream, interpreting the devil as being the pleasure of this world which sought to entice him, but St. Edmund embraced him because he desired him to become a monk of his Church.

Once when he was told that certain of the Convent murmured at something which he had done, he said to me as I sat beside him, ' God, God, it is most expedient that I should remember the dream that was dreamed before I became Abbot, to wit, that I should raven like a wolf. For assuredly this is what I fear most above all earthly things, namely that my Convent may say or do something that will make it my duty so to raven. But thus it is, when they say or do something contrary to my desire, I remember that dream and, though I raven in my heart, secretly roaring and gnashing my teeth, I force myself not to raven in word or deed ; and

> my pent-up grief
> Doth choke me and my heart within me boils.

F.131 Cum autem esset colericus naturaliter, et facile / accen-
deretur ad iram, iram tamen ratione dignitatis cum
magna lucta animi refrenabat sepius. De qua etiam re
aliquando se iactitabat, dicens : ' Hoc et illud uidi,
hoc et illud audiui, et tamen patienter sustinui.'

Dixit abbas aliquando, sedens in capitulo, quedam
uerba quibus uidebatur efficaciter uenari fauorem conuentus. ' Nolo,' inquit, ' ut aliquis ueniat ad me ad
accusandum alium, nisi palam idem dicere uoluerit ;
quod si aliquis aliter fecerit, nomen accusantis palam
manifestabo. Uolo eciam ut quilibet claustralis liberum
habeat accessum ad me, ut mecum loquatur de necessitate sua quando uoluerit.' Illud autem dixit quia
magnates nostri, tempore H. abbatis, uolentes nichil
agi in monasterio nisi per eos, decreuerunt nullum
monachum claustralem debere loqui cum abbate, nisi
prius ostenderet capellano abbatis quid et de qua re
uellet loqui cum abbate.

Quodam die iussit in capitulo, ut quicumque sigillum
proprium haberet, ei redderet ; et ita factum est, et
inuenta sunt triginta tria sigilla. Racionem huius
precepti ipse ostendit, prohibens ne aliquis officialis
appruntaret aliquod debitum ultra xx. solidos, sine
assensu prioris et conuentus, sicut solebat fieri. Priori
uero et sacriste reddidit sigilla sua, et cetera retinuit.
Alia die iussit sibi dari omnes claues cistarum et almari-
orum et hanepariorum, prohibens ne de cetero aliquis
haberet cistam nec aliquid obseratum, nisi per licentiam,
nec alias aliquid possideret, nisi quod regula permitteret.
Cuilibet tamen nostrum generaliter dedit licentiam

But though he was naturally quick to anger and easily kindled to wrath, yet more often, remembering his position, with a great struggle he curbed his wrath. And of this at times he boasted, saying, ' I have seen this thing and that, I have heard this and that, and yet have patiently endured it.'

The Abbot once, as he sat in Chapter, uttered certain words, in which he seemed to court the favour of the Convent. ' I do not desire,' he said, ' that anyone should come to me to accuse another, unless he is ready to say the same thing in public ; but if any should do otherwise, I shall make known the name of the accuser. I desire also that every cloister monk should have free access to me to speak with me concerning his need, whenever he wishes.' Now he said this because our chief men in the time of Abbot Hugh, wishing that nothing should be done in the monastery save through themselves, decreed that no cloister monk should speak with the Abbot, unless he first made known to the Abbot's chaplain what he desired to say to the Abbot and why.

One day he gave orders in the Chapter that anyone who possessed a seal of his own should deliver it up to him. His command was obeyed, and thirty-three seals were found. He himself revealed the reason for this command, and forbade any obedientiary to borrow more than twenty shillings, as was often done, without the assent of the Prior and Convent. But he gave back their seals to the Prior and the Sacrist, and kept the rest. On another occasion he ordered that all the keys of chests, aumbries and baskets should be given up to him, forbidding anyone in future to possess a chest or anything else under lock and key, save by his leave, or to own anything save what the Rule permitted. But he gave general permission to all of us to possess money to the

habendi denarios usque ad duos solidos, si forte nobis caritatiue darentur ; ita tamen ut in pauperes parentes uel in pios usus expenderentur. Alia uice dixit abbas se uelle conseruare antiquas consuetudines nostras de hospitibus suscipiendis ; scilicet, quando abbas est domi ipse recipiet omnes hospites cuiuslibet condicionis, preter uiros relligiosos, et preter presbiteros secularis habitus, et preter eorum homines, qui per eos se aduocauerunt ad portam curie ; si uero abbas non fuerit domi, omnes hospites cuiuslibet condicionis recipientur a celerario usque ad tredecim equos. Si uero laicus uel clericus uenerit cum pluribus equis quam tredecim, recipientur a seruientibus abbatis, uel intra curiam uel extra, ad expensas abbatis. Omnes uiri religiosi, etiam episcopi, si ipsi forte fuerint monachi, pertinent ad celerarium et ad expensas conuentus, nisi abbas uoluerit eum honorare, et ad expensas suas in sua aula recipere.

Abbas Samson mediocris erat stature, fere omnino caluus, uultum habens nec rotundum nec oblongum, naso eminente, labiis grossis, oculis cristallinis et penetrantis intuitus, auribus clarissimi auditus, superciliis in altum crescentibus et sepe tonsis ; ex paruo frigore F.131v cito / raucus ; die eleccionis [1] sue quadraginta et septem annos etatis habens, et in monachatu decem et septem annos ; paucos canos habens in rufa barba, et paucissimos inter capillos nigros, et aliquantulum crispos ; set infra xiiii^{or} annos post eleccionem suam totus albus efficitur sicut nix ; homo supersobrius, nunquam desidiosus, multum ualens, et uolens equitare uel pedes ire, donec senectus preualuit, que talem uoluntatem temperauit ; qui, audito rumore de capta cruce et perdi-

---

[1] This gives us the date of his birth (1135) and of his profession (1165 or 1166 ; cp. *Mem.* II, p. 5).

THE CHRONICLE OF JOCELIN OF BRAKELOND

amount of two shillings, if it were given to us out of
charity, yet on this condition that it should be expended
on poor kinsfolk or pious purposes. At another time the
Abbot said that he desired to keep our ancient customs
concerning the entertainment of guests, to wit, that when
the Abbot was at home, he should receive all guests of
every kind saving the religious and secular priests, and
their men who invited themselves to the court-gate under
cover of their masters ; but if the Abbot should be away
from home, then all guests of every condition should be
received by the Cellarer, up to the number of thirteen
horses. But if a layman or a clerk should come with more
than thirteen horses, he should be received by the servants
of the Abbot, either within the court or without, at the
Abbot's expense. All religious, even Bishops, should they
chance to be monks, fall to the care of the Cellarer at
the Convent's expense, unless the Abbot should desire
to do them honour and to receive them in his hall at his
own expense.

Abbot Samson was of middle height, and almost en-
tirely bald ; his face was neither round nor long, his nose
prominent, his lips thick, his eyes clear as crystal and of
penetrating glance ; his hearing of the sharpest ; his eye-
brows grew long and were often clipped ; a slight cold
made him soon grow hoarse. On the day of his election
he was forty-seven years old, and had been a monk for
seventeen. He had a few white hairs in a red beard and
a very few in the hair of his head, which was black and
rather curly ; but within fourteen years of his election he was white as snow. He was a man of extreme
sobriety, never given to sloth, extremely strong and ever
ready to go either on horseback or on foot, until old age
prevailed and tempered his eagerness. When he heard
of the capture of the Cross and the fall of Jerusalem, he

cione Jerusalem, femoralibus cilicinis cepit uti, et cilicio
loco staminis, et carnibus et carneis abstinere ; carnes
tamen uoluit sibi anteferri sedens ad mensam, ad
augmentum scilicet elemosine.[1] Lac dulce et mel et
consimilia dulcia libencius quam ceteros cibos comedebat.
Mendaces et ebriosos et uerbosos odio habuit ; quia
uirtus sese diligit, et aspernatur contrarium. Murmuratores cibi et potus, et precipue monachos murmuratores
condempnans, tenorem antiquum conseruans quem olim
habuit dum claustralis fuit : hoc autem uirtutis in se
habuit quod nunquam ferculum coram eo positum uoluit
mutare. Quod cum ego nouicius uellem probare si hoc
esset uerum, forte seruiui in refectorio, et cogitaui penes
me ut ponerem coram eo ferculum quod omnibus aliis
displiceret in disco nigerimo et fracto. Quod cum ipse
uidisset, tanquam non uidens erat ; facta autem mora,
penituit me hoc fecisse, et statim, arepto disco, ferculum
et discum mutaui in melius et asportaui : ille uero
emendacionem talem moleste tulit iratus et turbatus.
Homo erat eloquens, Gallice et Latine, magis rationi
dicendorum quam ornatui uerborum innitens. Scriptu-
ram Anglice scriptam legere nouit elegantissime, et Anglice sermocinare solebat populo, set secundum linguam
Norfolchie, ubi natus et nutritus erat, unde et pulpi-
tum iussit fieri in ecclesia et ad utilitatem audiencium
et ad decorem ecclesie. Uidebatur quoque abbas ac-
tiuam uitam magis diligere quam contemplatiuam, quia
bonos obedienciales magis commendauit quam bonos
claustrales ; et raro aliquem propter solam scientiam
literarum approbauit, nisi haberet scientiam rerum
secularium ; et cum audiret forte aliquem prelatum

---

[1] The food which he had left untouched would be given to the poor
with the broken meats of the convent.

began to wear drawers of haircloth, and a shirt of hair instead of wool, and to abstain from flesh and meat ; none the less he desired that meat should be placed before him when he sat at table, that so our alms might be increased. He preferred fresh milk and honey and the like to any other food. He hated liars and drunkards and wordy fellows, since virtue loves itself and hates its opposite. He condemned those who murmur at their food and drink, especially if they were monks, and preserved the old way of life that he had followed as a cloister monk ; but he had this virtue, that he never liked to have a dish changed when it had once been placed before him. When I was a novice, I wished to try if this were true and, chancing to be a server in the refectory, I thought in my heart that I would place before him a dish, which displeased all the rest, on a platter that was very black and broken. And when he saw this, he was as one that saw not. But after a time I repented that I had done this, and forthwith seizing the platter, I changed both dish and platter for the better and carried them away ; but he was angry and vexed and took the improvement ill. He was eloquent both in French and Latin, having regard rather to the sense of what he had to say than to ornaments of speech. He read English perfectly, and used to preach in English to the people, but in the speech of Norfolk, where he was born and bred, and to this end he ordered a pulpit to be set up in the church for the benefit of his hearers and as an ornament to the church. The Abbot seemed also to love the active life better than the contemplative ; he had more praise for good obedientiaries than for good cloister monks ; and rarely did he approve of any man solely for his knowledge of literature, unless he were also wise in worldly affairs. And when he heard of any

cedere oneri pastorali et fieri anachoritam, in hoc eum
non laudauit. Homines nimis benignos laudare noluit,
dicens : ' Qui omnibus placere nititur, nulli placere
debet.' Primo ergo anno suscepte abbatie omnes adulatores quasi odio habuit, et maxime monachos ; set in
processu temporis uidebatur eos quasi libentius audire
et magis familiares habere. Unde contigit quod, cum
quidam frater noster, hac arte peritus, curuasset genua
ante eum, et sub optentu consilii dandi auribus eius
F.132 adulacionis oleum infudisset, /subrisi ego stans a longe :
eo uero recedente, uocatus et interrogatus quare riserim,
respondi mundum plenum esse adulatoribus. Et abbas :
' Fili mi, diu est quod adulatores noui, et ideo non
possum adulatores non audire. Multa sunt simulanda
et dissimulanda, ad pacem conuentus conseruandam.
Audiam eos loqui, set non decipient me, si possum, sicut
predecessorem meum, qui consilio eorum ita inconsulte
credidit, quod diu ante obitum suum nichil habuit quod
manducaret uel ipse uel familia sua, nisi a creditoribus
mutuo acceptum ; nec erat quod distribui potuit pauperibus die sepulture eius, nisi quinquaginta solidos, qui
recepti erant a Ricardo firmario de Palegraua, hac
occasione quod eadem die intrauit firmam de Palegraua ;
quos denarios idem Ricardus [1] alia uice reddidit bailiuis
regis, integram firmam exigentibus ad opus regis.' His
dictis confortatus fui. Ille uero studuit disciplinatam
domum habere, et familie magnitudinem set neces-
sariam, prouidens sibi quod firma ebdomade,[2] que pre-

---

[1] See p. 8
[2] *hebdomade* is genitive ; *firma* (sc. *pecunia*) means ' a fixed sum '

prelate that he grew faint beneath the burden of his pastoral cares and turned anchorite, he did not praise him for so doing. He was loth to bestow much praise on kindly men, for he said, ' He that seeks to please everyone, ought to please nobody.' So in the first year of his abbacy he regarded all flatterers with hatred, especially if they were monks. But in process of time he seemed more ready to give ear to them and to be more friendly toward them. Wherefore it came to pass that, when a certain brother skilled in this art kneeled before him, and under pretence of giving him some advice had poured the oil of flattery into his ears, I laughed softly as I stood afar off : but when the monk retired, he called me and asked me why I laughed, and I replied that it was because the world was full of flatterers. To which the Abbot made answer, ' My son, it is long since I have been acquainted with flatterers, and it is therefore that I cannot help listening to them. In many things I must feign, and in many I must dissemble, to maintain peace in the Convent. I shall not cease to listen to their words, but they will not deceive me, as they deceived my predecessor who was so foolish as to put faith in their counsels, so that long before his death neither he nor his household had aught to eat save what was borrowed from their creditors ; nor on the day of his burial was there anything that could be given to the poor save only fifty shillings, which were received from Richard the tenant of Palgrave because it was that very day when he entered on his tenancy at Palgrave ; and the said Richard afterwards repaid this sum to the King's bailiffs, who demanded the rent in its entirety on the King's behalf.' I was comforted by these words. And in truth the Abbot was at pains to have his house well-disciplined and a household that, although large,

decessori suo non sufficiebat ad expensam v. dierum,
ei suffecit octo diebus uel nouem uel decem, si esset ad
maneria sua sine magno aduentu hospitum. Singulis
uero ebdomadis, computacionem expense sue domus
audiebat, non per uicarium, set in propria persona, quod
antecessor eius nunquam solebat facere. Septem annis
primis quatuor fercula [1] in domo sua, postea nisi tria,
preter xenia et preter uenacionem de parcis suis uel
pisces de uiuariis suis. Et si forte aliquem retinuit ad
tempus in domo sua prece alicuius potentis uel alicuius
familiaris, uel nuncios uel citharedos uel aliquem huiusmodi, nacta opportunitate transfretandi uel longe eundi,
a talibus superfluis se prudenter exonerauit. Monachos
uero, quos socios abbas habuit ante abbaciam susceptam
magis dilectos et magis familiares, raro promouit ad
obedientias occasione pristine familiaritatis, nisi essent
idonei ; unde quidam ex nostris, qui ei erant propicii
ad eligendum eum abbatem, dixerunt eum minus quam
deceret diligere eos, qui eum antequam fuerat abbas
dilexerant, et eos plus ab eo amari, qui eum et aperte et
occulte deprauauerunt, et eum hominem iracundum,
non socialem, paltenerium [2] et baratorem de Norfolchia,
etiam in audientia multorum, publice nominauerunt.
Uerum, sicut ille pristinis amicis suis nichil amoris uel
honoris indiscrete exibuit post suscepcionem abbatie,
sic et pluribus aliis pro meritis suis nichil rancoris uel
odii exibuit, bonum aliquando reddens pro malo, et
benefaciens persequentibus eum. Habuit etiam in

---

[1] A verb must be supplied, such as *erant* or *habuit*. For an interesting
discussion of the number of dishes that should be served, cp. the strictures
passed on the monks of Canterbury and Winchester by Giraldus Cambrensis (RS I. 52).

[2] ' A proud fellow ' ; cp. Fr. *pautonnier* ; Eng. paltener

was all of it necessary, and he made provision for himself so that the weekly sum, which had served his predecessor only for the expenses of five days, served him for eight, or nine, or ten, if he was away at his manors and there was no large arrival of guests. And every week he heard the account of his expenditure, not by deputy, but in person, which had never been the custom of his predecessor. During the first seven years of his abbacy four dishes were served to him, but afterwards only three, except when he had received presents or venison from his parks or fish from his ponds. And if perchance he kept any man in his household at the request of some person of importance or of some familiar friend, or maintained messengers or harpers or any such persons, as soon as he had an opportunity to go overseas or on a long journey, he prudently discarded such burdensome superfluities. As for the monks who had been his comrades before he succeeded to the abbacy, and had stood high in his love and regard, he rarely promoted them to office on the strength of his former affection, unless they were fit ; wherefore some of our brethren, who had favoured his election as Abbot, said that he showed less regard than was seemly toward those who had loved him before he was Abbot, and that he loved those better who had both openly and in secret disparaged him, and had publicly and even in the hearing of many called him an angry and unsociable man, a haughty fellow and a barrator from Norfolk. But as after his succession to the abbacy he vouchsafed no indiscreet affection or honour to those who had once been his friends, even so he showed no sign of rancour or hatred to others, such as their conduct might seem to deserve, sometimes rendering good for evil and doing good to those who had persecuted him. He also had

F132 v consuetudine quiddam quod nunquam uidi/hominem
habere, scilicet quod multos affectuose dilexit, quibus
nunquam uel raro uultum amoris exibuit ; hoc quod
uulgus clamat, dicens, 'ubi amor ibi oculus.'[1] Et
aliud mirum fuit, quod dampnum suum in temporalibus
a seruientibus suis scienter sustinuit, et se sustinere confessus est : set, sicut credo, hoc fuit in causa, ut congruum
tempus expectaret quo rem consultius emendaret, uel ut
magnum dampnum dissimulando euitaret.

Parentes suos mediocriter dilexit, nec nimis uero
tenere sicut alii solent ; quia nullum infra tercium
gradum habuit, uel habere simulauit. Set audiui eum
dicentem quod habuit parentes nobiles et generosos,
quos nunquam inperpetuum ut parentes cognosceret ;
quia, ut aiebat, plus essent ei oneri quam honori, si hoc
scirent ; set eos uoluit consanguineos habere qui eum
consanguineum habuerunt quando fuit pauper claustralis. Quosdam eorum (eos secundum quod sibi utiles
et idoneos estimauit) diuersis officiis in domo sua, quosdam uillis custodiendis deputauit. Quos autem infideles
probauit, a se elongauit sine spe redeundi. Quendam
hominem medie manus,[2] qui patrimonium eius fideliter
seruauerat, et ei iuueni deuote seruierat, pro caro consanguineo habuit, et filio eius clerico primam ecclesiam
in abbatia sibi commissa uacantem dedit, et ceteros filios
eius omnes promouit. Capellanum quendam, qui eum

---

[1] The origin of this aphorism, well established by the twelfth century
is uncertain ; it occurs in the letters of John of Salisbury with the addition
of *ubi dolor ibi digitus*. Its existence in the eleventh century is proved by
the following lines from the *Fecunda Ratis* of Egbert of Liége : *Sicubi torret
amor. mirantur lumina formam ; crebra manus palpat, quo membra dolore coquuntur.*
[2] I can find no parallel ; presumably it means 'middle class.'

a habit, which I have never marked in any other man, namely, that he warmly loved many towards whom he never or rarely showed a loving countenance, nor conformed to the proverb ' where your love is, there your eye is also.' And he had another characteristic that calls for wonder, namely, that he wittingly put up with losses in temporal matters at the hands of his servants, and acknowledged that he did so ; but to my thinking the reason was this, that he might wait for a suitable occasion to set matters right with greater prudence or that by shutting his eyes to the offence he might avoid great loss.

He loved his kin in moderation, and not over tenderly, as others are wont to do. For he had no kin within the third degree or at any rate pretended that this was so. But I have heard him say that he had kinsfolk of high birth and noble blood, whom he would never recognise as kindred at any time, because, as he said, they would be more of an onus than an honour to him, if they were aware of it. But he desired to treat those as being of his blood, who had treated him as their kinsman when he was a poor cloister monk. Some of them, according as he thought them suitable and like to be of use to himself, he appointed to sundry offices in his house or to have charge of townships. But those whom he found untrustworthy he banished far from him without hope of return. A certain man of no high birth, who had faithfully preserved his patrimony and had served him devotedly in his youth, he treated as a dear kinsman and gave his son, a clerk, the first church that fell vacant after the abbey had been committed to his charge ; and to all his other sons he gave advancement. A certain chaplain, who had maintained him by the profits made from the sale of holy water, in the

sustinuerat in scolis Parisius[1] questu aque benedicte,[2] quando pauper fuerat, mandari fecit, et ei ecclesiasticum beneficium quo sustentari possit, affectu uicario, contulit. Cuidam seruienti predecessoris sui uictum et uestitum concessit omnibus diebus uite sue, qui imposuerat ei conpedes ad preceptum domini sui, quando fuit positus in carcere. Filio Elie, pincerne Hugonis abbatis, facienti ei homagium de terra patris sui, dixit in plena curia : ' Distuli jam capere homagium tuum vii. annis de terra quam H. abbas dedit patri tuo, quia illud donum erat in detrimentum aule de Elmeswell : modo uictus sum, memor beneficii quod pater tuus mihi fecit quando in uinculis eram, quia misit mihi porcionem de ipso uino, quod dominus suus biberat, mandando ut confortarer in Deo.' Magistro Waltero, filio magistri Willelmi de Dice, petenti caritatiue uicariam ecclesie de Cheuentona, respondit : ' Pater tuus magister scolarum erat ; et cum pauper clericus eram, concessit mihi introitum scole sue sine pacto et caritatiue, et usum discendi ; et ego, causa Dei, concedo tibi quod postulas.'

Duos etiam milites de Risebi, Willelmum et Normannum, cum iudicati essent forte in misericordia eius, ita allocutus est coram omnibus : ' Cum essem monachus claustralis missus Dunelmiam pro negociis ecclesie nostre, et illinc in redeundo per Risebi, uespere / obscuro interceptus, petissem hospicium a domino Normanno, omnino repulsam sustinui ; domum uero domini Willelmi adiens et hospicium postulans, ab eo honorifice susceptus

F.133

---

[1] ' At Paris ' ; a regular usage in Med. Latin ; probably a corruption of *Parisiis*. The Parisii were a Gallic tribe, and the old name of the town was *Lutetia Parisiorum*.

[2] After High Mass holy water was carried round the houses of parishioners and they and their family were sprinkled with it. The money collected on such occasions seems to have been used for the support of poor students. See Du Cange, *s.v.*, Benificia aquae benedictae. *questu = quaestu*.

days when he was a poor student in the schools of Paris,
he caused to be summoned to him, and as a token of his
affectionate gratitude conferred upon him an ecclesiastical
benefice sufficient to maintain him. To a certain servant
of his predecessor, who had at the bidding of his lord
fettered his feet when he was put in prison, he gave food
and clothing for all the days of his life. To the son of
Elias, the butler of Abbot Hugh, when he did homage to
him for his father's land, he said in full court; ' For
seven years have I put off your homage for the land
which Abbot Hugh gave your father, because the gift
of that land was to the detriment of the hall of Elmswell,
but now I give way, for I remember the kindness which
your father showed me when I was in chains ; for he
sent me a portion of that very same wine which his lord
was used to drink, bidding me to be comforted in God.'
To Master Walter, the son of Master William of Diss,
when he besought him of his charity that he might have
the vicarage of the church of Chevington, he replied ;
' Your father was master of the schools : and when I
was a poor clerk, he, out of pure charity and making no
conditions, gave me admission to his school and the
opportunity of learning ; and I now for God's sake grant
your desire.' When it chanced that two knights of Risby,
William and Norman were amerced in his court, he thus
addressed them in the presence of all, ' When I was
a cloister monk and having been sent to Durham on
business of our Church, I was returning home by Risby,
I was benighted and asked Lord Norman to give me
lodging ; but he utterly refused to take me in ; but
when I approached the house of Lord William and
asked for lodging, I was received by him with honour.
Wherefore from Norman I will recover twenty shillings,
to wit, the full amerciment without mercy. But to

sum : et ideo xx solidos, scilicet misericordiam, sine misericordia integram recipiam a Normanno ; Willelmo autem gratias ago et debitam miseracionem[1] xx. solidorum gratanter remitto.'

Quedam iuuencula uirguncula, hostiatim uictum querens, conquesta est abbati, quod unus ex filiis Ricardi filii Drogonis eam vi oppresserat ; que tandem, procurante abbate, pro bono pacis unam marcam accepit. Abbas autem iiii[or] marcas accepit ab eodem R. pro concessione concordie ; set omnes illas v. marcas iussit dari statim cuidam mercatori, hoc pacto, ut prefatam pauperculam duceret in uxorem.

In uilla Sancti Ædmundi domos lapideas[2] emit abbas, et eas scolarum regimini assignauit, hac occasione, ut pauperes clerici in perpetuum ibi quieti essent de conduccione domus, ad quam conducendam denarium uel obolum singuli scolares, tam inpotentes quam potentes, bis in anno conferre cogebantur.

Recuperacio manerii de Mildenhala[3] pro mille marculis[4] argenti et centum, et eiectio iudeorum de uilla Sancti Ædmundi, et fundatio noui hospitalis de Babbewell, magne probitatis sunt indicia.

Dominus abbas peciit a rege literas ut iudei[5] eicerentur a uilla Sancti Ædmundi, allegans quod quicquid est in uilla Sancti Ædmundi, uel infra bannam leucam,[6]

---

[1] *miseracionem = misericordiam* ('amercement')
[2] In School Hall Street, just outside the Abbey precincts ; see L p. 46
[3] See Appendix G
[4] The diminutive may mean no more than 'paltry marks,' or might conceivably be used to emphasize that they were silver marks as opposed to gold.   The diminutive is dropped on the next page.
[5] Fifty-seven Jews were killed on Palm Sunday, March 18, 1190, a year notorious for such massacres ; see *Mem.* II. 6 ; III. 7.   The ejection of the Jews may have been for their own good.   Their only hope was to take refuge in the castle of the town where they lived.   They would then

William I offer my thanks and gratefully remit the amerciment of twenty shillings which he owes me.'

A certain young maid, who begged her food from door to door, complained to the Abbot that one of the sons of Richard FitzDrogo had deforced her ; at length at the Abbot's suggestion, she accepted one mark for the sake of peace. But the Abbot took four marks from the said Richard for granting him his peace, and ordered all those five marks to be given at once to a certain merchant on condition that he took the aforesaid young girl to wife.

The Abbot bought some stone houses in the town of St. Edmund and assigned them to the master of the schools, in order that the poor clerks might be quit of hiring houses—for which each scholar, whether he could or could not, was forced to pay a penny or halfpenny twice a year.

The recovery of the manor of Mildenhall for eleven hundred paltry marks of silver, and the expulsion of the Jews from the town of St. Edmund, and the foundation of the new hospital of Babwell are all proofs of the Abbot's excellence.

The lord Abbot petitioned the King that he might have letters for the expulsion of the Jews from the town of St. Edmund, alleging that everything that is in the town of St. Edmund or within its liberties belongs of right to St. Edmund : therefore the Jews must either

---

be protected as being the property of the King. But there was no castle at Bury, and there were obvious difficulties about harbouring them in the Abbey ; as Samson's argument puts it, they could not be St. Edmund's men.

[8] See p. 6o. The area is given in DB as a league and a half by a league and a half. The word means jurisdiction over a league (cp. Fr. *banlieue*, Ger. *Banmeile*).

de iure Sancti Ædmundi est : ergo, uel iudei debent
esse homines Sancti Ædmundi, uel de uilla sunt eiciendi.
Data est ergo licentia, ut eos eiceret, ita tamen quod
haberent omnia katalla,[1] scilicet et precia domorum
suarum et terrarum. Et cum emissi essent, et armata
manu conducti ad diuersa oppida, abbas iussit sollempniter excomunicari per omnes ecclesias et ad omnia
altaria omnes illos, qui de cetero receptarent iudeos uel
in hospicio reciperent in uilla Sancti Ædmundi. Quod
tamen postea dispensatum est per iusticiarios regis,
scilicet, ut si iudei uenerint ad magna placita [2] abbatis
ad exigendum debita sua a debitoribus suis, sub hac
occasione poterunt duobus diebus et ii. noctibus hospitari
in uilla, tercio autem die libere discedent.

Abbas optulit regi Ricardo quingentas marcas pro
manerio de Mildenhala,[3] dicens illud manerium lx.
librarum et decem, et pro tanto esse rollatum in magna
rolla de Wincestria. Et cum ita spem uoti sui concepisset,
cepit res dilacionem usque in crastinum. Interim uenit
F.133v aliquis dicens regi, manerium illud bene / ualere c. libras.
In crastino ergo abbate petitioni sue instante, dixit rex :
' Nichil est, domine abbas, quod queris ; uel mille marcas
dabis, uel manerium non habebis.' Cum autem regina
Alienor [4] secundum consuetudinem regni deberet accipere
c. marcas ubi rex cepit mille, accepit a nobis calicem
magnum aureum in precium c. marcarum, et eundem
calicem nobis reddidit pro anima domini sui regis Henrici, qui eum primo dederat Sancto Ædmundo. Alia

---

[1] Here it means ' chattels.' See p. 2
[2] ' The great pleas ' ; *i.e.* at the central court of the Liberty of St.
Edmund, held at Cateshill about 2 miles east of Bury, the Abbot himself
presiding in lieu of the Sheriff.
[3] See Appendix G
[4] See Appendix H

be St. Edmund's men or be expelled from the town. Leave was therefore given him to expel them, but on this condition, that they should keep all their chattels and have the value of their houses and lands as well. And when they had been sent forth and conducted under armed escort to other towns, the Abbot ordered that all those who from that time forth should receive Jews or harbour them in the town of St. Edmund should be solemnly excommunicated in every church and at every altar. Nevertheless afterwards the King's justices ordained that, if Jews came to the Abbot's great pleas to exact the money owed them from their debtors, they should under those circumstances have leave to be lodged in the town for two nights and two days, and on the third day should depart in freedom.

The Abbot offered King Richard five hundred marks for the manor of Mildenhall, saying that the manor was worth seventy pounds and was enrolled at this value in the Great Roll of Winchester. And when for this reason he had conceived the hope that his desire would be fulfilled, the matter was postponed till the next day. In the meantime someone approached the King and told him that the manor was worth at least a hundred pounds. On the morrow therefore, when the Abbot pressed his petition, the King said, ' My Lord Abbot, what you ask is impossible. Either you shall give a thousand marks or you shall not have the manor.' But since Queen Eleanor, according to the custom of the realm, had the right to receive a hundred marks when the King received a thousand, she received from us a great golden cup worth a hundred marks ; and she returned the said cup to us on behalf of the soul of her Lord King Henry, who had first given it to St. Edmund. On another occasion when the treasure of our Church

quoque uice, cum thesaurus ecclesie nostre portaretur
Lundonias ad redempcionem regis Ricardi, eadem regina
eundem calicem adquietauit pro c. marcis et nobis
reddidit, accipiens cartam nostram a nobis in testimonium promissionis nostre facte in uerbo ueritatis, quod
calicem illum nunquam pro aliquo casu ab ecclesia nostra
alienabimus. Cum autem persoluta esset tanta pecunia
cum magna difficultate adquisita, sedit abbas in capitulo,
dicens se habere aliquam porcionem de tanto questu
tanti manerii. Et responsum est a conuentu quod hoc
iustum est, et ad uoluntatem uestram fiat. Et dixit
abbas, se posse uendicare de iure dimidiam partem,
ostendens se plusquam cccc. marcas cum magnis laboribus expendisse, set dixit se esse contentum quadam porcione illius manerii, que dicitur Ikelingham ; quod
concessum est ei libentissime a conuentu.[1] Abbas uero
hoc audiens, dixit : ' Et ego illam partem terre recipio
ad meum opus, non ut retineam in manu mea, uel ut
parentibus meis donem, set pro anima mea et pro anima-
bus uestris communiter dono illam nouo hospitali de
Babbewell, in sustentacionem pauperum et usum hospitalitatis.' Dixit, et ita factum est, et carta regis postea
confirmatum. Hec et consimilia facta, scriptis et laudibus eternanda, fecit abbas Samson. Nichil tamen se
dixit agere, nisi posset facere in diebus suis dedicari.[2]
ecclesiam nostram ; post quod factum, asseruit se uelle

---

[1] On November 12, 1189. The charter having been lost, the King
gave another confirming Mildenhall to the Abbey, and with it another
charter placing the manor, less Icklingham, at the disposal of the sacrist,
on condition of his paying £12 annually to the Hospital of St. Saviour
(July 18, 1198). The Abbot in 1199 bestowed further endowments on
the Hospital.

[2] The church had been dedicated on the completion of the choir by
Abbot Baldwin (see p. xix). Samson aimed at the completion of the whole

was carried to London for the ransom of King Richard, the said Queen redeemed the same cup for a hundred marks and sent it back to us, receiving a charter from us in token of our promise on the word of truth, that we would never alienate that cup from our Church under any circumstances whatsoever. Now when we had paid this great sum of money, which had only been raised with great difficulty, the Abbot, sitting in Chapter, said that he claimed a certain portion of the large profit derived from so great a manor. And the Convent replied that this was just, and bade him do as he thought good. And the Abbot said that he might with justice claim a half, and made it clear to us that he had by a great effort paid four hundred marks of the purchase money ; but he said that he was content to have a cer- tain portion of the manor named Icklingham. And this was gladly granted him by the Convent. But when he heard this, he replied, ' I take that portion of land for my own purposes, but not that I may keep it in my own hands or give it to my kin ; but for my soul's sake and for your souls likewise, I give it to the new hospital of Babwell, for the maintenance of the poor and the entertainment of strangers.' So said he and thus it was done, and afterwards confirmed by a charter from the King. Such were the deeds of Abbot Samson, deeds worthy of immortal record and renown. Yet he said that all this was naught, unless he could in his lifetime carry out the dedication of our Church, which once done, he declared himself ready to die, and for the

---

church, and seems to have accomplished his desire, but there is no record of any such dedication, although as early as 1198 Innocent III gave him leave to make arrangements for it. See Cal. Pap. Letters I, December 1, 1198.

mori : ad cuius facti sollemnitatem dixit se esse paratum
expendere duo milia marcarum argenti, dummodo
dominus rex ibi esset presens et res debito honore peragi
possit.

Nuntiatum est abbati, quod ecclesia de Wlpet [1]
uacaret, Waltero de Constantiis electo ad episcopatum
de Lincolnia. Mox conuocauit priorem et magnam
partem conuentus, et incipiens narracionem suam, et
ait : ' Bene scitis quod multum laboraui propter ecclesiam de Wlpet, propter quam habendam in proprios usus
uestros, iter arripui uersus Romam per consilium uestrum,
tempore scismatis inter papam Allexandrum et Octauia-
F.134 num,[2] transiuique per Italiam, illa tempestate / qua omnes
clerici qui portabant literas domini pape Allexandri
capiebantur, et quidam incarcerabantur, quidam sus-
pendebantur, quidam truncatis naso et labiis remitte-
bantur ad papam in dedecus et confusionem ipsius. Ego
uero simulaui me esse Scottum, et Scotti habitum induens
et gestum Scotti habens, sepe illis qui mihi illudebant
baculum meum excussi ad modum teli quod uocatur
gaueloc, de more Scottorum uoces comminatorias pro-
ferens. Obuiantibus et interrogantibus quis essem nichil
respondi, nisi : ' *Ride, ride Rome, turne Cantwereberei.*' [3]
Sic feci, ut me et propositum meum celarem, ' tucius et
peterem Scotti sub ymagine Romam.' [4] Impetratis autem
literis a domino papa pro uoto meo, in redeundo transiui
per quoddam castellum, sicut ' uia me ducebat ab urbe ; '
et ecce ministri de castro circumdederunt me, capientes
et dicentes : ' Iste soliuagus, qui Scottum se facit, uel
explorator est uel portitor literarum falsi pape Allexandri.'

---

[1] See Appendix I
[2] See Appendix J
[3] This must mean, ' I am riding to Rome and turning away from
Canterbury.' The Scots supported Octavian. Hence Samson's disguise.
[4] A hexameter verse, probably of Samson's composition

celebration of this he said that he was ready to expend two thousand marks of silver, provided that the King should be present in person, and that the ceremony could be performed with all due honour.

It was reported to the Abbot that the church of Woolpit was now vacant, Walter of Coutances having been elected to the Bishopric of Lincoln. Soon afterwards he summoned the Prior and a great part of the Convent, and beginning his story, he said, ' You are well aware that I have laboured much for the church of Woolpit ; for, that I might recover it for your own use, I journeyed to Rome in obedience to your counsel, at the time of the schism between Pope Alexander and Octavian and I passed through Italy at a time when all clerks carrying letters for the Lord Pope Alexander were seized and some of them imprisoned, some hanged, and others sent to the Pope with their lips and noses lopped off, to his great dishonour and confusion. But I pretended that I was a Scot, and putting on Scottish garb, and bearing myself after the fashion of a Scot, I often thrust out my staff as it were a javelin against those that mocked me, uttering threatening words after the fashion of the Scots. And when those that met me asked who I was, I answered nothing save ' Ride, ride Rome, turne Canterbury.' Thus did I that I might disguise myself and my purpose and that
in likeness of a Scot
I might more safely wend my way to Rome.

And when I had obtained letters from the Lord Pope such as I desired, on my homeward way from Rome I passed by a certain castle, and behold ! the servants of the castle surrounded me, seizing me and saying, ' This fellow that wanders all alone, pretending that he is a Scot, is either a spy or carries letters of the false

Et dum perscrutabantur panniculos meos et caligas et
femoralia et etiam sotulares ueteres, quos super humeros
portaui ad consuetudinem Scottorum, inieci manum
meam in peram quam portaui cuteam, in qua scriptum
domini pape continebatur, positum sub ciffo paruo, quo
bibere solebam : et Domino Deo uolente et sancto
Ædmundo, simul extraxi scriptum illud cum ciffo, ita
quod, brachium extendens in altum, breue tenui sub
ciffo. Ciffum quidem uiderunt, set breue non perceperunt. Et sic euasi manus eorum in nomine Domini.
Quicquid monete habui abstulerunt a me, unde oportuit
me hostiatim mendicare sine omni expensa, donec in
Angliam uenirem. Audiens autem quod ecclesia illa
data esset Galfrido Ridello, contristata est anima mea
eo quod in uanum laboraui. Ueniens ergo domum,
feretro Sancti Ædmundi latenter me supposui, timens
ne dominus abbas me caperet et incarceraret, qui nichil
mali merueram ; nec erat monachus qui mecum audebat
loqui, nec laicus qui michi auderet uictum ministrare,
nisi aliquis furtiue. Tandem, inito consilio, misit me
abbas apud Acram in exilium, ibique diu moram feci.
Hec et multa alia mala innumerabilia passus sum propter
ecclesiam de Wlpet ; set benedictus Deus, qui omnia
cooperatur in bonum,[1] Ecce ! ecclesia, pro qua tot mala
sustinui, data est in manu mea, et nunc potestatem
habeo donandi eam ubi uoluero, quia uacat. Et ego
eam conuentui reddo,[2] et in suos proprios usus assigno
antiquam consuetudinem uel pensionem x. marcarum,
quam perdidistis plus quam lx. annis. Integram libentius
F.134*v* uobis / eam darem, si possem ; set scio, quod episcopus

---

[1] Rom. viii. 28
[2] Only as far as the *pensio* of ten marks is concerned. The Abbot retained the advowson.

Pope Alexander.' And while they searched my rags and boots and drawers, and even my old shoes, which I carried hung over my shoulders after the fashion of the Scots, I thrust my hand into my leathern wallet which contained the writing of the Lord Pope, placed beneath a small cup, from which I used to drink ; and by the will of God and of St. Edmund, I pulled out the writing together with the cup, so that when I raised my arm on high, I held the letter under the cup. The cup they saw, but not the letter. And thus I escaped from their hands in the name of the Lord. Whatever coin I had they took from me, so that I had to beg from door to door, without any money to spend, until I came to England. But when I heard that the church had been given to Geoffrey Ridell, my soul was filled with sorrow for that I had laboured all in vain. So when I came home, I hid myself secretly beneath the feretory of St. Edmund, fearing lest the lord Abbot should seize me and put me in prison, though I had deserved no such thing ; nor was there a monk dared speak with me nor any layman feed me, save by stealth. At length, after he had taken counsel, the Abbot sent me into exile at Acre, and there I remained for a long time. These and many other ills beyond number I have suffered for the church of Wool-pit. But now—blessed be God, who worketh all things for good !—behold ! the church for which I have endured so many ills, has been given into my hands ; and now, since it is vacant, I have power to bestow it as I will. And I restore it to the Convent, and assign to its proper use the ancient custom or pension of ten marks, which you have lost for more than sixty years. I would gladly give you the church in its entirety ; but I know

Norwicensis [1] michi contradiceret, uel si hoc concederet,
tali occasione subieccionem et obedientiam de uobis sibi
uendicaret, quod est inconsultum et inconueniens.
Faciamus ergo quod de iure possumus facere ; ponamus
clericum uicarium, qui episcopo respondeat de spiritualibus, et uobis de decem marcis ; et uolo, si uos consulitis,
ut uicaria illa donetur alicui consanguineo R. de Heng-
heham, monachi et fratris uestri, qui michi fuit consors
in illo itinere uersus Romam, et eisdem periculis expositus
et propter idem negocium.' His dictis omnes surreximus
et gratias egimus ; et receptus est Hugo clericus frater
predicti Rogeri ad predictam ecclesiam, salua nobis
annua pensione x^{cem} marcarum.

In manerio monacorum Cantuariensium, quod dicitur
Illegga, et quod est in hundredo abbatis, contigit fieri
homicidium.   Homines uero archiepiscopi noluerunt
pati, ut illi homicide starent ad rectum in curia sancti
Ædmundi.   Abbas uero conquestus est regi Henrico
dicens, quod archiepiscopus Baldewinus uendicabat sibi
libertates ecclesie nostre, optentu carte noue quam rex
dederat ecclesie Cantuariensi post mortem sancti Thome.
Rex autem respondit, se nunquam fecisse cartam aliquam
in preiudicium ecclesie nostre, nec aliquid sancto
Ædmundo uelle aufferre, quod habere solebat.   Quo
audito, dixit abbas consiliariis priuatis suis : ' Sanius
consilium est, ut archiepiscopus conqueratur de me
quam ego de archiepiscopo.   Uolo me ponere in saisinam
huius libertatis, et post me defendam cum auxilio sancti
Ædmundi, cuius ius hoc esse carte nostre testantur.'

---

[1] Samson follows the injunction contained in the Pope's letter (No. 2)
given in Appendix J.   He clearly felt that he was better able to deal with the
Bishop than the Convent would have been.   But he realises that the Bishop
might object if the church was served by a monk, while the revenues were
taken by the Convent, or alternatively, if a secular were put in with an
inadequate stipend, the Convent pocketing the balance.

that the Bishop of Norwich would say me nay, or, if he permitted it, would avail himself of the opportunity to claim submission and obedience from you, which it is unwise and unbecoming for us to give. Let us therefore do what we have the right to do ; let us appoint a clerk as vicar, who will be answerable to the Bishop for things spiritual, and to you for the ten marks ; and I desire, if you think good, that the vicarage should be given to some kinsman of Roger of Hingham, your monk and brother, who was my comrade on that journey to Rome and was exposed to the same perils on behalf of the same cause.' When he had said this, we all rose and thanked him, and Hugh, a clerk and brother of the said Roger, was accepted for the aforesaid church, saving always our yearly pension of ten marks.

In the manor of the monks of Canterbury named Eleigh, which is in the Abbot's hundred, it chanced that a man was slain. But the Archbishop's men refused to allow those that killed him to be brought to trial in the court of St. Edmund. The Abbot, however, complained to King Henry, saying that Archbishop Baldwin claimed for himself the liberties of our Church, on the pretext of a new charter which the King had given to the Church of Canterbury after the death of St. Thomas. But the King replied that he had never given any charter to the prejudice of our Church, and that he did not desire to deprive St. Edmund of any of his ancient rights. On hearing this the Abbot said to his private counsellors, ' It is better policy that the Archbishop should complain of me than that I should complain of the Archbishop. I therefore desire to place myself in seizin of this liberty, and will afterwards defend myself with the

Subito ergo summo mane, procurante Roberto de Cokefeld, missi sunt circiter quater xx. homines armati ad
uillam de Illegga, et ex inopinato ceperunt illos tres
homicidas et ligatos duxerunt ad Sanctum Ædmundum,
et in fundum carceris proiecerunt. Conquerente inde
archiepiscopo, Ranulfus de Glanuilla iusticiarius precepit, ut homines illi ponerentur per uadium et plegios
ad standum ad rectum in curia qua deberent stare,
et summonitus est abbas, ut ueniret ad curiam regis
responsurus de ui et iniuria, quam dicebatur fecisse
archiepiscopo. Abbas uero sine omni exonio se pluries
presentauit. Tandem in capite ieiunii steterunt coram
rege in capitulo Cantuariensi, et lecte sunt palam carte
ecclesiarum hinc et inde. Et respondit dominus rex :
' Iste carte eiusdem antiquitatis sunt et ab eodem rege
Ædwardo [1] emanant. Nescio quid dicam, nisi ut carte
ad inuicem pugnent.' * Cui abbas dixit : ' Quicquid
de cartis dicatur, nos in saisina sumus, et hucusque
fuimus, et de hoc ponere me uolo in uerumdictum
duorum comitatuum, scilicet, Norfolchie et Suthfolchie,/
F.135 se hoc concedere.' [2] Set archiepiscopus Baldwinus,[3]

---

[1] The manor of Monk's Eleigh belonged to the Archbishop, but lay
within the Liberty of St. Edmund, and the Abbot claims that it comes
under his jurisdiction. Cp. Baldwin's Feudal Book (FD p. 9) : ' En descrip-
tos hic habes quicunque hec uides VIII hundretos et dimidium in quibus
tota saca et soca et regales omnes consuetudines sunt Sancti Ædmundi
super uniuscuiusque terram quicumque ibi possideat.'

[2] See Appendix K

[3] Archbishop of Canterbury (1184–90). The date of this dispute would
appear to be 1186 ; cp. *tandem in capite ieiunii* ; *i.e.* when the king went to
Canterbury on February 11, 1187, to settle disputes between the Archbishop and his monks (Gervase, RS I. 353), see below.

* In the margin there is the following note : ' Quia carta quam habemus
de sancto Ædwardo antiquior est, quam carta quam habent monachi
Cantuarienses. Quia carta, quam habent, non dat eis libertatem, nisi
inter homines suos tantum : et carta nostra loquitur de tempore regis
Ædwardi et de tempore matris sue regine Emme, que habuit viii. hundredos et dimidium in dotem, ante tempora sancti Ædwardi, et Milden-
hale insimul.'

help of St. Edmund, to whose right in this matter our charters bear witness.' So, early in the morning, Robert de Cockfield being in charge of the enterprise, about four score armed men were suddenly despatched to the township of Eleigh, and taking them by surprise, they seized the three man-slayers in question and brought them bound to St. Edmund's and cast them into the lowest dungeon. When the Archbishop complained of this, Ranulph de Glanvill the Justiciar gave orders that those men should be bound by gage and pledge to stand their trial in that court where they ought so to stand ; and the Abbot was summoned to come to the King's court to answer the charge of violence and injury which he was said to have done to the Archbishop. Now the Abbot presented himself many times without making an excuse that he was unable to attend. And at length at the beginning of Lent they stood before the King in the chapterhouse of Canterbury, and the charters of both Churches were read aloud by the parties. And our lord the King replied, ' These charters are of the same age and both were issued by the same King Edward. I know not what to say save that the charters contradict each other.' * The Abbot replied, ' Whatever may be said of the charters, we are in seizin and have been so up to this time, and on this matter I desire to place myself on the verdict of two counties, to wit, Norfolk and Suffolk, that they allow this to be true.' But Archbishop Baldwin,

---

* Because the charter we hold from St. Edward is older than that held by the monks of Canterbury. Because the charter which they hold, gives them no liberty save among their own men : and our charter speaks of the time of King Edward and that of his mother Queen Emma, who had eight and a half hundreds for her dowry before the times of St. Edward, and had Mildenhall as well.

habito prius consilio cum suis, dixit homines Norforchie
et Suthfolchie multum diligere Sanctum Ædmundum, et
magnam partem illorum comitatuum esse sub dictione
abbatis, et ideo se nolle stare illorum arbitrio. Rex uero
iratus inde et indignans surrexit, et recedendo dixit :
' Qui potest capere capiat ; ' [1] et sic res cepit dilacionem,
' et adhuc sub iudice lis est.' [2] Uidi tamen, quod quidam
homines monacorum Cantuariensium uulnerati fuerunt
usque ad mortem a rusticis de uilla de Meldingis, que
sita est in hundredo Sancti Ædmundi ; et quia sciuerunt
quod actor forum rei sequi debet,[3] maluerunt silere et
dissimulare, quam inde clamorem facere abbati siue
bailliuis eius, quia nullo modo uoluerunt uenire in
curiam Sancti Ædmundi ad placitandum.   Postea
leuauerunt homines de Illegga quoddam trebuchet,[4] ad
faciendam iusticiam pro falsis mensuris panis uel bladi
mensurandi, unde conquestus est abbas domino Eliensi
episcopo,[5] tunc iusticiario et cancellario. Ille uero
abbatem audire nolebat, quia dicebatur olfacere archie-
piscopatum, qui uacabat tunc temporis.[6] Cum autem
uenisset apud nos, et susceptus esset ut legatus,[7] antequam
recederet, orationem fecit ad feretrum sancti martiris ;
abbasque nacta oportunitate dixit, cunctis audientibus
qui aderant : ' Domine episcope, libertas, quam sibi
uendicant monaci Cantuarienses, est ius sancti Ædmundi,
cuius corpus presens est, et quia non uis me adiuuare
ad tuendam libertatem ecclesie sue, pono loquelam inter

---

[1] Matt. xix. 12. Here not in the Biblical sense, but meaning ' Let him
take who can ! '
[2] Horace, *Ars Poetica*, 78
[3] Cp. Gratian, pars 2, caus. 3, quaest. 6, canon 16
[4] ' weigh-beam.' The Archbishop as Lord of the Manor claims to deal
with cases of false weight or measure, and presumably to make a charge
for weighing (tronage). The Bishop of Ely later made the same claim for
his manors lying within the Liberty of St. Edmund ; see p. 132 sqq.

after consultation with his folk, said that the men of
Norfolk and Suffolk had a great love for St. Edmund
and that a great part of those counties was under the
Abbot's jurisdiction, wherefore he refused to stand by
their testimony. The King, however, was angry and
rose in indignation, and said as he departed, ' Let him
take who can ! ' And so the matter was postponed
' and the suit is still unjudged.' But I noted that certain men of the monks of Canterbury were wounded,
even unto death, by country folk of the township of
Milden, which lies in the hundred of St. Edmund ; and
because they knew that the complainant must sue in the
court of the accused, the monks, being unwilling to come
to the court of St. Edmund to plead, preferred to say
nothing and shut their eyes, sooner than make any complaint to the Abbot or his bailiffs. Afterwards the men
of Eleigh set up a weigh-beam to do justice on false
measure of bread and corn, and the Abbot therefore
complained to the Lord Bishop of Ely, who was then Justiciar and Chancellor. But since he was said to be sniffing
after the Archbishopric which was at that time vacant,
he refused to hear the Abbot. But when he came to us
and was received as legate, before he departed, he prayed
at the feretory of the holy Martyr ; and the Abbot, seizing the opportunity, said to him in the hearing of all pre-
ent, ' My lord Bishop, the liberty, which the monks of
Canterbury claim for themselves, is the right of St.
Edmund, whose body is here present ; and because you

---

[5] William Longchamp, consecrated December 31, 1189, as Bishop and
appointed Chancellor in the same year.

[6] The see became vacant by Archbishop Baldwin's death at the siege
of Acre on November 19, 1190.

[7] He was appointed *legatus a latere* on June 5, 1190

te et ipsum. Ipse de cetero procuret ius suum.' Cancellarius nichil dignatus est respondere ; qui infra annum
Angliam exire compulsus est, et diuinam ulcionem
expertus est. Cum autem idem cancellarius redisset de
Almannia,[1] et applicuisset apud Gippewic, et pernoc-
tasset apud Heggham, uenit rumor ad abbatem quod
cancellarius uellet transire per Sanctum Ædmundum,
apud nos missam in crastino auditurus. Prohibuit ergo
abbas, ne celebrarentur diuina, dum cancellarius esset
in ecclesia presens, quia dixit se audisse apud Londonias
Londoniensem episcopum pronuntiasse cancellarium esse
excommunicatum,[2] et excommunicatum recessisse ab
Anglia, coram sex episcopis, et nominatim pro uiolentia
illata Archiepiscopo Eboracensi apud Doffram.[3] Ueniens
ergo in crastino cancellarius apud nos, non inuenit qui
missam ei cantaret, nec clericum nec monachum. Immo
sacerdos stans ad primam missam ad canonem misse et
ceteri sacerdotes ad altaria cessauerunt, stantes inmotis
labiis, donec nuntius ueniret dicens, illum recessisse ab
ecclesia. Cancellarius omnia dissimulans, multa graua-
mina intulit abbati, donec, procurantibus amicis, hinc
F.135*v* et inde / ad pacis osculum reuersi sunt.

    Cum rex Henricus accepisset crucem [4] et uenisset
infra mensem ad nos orationis gratia, abbas ipse sibi
fecit crucem occulte de lineo panno, et tenens in una
manu crucem et acum et filum, petiuit licenciam a rege

----

[1] He visited King Richard in his captivity and returned with a letter
from the Emperor in the spring of 1193.
[2] October 6, 1191 (Gervase RS VIII. 507)
[3] Geoffrey, Archbishop of York, illegitimate son of Henry II, was
arrested by order of Longchamp near Dover on September 16, 1191.
[4] At Gisors, January 21, 1188. On 11th February he held a great council
at Geddington in Northamptonshire at which the Bishop of Norwich took
the cross. The king therefore came to St. Edmunds on his way from
Geddington.

refuse to defend the right of his Church, I place my complaint between him and you. Let him henceforth watch over his own right.' To this the Chancellor deigned not reply, and before a year was out, he was forced to fly from England and felt the vengeance of God. But when the said Chancellor had returned from Germany and, after landing at Ipswich, had spent the night at Hitcham, news reached the Abbot that the Chancellor desired to pass through St. Edmund's and hear mass in our Church on the morrow. The Abbot therefore forbade the celebration of divine office, while the Chancellor was present in the church ; for he said that he had heard in London that the Bishop of London had pronounced the Chancellor to be excommunicate, and that he had left England after being excommunicated in the presence of six Bishops, on account of the violence which he had offered the Archbishop of York at Dover. When therefore the Chancellor came to us on the morrow, he found no one to sing mass for him, neither clerk nor monk. Nay more, the priest who was celebrating the first mass and had already reached the canon of the mass, and the other priests at the altars, ceased to celebrate and stood with lips unmoved, until a messenger came announcing that he had departed from the church. The Chancellor pretended to be blind to all this, but caused the Abbot many annoyances, until at the instance of their friends they both returned to the kiss of peace.

When King Henry had taken the Cross and within a month came to us to pray, the Abbot himself secretly made a cross of linen cloth, and holding the cross in one hand together with a needle and thread, he asked leave

ut acciperet crucem ; set denegata est ei licentia, procurante episcopo Norwicensi Johanne et dicente, quia
non expediret patrie nec tutum esset comitatibus Norfolchie et Sutfolchie, si episcopus Norwicensis et abbas
Sancti Ædmundi simul recederent.

Cum rumor uenisset Lundoniis de capcione regis
Ricardi et incarceracione eius in Alemannia, et barones
conuenissent pro consilio accipiendo, prosiliit abbas
coram omnibus dicens, se esse paratum querere dominum
suum regem, uel in tapinagio ¹ uel alio modo, donec
eum inueniret et certam noticiam de eo haberet ; ex
quo uerbo magnam laudem sibi adquisiuit.

Cum cancellarius, episcopus scilicet Eliensis, legati
fungeretur officio et concilium celebraret apud Lundoniam,² et quedam decreta proposuisset contra nigros
monacos,³ loquens de uagacione eorum ad sanctum
Thomam et ad sanctum Ædmundum peregrinacionis
optentu, et contra abbates loquens, prefiniens eis certum
numerum equorum : respondit abbas Samson : ' Nos
non recipimus aliquod decretum contra regulam sancti
Benedicti, que permittit abbatibus liberam disposi-
cionem habere de monachis suis. Ego uero baroniam
sancti Ædmundi seruo et regnum eius ; nec sufficiunt
michi tredecim equi, sicut quibusdam aliis abbatibus,
nisi plures habeam ad execucionem regie iustitie con-
seruande.'

Cum esset werra ⁴ in tota Anglia, capto rege Ricardo,
abbas cum toto conuentu sollempniter excomunicauit
omnes factores werre et pacis turbatores, non timens

---

¹ ' On the quiet,' cp. Fr. *en tapinois*
² Longchamp held a council at Westminster on October 13, 1190.
³ Benedictines and Cluniacs
⁴ John, asserting that Richard was dead, attempted to seize the throne

of the King to take the Cross. But such leave was refused
him, at the instance of John, Bishop of Norwich, who
said it would not be expedient for the country nor safe
for the counties of Norfolk and Suffolk, if both the Bishop
of Norwich and the Abbot of St. Edmund departed at
the same time.

When news reached London of the capture of King
Richard and his imprisonment in Germany, and the
Barons had met to take counsel, the Abbot sprang forth
before them all, saying that he was ready, secretly or
otherwise, to seek his lord the King until he found him
and had sure knowledge of him ; from which saying he
won much praise.

When the Chancellor, to wit, the Bishop of Ely, in
virtue of his authority as legate, held a council at London,
he proposed certain decrees against the black monks,
holding forth about their wandering off to the shrines of
St. Thomas and St. Edmund on the pretext of a pilgrim-
age, and denouncing their Abbots and restricting them
to a fixed number of horses ; whereupon the Abbot
replied, ' We refuse to accept any decree that is contrary
to the Rule of St. Benedict, which grants Abbots the free
disposal of their monks. As for myself, I hold the barony
of St. Edmund and his realm, and thirteen horses are
not enough for me as they are for certain other Abbots,
but I must have more for the execution of the King's
justice.'

When there was war in all England after the capture
of King Richard, the Abbot with the whole Convent
solemnly excommunicated all makers of war and dis-

---

and occupied Windsor and Wallingford Castles. There was a general
rising against him, the castles were recaptured, and a truce was made
(May 1193). In July the news arrived of Richard's release.

comitem Johannem fratrem regis nec alium, unde
abbas magnanimus dicebatur. Post quod factum iuit
ad obsidionem de Windleshor, ubi armatus cum
quibusdam aliis abbatibus Anglie, uexillum [1] proprium
habens, et plures milites ducens ad multas expensas,

plus ibi consilio quam probitate nitens.

Nos uero claustrales tale factum periculosum iudicauimus,
timentes consequentiam, ne forte futurus abbas cogatur
in propria persona ire in expedicionem bellicam. Datis
induciis illo tempore iuit in Alemanniam, et ibi uisitauit
regem cum donis plurimis.

Post redditum regis Ricardi in Angliam, data est
licentia torneandi [2] militibus. Ad quod faciendum conuenerunt multi inter Theford et Sanctum Ædmundum,
F.136 set prohibuit / eos Abbas ; qui resistentes, uotum suum
impleuerunt. Alia uice uenerunt quater uiginti iuuenes
cum sectis suis, filii nobilium, ad uindicium faciendum
cum plenis armis ad predictum locum. Quo perfecto,
redierunt in uillam istam causa hospitandi. Abbas uero
hoc audiens, portas iussit obserari et eos omnes includi.
Crastinus dies erat uigilia apostolorum Petri et Pauli.
Fide ergo interposita, promittentes se non exire, nisi
per licenciam, manducauerunt omnes cum abbate illo
die ; set post prandium, abbate eunte in talamum
suum, surrexerunt omnes et inceperunt carolare et cantare, mittentes in uillam propter uinum, bibentes et
postea ululantes, abbati et conuentui somnum suum au-
ferentes, et omnia in derisum abbatis facientes, et diem

---

[1] In MS Harley 2278, this standard is depicted in brilliant colours
showing a golden lamb above the Tree of Life, on a field gules sprinkled
with stars and crescents of gold. On each side of the tree stand Adam
and Eve, while the serpent is twined about its trunk.

[2] The alleged aim was military efficiency, the real aim the raising of
money (1194). The charge was 20 marks for an earl, 10 for a baron, 4 for

turbers of the peace, fearing not Earl John, the King's
brother nor any other ; for which men called the Abbot
a man of high spirit. And after doing this he went to
the siege of Windsor, at which, with certain other
Abbots of England, he carried arms having his own
standard and leading a number of knights at great expense, though shining rather in counsel than in prowess.
But we cloister monks judged that such conduct was
hazardous, for we feared that in consequence some
future Abbot might perchance be constrained to go
forth in person on some warlike expedition. When a
truce was concluded on that occasion, he went to Germany and visited the King, bringing him many gifts.

After the return of King Richard to England, licenses
for tournaments were granted to knights. And a number
gathered for this purpose between Thetford and St.
Edmund's. The Abbot forbade them, but they resisted
his authority and fulfilled their desire. On another
occasion fourscore young men, the sons of nobles, came
with their followers to the same place fully armed for
a return match. This accomplished, they came to this
town to find lodging. But the Abbot, hearing this, gave
orders that the gates should be barred and all of them
shut in. The next day was the vigil of the Feast of
St. Peter and St. Paul. So, when they had promised
him that they would not go forth without his leave, they
all ate with the Abbot that day ; but after dinner, when
the Abbot retired to his lodgings, they all arose and
began to dance and sing, and sending into the town to
fetch wine, they drank, and after that they yelled, rob-

---

a knight with land, 2 for a knight with none. See Rymer's *Foedera*, I. i. 65,
where a writ licensing tournaments in various places is given (1194).

usque ad uesperam hoc modo deducentes, nec propter
mandatum abbatis uoluerunt desistere. Uespere uero
adueniente, seras portarum uille fregerunt, et ui exierunt. Abbas uero omnes sollemniter excomunicauit,
per consilium tamen archiepiscopi Huberti iusticiarii
tunc temporis ; quorum multi uenerunt ad emendacionem, absolucionem petentes.

Romam misit abbas sepius nuntios suos, non uacuos.
Primi [1] quos misit, statim postquam fuit benedictus,
impetrauerunt in genere omnes libertates et consuetudines que concesse fuerant prius, eciam tempore scismatis,
predecessoribus suis ; postea impetrauit, primus inter
abbates Anglie, quod dare posset episcopalem benedictionem [2] sollempniter ubicunque fuerit ; et hoc est
impetratum sibi et successoribus suis. Postea impetrauit
exempcionem [3] generalem sibi et successoribus suis ab
onmibus archiepiscopis Cantuariensibus, quam abbas
H. predecessor suus specialiter sibi adquisierat. Plures
et nouas libertates in illis confirmacionibus apponi fecit
abbas Samson ad maiorem libertatem et securitatem
ecclesie nostre. Uenit quidam clericus ad abbatem
portans literas petitorias de redditu ecclesiastico habendo.
Et abbas extrahens de scrinio suo septem scripta apostolica
cum bullis pendentibus, ita respondit : ' Ecce scripta
apostolica, quibus diuersi apostolici diuersis clericis eccle-
siastica beneficia petunt dari. Cum ergo illos pacauero
qui preuenerunt, tibi redditum dabo, quia qui prius
uenit ad molendinum prius molere debet.'

---

[1] These obtained renewal of liberties and customs of the Abbey from
Lucius III (1181–85) on March 31, 1182. A matter of routine, similar
charters being obtained from Urban III (1185–87), Celestine III (1191–98),
and Innocent III (1198–1216). See *Pinchbeck Register, ad init.*
[2] This privilege was granted by Urban III
[3] Granted by Clement III (1187–91) in 1188

bing the Abbot and the whole Convent of their sleep, and doing everything they could to make a mockery of the Abbot ; and they continued thus till evening and refused to obey the Abbot when he ordered them to desist. But when evening was come, they broke the gates of the town and forced their way out. But the Abbot solemnly excommunicated them all, by the advice of Hubert, Archbishop of Canterbury, who was then Justiciar. And many of them came to make amends, and begged for absolution.

The Abbot often sent his messengers to Rome, nor did they go empty-handed. The first whom he sent, immediately after his benediction, secured a general confirmation of all the liberties and customs granted aforetime to his predecessors, even in time of schism. Afterwards he, first among all the Abbots of England, secured the privilege of giving solemn episcopal benediction, wheresoever he might be ; and this was secured both for himself and those who should come after him. Later he obtained for himself and his successors a general exemption from the authority of all Archbishops of Canterbury, an exemption which Abbot Hugh had secured as a special privilege for himself. Abbot Samson also caused a number of fresh liberties to be added in these confirmations for the greater freedom and security of our Church. A certain clerk came to him bearing letters petitioning that he might be granted some ecclesiastical benefice. And the Abbot drawing from his case seven letters apostolic with their bulls still attached, replied, ' Behold these letters apostolic in which divers Popes ask that ecclesiastical benefices should be given to sundry clerks. When I have appeased them, and then only, I will give you a benefice : for he who comes first to the mill ought to have first grind.'

Facta est summonicio magna in hundredo de Rise-
brigga,[1] ut audiretur querela et rectum comitis de Clara
F.136v apud Witham.[2]/ Ipse uero constipatus multis baronibus
et militibus, comite Alberico et multis aliis assistentibus,
dixit quod balliui sui fecerunt ei intelligere, quod ipsi
solebant annuatim accipere ad opus suum v. solidos de
hundredo et balliuis · hundredi, et nunc detinerentur
iniuste ; et allegabat, quod predecessores sui fuerunt
feffati ad capcionem Anglie de terra Alfrici filii Withari,
qui quondam fuerat dominus illius hundredi. Abbas
uero sibi consulens, nec de loco se mouens, respondit :
' Mirum uidetur, domine comes, quod dicis ! deficit.
Rex Ædwardus dedit Sancto Ædmundo et carta sua
confirmauit hunc hundredum integre, etiam de illis v.
solidis nulla fit ibi mencio. Dicendum est tibi, pro quo
seruicio, uel qua ratione exigis illos v. solidos.' Et comes,
habito consilio suorum, respondit se debere portare uexillum Sancti Ædmundi in exercitu, et ob hanc causam illos
v. solidos sibi deberi. Et respondit abbas : ' Certe
inglorium esse uidetur si tantus uir, utpote comes
Clarensis, tam paruum donum pro tali seruicio recipiat :
abbati autem Sancti Æmundi paruum grauamen est
dare v. solidos. Comes R. Bigot se saisiatum tenet, et
saisiatum se asserit officio portandi uexillum Sancti
Ædmundi, qui illud portauit quando comes Lehecestrie
fuit captus et Flandrenses destructi. Thomas eciam de
Mendham dicit hoc esse ius suum. Cum uero dirationa-
ueris uersus eos hoc esse ius tuum, ego libenter v. solidos,

---

[1] Risbridge, the south-west hundred of the Liberty of St. Edmund,
contained many manors of the Earl of Clare, including Clare itself. The
Earl of Cornwall also held wide possessions both in Norfolk and Suffolk, their
administrative centre being Eye. Cp. H. M. Cam, *Hundred and Hundred
Rolls* (1930), pp. 206ff.
[2] Wickhambrook in the centre of the hundred. Is it a coincidence
that just to the north there is a spot called Meeting Green ?

A general summons was made in the hundred of Risbridge that the complaint and claim of the Earl of Clare might be heard at Wickhambrook. He himself came surrounded by a throng of barons and knights, Earl Aubrey and many others supporting him ; and he said that his bailiffs gave him to understand that they used formerly to receive five shillings a year on his behalf from the hundred and its bailiffs, but that now this sum was unjustly denied them ; and he alleged that his predecessors at the time of the conquest of England had been enfeoffed of the land of Alfric the son of Withar, who was once the lord of that hundred. But the Abbot, consulting his own good and yielding no ground, made answer, ' My Lord Earl, I marvel at your words. Your claim fails ! King Edward gave this hundred to St. Edmund in its entirety and confirmed his gift by charter ; and there is no mention therein of those five shillings. You must tell me for what service or cause you demand these five shillings.' And the Earl, after consulting his friends, replied that it was his duty to carry the standard of St. Edmund in the army, and that it was for this that the five shillings were due to him. And the Abbot made answer, ' In truth five shillings is but a paltry sum for a man so great as the Earl of Clare to receive for such service : but it is no great burden for the Abbot of St. Edmund to give five shillings. Earl Roger Bigot maintains and asserts that he is seized of the duty of carrying the standard of St. Edmund ; for he carried it when the Earl of Leicester was taken and the Flemings destroyed. Thomas of Mendham also says this is his right. When you have made good your claim against these two, I will gladly pay you the five shillings which

quos queris, persoluam.' Comes uero respondit, se esse
locuturum inde cum comite R. cognato suo, et sic res
cepit dilacionem usque hodie.

Mortuo Roberto de Kokefeld, uenit Adam filius eius
et eum eo parentes sui, comes R. Bigot, et alii multi
potentes, et sollicitantes abbatem de tenementis predicti
Ade, et precipue de dimidio hundredo de Cosford tenendo
per annuum censum c. solidorum, tanquam hoc esset
ius suum hereditarium, et dicentes quod pater eius et
auus eius tenuerunt illud quater xx. annis retro et plus.
Abbas uero, nacta oportunitate loquendi, apponens
duos digitos suos ad duos occulos suos, dixit : ' Illa die
et illa hora perdam oculos istos, qua alicui concedam
hundredum hereditarie tenendum, nisi rex inde uim
mihi faciat, qui mihi potest auferre abbatiam et uitam.'
Ostendensque racionem dicti ait : ' Si aliquis teneret
hundredum hereditarie, et ipse forisfaceret uersus regem
aliquo modo ita quod exhereditari deberet, statim uicecomes Sutfolchie et balliui regis saisiarent hundredum,
F.137 et excercerent / potestatem suam infra terminos nostros ;
et si haberent custodiam hundredi, periclitaretur libertas
octo hundredorum et dimidii.' Conuertensque sermonem ad Adam, ait : ' Si tu, qui clamas hereditatem in
illo hundredo, acciperes in uxorem aliquam liberam femi-
nam, que teneret saltem unam acram terre de rege in
capite, rex post mortem tuam saisiaret totum tenemen-
tum tuum et wardam filii tui, si esset infra etatem ; et
ita balliui regis intrarent in hundredum Sancti Ædmundi in preiudicium abbatis. Ad hoc, pater tuus recognouit mihi, se nichil iuris hereditarii uendicare de

you demand.' The Earl replied that he would talk over
the matter with his kinsman Earl Roger, and thus the
affair was put off even to this day.

Robert de Cockfield having died, his son Adam came,
and with him his kinsfolk, Earl Roger Bigot and many
other great men, soliciting the Abbot concerning the
holdings of the aforesaid Adam and more especially
concerning the holding of the half-hundred of Cosford
for an annual rent of a hundred shillings, on the ground
that it was his by hereditary right ; for they said that his
father and grandfather had held it for eighty years past
and more. But the Abbot, when he got a chance to
speak, put two fingers against his two eyes and said,
' May I lose these eyes on that day and in that hour,
when I grant any hundred to be held by hereditary right,
unless the King, who has power to take away my Abbey
and my life, should force me to do so.' And then setting
forth the reason for what he had said, he continued, ' If
any man should hold a hundred by hereditary right,
and should commit an offence against the King of such
a kind that he ought to be disinherited, the Sheriff of
Suffolk and the King's bailiffs would forthwith seize the
hundred and exercise their power within our bounds ;
and if they had the custody of that hundred, the liberty
of the eight and a half hundreds would be in peril.' And
then, turning to Adam, he said, ' If you, who claim to
be the heir of that hundred, should take to wife some
free woman, who held at least one acre of land as tenant
in chief of the King, the King after your death would
seize your entire holding and the wardship of your son,
if he were under age ; and so the bailiffs of the King
would enter into St. Edmund's hundred, to the prejudice of the Abbot. Moreover, your father acknowledged
to me that he claimed no hereditary right to the hundred ;

hundredo ; et, quia seruicium suum mihi placuit, permisi eum tenere omnibus diebus uite sue, meritis suis exigentibus.' Hiis dictis, oblata est abbati pecunia multa : set nec potuit flecti nec prece nec precio. Conuenit tandem inter eos ita : Adam renuntiauit iuri suo [1] quod ore dicebat se habere in hundredo, et abbas confirmauit ei omnes alias terras suas. Set de uilla nostra de Cokefeld nulla fuit facta mencio, nec cartam creditur inde habere ; Semere et Grotene tenebit ad tempus uite sue.

Herbertus decanus [2] leuauit molendinum ad uentum super Hauberdun : [3] quod cum audisset abbas, tanta ira excanduit, quod uix uoluit comedere, uel aliquod uerbum proferre. In crastino, post missam auditam, precepit sacriste ut sine dilacione faceret carpentarios suos illuc ire et omnia subuertere, et materiam lignorum in saluam custodiam reponere. Audiens hoc decanus, uenit dicens se hoc de iure posse facere super liberum feudum suum, nec beneficium uenti alicui homini debere denegari, et dixit se uelle suum proprium bladum ibi molere, non alienum, ne forte putaretur hoc facere in uicinorum molendinorum detrimentum. Et respondit abbas adhuc iratus : ' Gratias tibi reddo ac si ambos pedes meos amputasses ; per os Dei, nunquam panem manducabo, donec fabrica illa subuertatur. Senex es, et scire debuisti, quod nec regi

---

[1] In 1192 Adam in an Assize of Mort d'Ancestor before the King's Justices at Westminster renounced his claim to the half-hundred of Cosford, and the Abbot confirmed to him certain hereditaments held of the Abbey, and leased to him Semer and Groton for life (Pipe Rolls, Norf., Suff., 2. Rich. I).

[2] *decanus* would normally mean 'rural dean,' but an official known as *decanus Christianitatis* is found at a later date, serving as the Sacrist's deputy in the administration of the town. See L p. 46.

and because his service was acceptable to me, I permitted him as a reward of his merits to hold it all the days of his life.' When he had said this, a large sum of money was offered to the Abbot ; but he could not be moved either by bribe or entreaty. At length they came to an agreement on the following terms : Adam renounced the right in the hundred which he alleged that he possessed, and the Abbot confirmed to him all his other lands ; but no mention was made of our township of Cockfield, nor is it thought that he has any charter for it : Semer and Groton he will hold for his lifetime.

Herbert the Dean set up a windmill on Haberdun ; and when the Abbot heard this, he grew so hot with anger that he would scarcely eat or speak a single word. On the morrow, after hearing mass, he ordered the Sacrist to send his carpenters thither without delay, pull everything down, and place the timber under safe custody. Hearing this, the Dean came and said that he had the right to do this on his free fief, and that free benefit of the wind ought not to be denied to any man ; he said also that he wished to grind his own corn there and not the corn of others, lest perchance he might be thought to do this to the detriment of neighbouring mills. To this the Abbot, still angry, made answer, ' I thank you as I should thank you if you had cut off both my feet. By God's face, I will never eat bread till that building be thrown down. You are an old man, and you ought to know that neither the King nor his Justiciar can

---

[3] The name of the land lying between Southgate Street and the River Lark, and bordering on the parish of Rougham. It lay well within the *bannaleuca*, and was strictly within the Sacrist's domain. Neither the Dean nor the Cellarer had any right to erect mills within the *bannaleuca* without the consent of the Abbot and the Convent.

nec iustitiario licet aliquid immutare uel constituere infra
bannam leucam sine abbate et conuentu ; et tu tale quid
presumsisti ? Nec hoc sine detrimento meorum molendinorum est, sicut asseris, quia ad tuum molendinum
burgenses concurrent, et bladum suum molerent pro
beneplacito suo, nec eos possem de iure aduertere, quia
liberi homines sunt. Nec etiam molendinum celerarii
nouiter leuatum stare sustinerem, nisi quia leuatum fuit
antequam fui abbas. Recede, inquit, recede; antequam/
F.137ᵥ domum tuam ueneris, audies quid fiet de molendino tuo.'
Decanus autem timens a facie [1] abbatis, consilio filii sui
magistri Stephani, famulos sacriste preueniens, molendinum illud eleuatum a propriis famulis suis sine omni
mora erui fecit ; ita quod, uenientibus seruientibus
sacriste, nichil subuertendum inuenerunt.

Quarumdam ecclesiarum aduocacionem calumpniatus est [2] abbas et optinuit. Quasdam etiam calumpniatas retinuit, ecclesiam de Westle, de Meringetorp, de
Brethenham, de Weneling, de Pakeham, de Neutona,
de Bradefelda in Norfolcia, medietatem ecclesie de
Bocsford, ecclesiam de Scaldewella, et ecclesiam de
Endegate, omnes ab aliis calumpniatas retinuit, et tres
porciones de ecclesia de Diccleburcha ad ius aduocacionis sue reuocauit, et illarum porcionum tenementa
ad liberum feudum ecclesie reduxit, saluo seruicio quod
inde debetur aule de Tiueteshala. Ecclesia uero de
Bocsford uacante, cum summonita fuisset inde recog-

---

[1] Jer. xlii. 11
[2] He claimed the advowson of the churches here mentioned under the
procedure known as the Assize of Darrein Presentment (see PM I. 148),
introduced by Henry II. The principle is ' He that presented last time,
let him present this time.' The jury was sworn as to the last presentment.
If the church remained two months vacant, the presentment passed to

change or set up anything within the liberties of this town without the assent of the Abbot and the Convent. Why have you then presumed to do such a thing ? Nor is this thing done without detriment to my mills, as you assert. For the burgesses will throng to your mill and grind their corn there to their heart's content, nor should I have the lawful right to punish them, since they are free men. I would not even allow the Cellarer's mill, which was built of late, to stand, had it not been built before I was Abbot. Go away,' he said, ' go away ; before you reach your house, you shall hear what will be done with your mill.' But the Dean, shrinking in fear from before the face of the Abbot, by the advice of his son Master Stephen, anticipated the servants of the Abbot and caused the mill which he had built to be pulled down by his own servants without delay, so that, when the servants of the Sacrist came, they found nothing left to demolish.

The Abbot claimed and secured the advowson of certain churches ; some too, which were claimed by others, he retained in his possession : the churches of Westley, Morningthorpe, Brettenham, Wendling, Pakenham, Nowton, and Bradfield in Norfolk, half the church of Boxford, the church of Scaldwell, and the church of of Endgate, all these, though claimed by others, he retained, and he recovered three-quarters of the church of Dickleborough, and brought back the holdings of those portions into the free fee of the church, saving the service which is owed therefrom to the hall of Tivetshall. But when the church of Boxford was vacant, and a recognition had been summoned to deal with the matter,

---

the diocesan bishop. Documents dealing with the settlement of these claims exist in all these cases except Bradfield, Honington, and Tivetshall. See Rokewode.

nicio, uenerunt quinque milites temptantes abbatem, et
querentes quid inde deberent iurare. Abbas autem
noluit eis aliquid dare uel promittere, set dixit : ' Cum
ad iuramentum peruentum fuerit, dicite rectum secundum conscientiam uestram.' Ipsi uero indignantes recesserunt, et ei per iuramentum suum aduocacionem
illius ecclesie, scilicet ultimam presentacionem, abstulerunt ; quam tamen postea recuperauit, multis factis
expensis et datis decem marcis.

Ecclesiam de Hunegetona non uacantem set calum-
niatam retinuit abbas, tempore Durandi de Hostesli,
licet ipse monstrauerit in testimonium iuris sui cartam
W. Norwicensis episcopi, qua continetur, quod Robertus
de Valoniis socer eius dederit illam ecclesiam Ærnaldo
Luuello.

Uacante medietate ecclesie de Hopetuna,[1] mota est
controuersia inde inter abbatem et Robertum de Ulmo,
positoque die concordie apud Hopetonam, post multas
altercaciones dixit abbas ad predictum R., nescio quo
impetu animi ductus : ' Tu iura in propria persona
quod hoc tuum ius est, et ego concedo quod tuum sit.'
Cumque miles ille renuisset iurare, delatum est iuramentum per consensum utriusque partis sexdecim legalibus
de hundredo, qui iurauerunt hoc esse ius abbatis. Gilbertus filius Radulfi et Robertus de Cokefeld, domini
illius feudi, affuerunt et consenserunt. Prosiliens ibi
magister Iordanus de Ros, habens tam cartam H.
abbatis, quam predicti R. et hinc inde ut uter eorum
diracionaret ecclesiam, ipse personatum haberet, dixit
se esse personam tocius ecclesie et clericum proximo
mortuum fuisse uicarium eius, reddendo ei annuam /
F.138 pensionem de illa medietate, et inde ostendit cartam

---

[1] See Appendix L

five knights came, tempting the Abbot and asking him
what they should swear concerning it.   The Abbot,
however, refused to give or promise them anything, but
said, ' When it comes to making oath, say what is right
according to your conscience.'   But they retired in
indignation, and by their oath deprived him of the
advowson of that church—that is, the last presentation ;
yet later he recovered it after much expense and the
payment of ten marks.

The Abbot retained the church of Honington, which
was not vacant, but was claimed, in the time of Durand
of Hostesli, though the latter in evidence of his right
produced a charter of William, Bishop of Norwich,
containing the statement that Robert of Valognes his
father-in-law gave that church to Arnold Lovell.

When half the church of Hopton fell vacant, a dispute
arose between the Abbot and Robert de Ulmo, and a day
of settlement having been appointed, after much debate
the Abbot, led by I know not what impulse, said to this
same Robert, ' Do you swear in person that this is your
right, and I will allow it to be so.'   And when that knight
had refused to swear, with the consent of both parties
the oath was put to sixteen law-worthy men of the
hundred, who swore that the right of presentation belonged to the Abbot.   Gilbert FitzRalph and Robert
de Cockfield, the lords of that fief, were present and
agreed.   Thereupon Master Jordan of Ros started up,
holding a charter from Abbot Hugh and another from
the aforesaid Robert, to the effect that whichever of the
two might make good his claim, he should have the
victory, and said that he himself was the rector of
the whole church, while the clerk lately deceased was
his vicar paying him a yearly pension for that half, and
in support of this he produced a charter of Archdeacon

Walchelini archidiaconi. Abbas uero turbatus et iratus
erga eum, nunquam eum in gratiam amicitie recepit,
donec ipse Iordanus in capitulo monacorum de Theford,
instante abbate, reconsignauit in manus episcopi ibi
presentis illam medietatem precise, sine omni conditione
et spe recuperandi eam, coram multitudine clericorum.
Quo facto, dixit abbas : ' Domine episcope, ego ex
promisso teneor dare redditum alicui clerico uestro :
et ego dabo hanc medietatem huius ecclesie cui ex
uestris uolueritis.' Et episcopus petiuit, ut amicabiliter
redderetur eidem magistro Iordano, et sic ex presenta-
cione abbatis eam suscepit Iordanus. Postea mota est
controuersia inter abbatem et eundem Iordanum de
terra Herardi in Herlaua,[1] utrum esset liberum feudum
ecclesie an non. Cumque inde summonita esset recognicio duodecim militum in curia regis facienda, facta
est in curia abbatis apud Herlauam per licentiam
Rannulfi de Glanuilla, et iurauerunt recognitores se
nunquam sciuisse illam terram fuisse separatam ab
ecclesia, set tamen illam terram debere abbati tale seruitium quale debet terra Eustachii, et quedam alie terre
laicorum in eadem uilla. Tandem conuenit inter eos
ita : magister Iordanus in plena curia recognouit illam
terram esse laicum feudum, et se nichil inde uendicare,
nisi per gratiam abbatis ; et illam terram tenebit omnibus diebus uite sue, reddendo inde annuatim abbati
xii. denarios pro omnibus seruitiis.

Cum iuxta consuetudinem Anglorum multi multa
darent munera abbati ut domino, die Circumcisionis
Dominice,[2] cogitaui ego Iocelinus quid dare possem.
Et incepi in scriptum redigere omnes ecclesias, que

---

[1] See Appendix M
[2] New Year's Day

Walchelin. But the Abbot was vexed and angry with him, and did not take him back into his friendship, until Jordan himself in the chapterhouse of the monks at Thetford, at the instance of the Abbot, absolutely and unconditionally and without any hope of recovery resigned that half of the church into the hands of the Bishop there present before a multitude of clerks. This done, the Abbot said, ' My Lord Bishop, I am bound by my promise to give a benefice to some one of your clerks ; and I will give this half of this church to anyone you may choose.' And the Bishop asked that it might in all friendship be restored to Master Jordan, and so Jordan received it at the Abbot's gift. Afterwards a dispute arose between the Abbot and the same Jordan concerning the land of Herard at Harlow, as to whether it was a free fief of the church or not. And when a recognition had been summoned to be made by twelve knights in the King's court, it was, by leave of Ranulph de Glanvill, held in the Abbot's court at Harlow ; and the recognitors swore that that they had never known that land to be separated from the church, but that nevertheless it owed the Abbot the same service that was owed by the land of Eustace and certain other lands of laymen in the same township. At length they came to an agreement on the following terms : Master Jordan in full court recognised that the land was a lay fief and that he had no claim therein, save by grant of the Abbot ; and he should hold that land all the days of his life, on an annual payment of twelve pence to the Abbot in lieu of all services.

Since according to the custom of the English many persons gave many gifts to the Abbot, as their lord, on the Feast of our Lord's Circumcision, I Jocelin pondered what I might give him : and I began to set down in

sunt in donacione abbatis, tam de nostris maneriis quam
de suis, et rationabilia precia earum, sicut possent poni
ad firmas, tempore quo bladus mediocriter uenditur.
Et intrante anno subsequente, dedi abbati sedulam illam
pro munere eius, quam ualde gratanter accepit. Ego
uero, quia placui tunc temporis in conspectu [1] eius,
cogitaui in corde meo [2] quod dicerem ei, ut aliquam
ecclesiam daret conuentui et assignaret in usum hospitalitatis, sicut desiderauit quando pauper monachus
claustralis fuit, et sicut ipse uoluit ante electionem suam,
ut fratres iurarent, ut super quemcumque sors abbatie
caderet, hoc faceret. Set dum hoc cogitaui, occurrit /
F.138v mihi memorie, quod quidam alius prius dixerat ei idem
uerbum, et audieram abbatem respondentem, se non
posse demembrare baroniam, scilicet nec debere minuere
libertatem et dignitatem, quam H. abbas et ceteri predecessores sui habuerunt de ecclesiis donandis, qui nullam uel uix contulerunt conuentui : et icirco tacui.
Scriptum tale fuit :

' Hee sunt ecclesie de maneriis et sochagiis abbatis.
Ecclesia de Meleford ualet xl. libras, Geuentona x.
marcas, Saxham xii. marcas, Hargraua v. marcas, Brethenham v. marcas, Bocsford centum solidos, maior
Fornham c. solidos, Stowa c. solidos, Hunegetona v.
marcas, Helmeswella tres marcas, Cottuna xii. marcas,
Brocford v. marcas, Palegraua x. marcas, maior Horninge-
sherd v. marcas, Cunegestuna iiii[or] marcas, Herlaua
xix. marcas, Stapelforda tres marcas, Tiueteshala c.
solidos, Wirlingworda cum Bedingfelda xx. marcas,
Saham vi. marcas, medietas ecclesie de Wortham c.
solidos, Rungetona xx. marcas, Torp vi. marcas, Wlpet
preter pensionem [3] c. solidos, Ressebroc v. marcas,

[1] Deut. xii. 25
[2] Eccles. ii. 3
[3] See Appendix I

writing all the churches which are in the gift of the
Abbot, both of our manors and of his, and their reasonable value, at the rate at which they might be put to
farm in a season when corn is sold at a moderate price.
And at the beginning of the next year, I gave the sheet,
whereon I had written, as a gift to the Abbot, who
accepted it with gratitude. But I, since I was then
pleasing in his sight, thought in my heart that I would
say to him that he should give some church to the Convent and assign it for the purpose of entertainment of
guests, as he desired when he was a poor cloister monk,
and as he himself before his election desired the brethren
to swear, that whosoever was elected Abbot should do
this. But while I pondered this, it came to my memory
that a certain other person had said the same thing to
the Abbot, and I had heard the Abbot reply that he
could not dismember his barony, and that he ought not
to diminish the liberty and the dignity, which Abbot
Hugh and the rest of his predecessors possessed in respect
of the giving of churches ; and that they had given no
church or scarcely any to the Convent ; and so I said
nothing. Now the writing was as follows :

'These are the churches of the manors and socages
of the Abbot : Melford worth forty marks, Chevington
ten marks, Saxham twelve marks, Hargrave five marks,
Brettenham five marks, Boxford a hundred shillings,
Fornham Major a hundred shillings, Stowe a hundred
shillings, Honington five marks, Elmswell three marks,
Cotton twelve marks, Brockford five marks, Palgrave ten
marks, Horningsheath Major five marks, Coney Weston
four marks, Harlow nineteen marks, Stapleford three
marks, Tivetshall a hundred shillings, Worlingworth cum
Bedingfield twenty marks, Soham six marks, half the
church of Wortham a hundred shillings, Runcton twenty

medietas ecclesie de Hopetona lx. solidos, Richinghale
vi. marcas, tres partes ecclesie de Dicleburch quelibet
pars ualet xxx. solidos et plus, medietas ecclesie de
Gislingham quatuor marcas, Ichelingham vi. marcas,
de ecclesia de Mildenhala, que ualet xl. marcas, et de
medietate ecclesie de Wederdena quid dicam ? ¹ Wene-
linge c. solidos, ecclesia de Len x. marcas, ecclesia de
Scaldewelle v. marcas, de Werketona—.

'Hee sunt ecclesie de maneriis conuentus : Mildenhala, Bertona, et Horningeshertha xxv. marcas preter
pensionem, Rutham xv. marcas preter pensionem,
Bradefeld v. marcas, Pakeham xxx. marcas, Suthreia
c. solidos, Riseby xx. marcas, Neutona iiii°ʳ marcas,
Wepsteda xiiii. marcas, Forham Sancte Genouefe xv.
marcas, Herningeswella ix. marcas, Fornham Sancti
Martini iii. marcas, Ingham x. marcas. Lacforda c.
solidos, Aluedena x. marcas, Kokefelda xx. marcas,
Semere xii. marcas, Grotone v. marcas, medietas ecclesie
de Frisingfeld xiiii. marcas, Beccles xx. marcas, Broc xv.
marcas, Hildercle x. marcas, Werketona x. marcas,
Scaldewella v. marcas, Westle v. marcas, ecclesia in
Norwico duas marcas preter pensionem allec, et due
ecclesie in Colecestria iii. marcas preter pensionem iiii.
solidorum, Chelesworda c. solidos, Meringetorp iiii.
marcas, medietas ecclesie de Bradefeld in Norfolchia tres
marcas : staffacres et foracres,² et tercie partes deci-
marum dominiorum Wrabenesse, vi. marcas.

Duo comitatus Norfolchia et Suthfolchia positi fue-
F.139 runt in misericordia / regis a iusticiariis errantibus propter
quoddam forisfactum, et posite fuerunt l. marce super
Norfolchiam, et xxx. super Sutfolciam. Et cum quedam

¹ See p. 95
² See Appendix N

marks, Thorpe six marks, Woolpit excluding pension a hundred shillings, Rushbrook five marks, half the church of Hopton sixty shillings, Rickinghall six marks, three quarters of the church of Dickleburgh thirty shillings and more for each quarter, half the church of Gislingham four marks, Icklingham six marks ; concerning the church of Mildenhall, which is worth forty marks, and half the church of Wetherden what shall I say ? Wendling a hundred shillings, the church of Lynn ten marks, the church of Scaldwell five marks, Warkton.

' These are the churches of the manors of the Convent : Mildenhall, Barton and Horningsheath twenty-five marks excluding pension, Rougham fifteen marks excluding pension. Bradfield five marks, Pakenham thirty marks, Southrey a hundred shillings, Risby twenty marks, Nowton four marks, Whepstead fourteen marks, Fornham St. Genevieve fifteen marks, Herringswell nine marks, Fornham St. Martin three marks, Ingham ten marks, Lackford a hundred shillings, Elveden ten marks, Cockfield twenty marks, Semer twelve marks, Groton five marks, half the church of Fressingfield fourteen marks, Beccles twenty marks, Brooke fifteen marks, Hinderclay ten marks, Warkton ten marks, Scaldwell five marks, Westley five marks, the church in Norwich two marks excluding pension of herrings, and two churches in Colchester three marks excluding pension of four shillings, Chelsworth a hundred shillings, Morningthorpe four marks, half the church of Bradfield in Norfolk three marks, staffacres and foracres and a third of the tithes of the domains of Wrabness six marks.'

The two counties of Norfolk and Suffolk were placed in the King's mercy by the Justices in eyre on account of a certain offence, the amercement of Norfolk being fifty marks and of Suffolk thirty marks. And when a

porcio de illa communi misericordia poneretur super
terras Sancti Ædmundi et acriter exigeretur, abbas sine
omni mora adiit dominum regem, et inuenimus eum
apud Clarendonam [1] ; ostensaque ei carta regis Ædwardi, que liberas facit terras Sancti Ædmundi de omnibus geldis et scottis,[2] precepit rex per literas suas, ut sex
milites de comitatu de Norforchia et sex de Sutfolchia
summonerentur ad recognoscendum coram baronibus
scaccarii, utrum dominia Sancti Ædmundi deberent esse
quieta de communi misericordia ; et electi sunt tantum
sex milites, ut ita parceretur laboribus et expensis, et
ideo quia habuerunt terras in utroque comitatu, scilicet
Hubertus de Briseworda, W. filius Heruie, et Willelmus
de Francheuilla, et tres alii, qui Lundonias iuerunt nobiscum, et ex parte duorum comitatuum libertatem ecclesie
nostre recognouerunt. Iustitiarii autem assidentes uerumdictum illorum inrollauerunt.

Abbas Samson iniit certamen cum militibus suis,[3] ipse
contra omnes, et omnes contra eum. Proposuit eis quod
deberent ei facere integre seruicium quinquaginta militum in scutagiis et in auxiliis et in consimilibus, quia,
ut aiebat, feudos tot militum tenebant ; quare decem ex
illis quinquaginta [4] militibus essent sine seruicio, uel qua
ratione uel cuius auctoritate illi quadraginta reciperent
seruicium decem militum. Responderunt omnes una
uoce talem fuisse consuetudinem, ut decem ex illis
semper adiuuarent quadraginta, nec se uelle inde, nec
debere inde respondere, nec in placitum intrare. Cum

---

[1] Henry II was in England between April 27, 1186, and February 27,
1187, and was at Clarendon, his favourite palace near Salisbury, at the
close of that period.

[2] See Appendix K. *geldis et scottis*, used in the general sense of contributions due to the Crown

[3] See Appendix O

certain portion of that common amercement was placed upon the lands of St. Edmund and sharply demanded, the Abbot without delay went to our lord the King, and we found him at Clarendon. And when the charter of King Edward, which makes the lands of St. Edmund free of all geld and scot, was shown to the King, he gave orders by his letters that six knights of the county of Norfolk and six of Suffolk should be summoned to recognize before the Barons of the Exchequer, whether the domains of St. Edmund should be quit of the common amercement. Only six knights were chosen, to save labour and expense and because they had lands in both counties, to wit Hubert de Braiseworth, William FitzHervey, William de Francheville and three others, who went to London with us, and on behalf of the two counties recognised the liberty of our Church. And the justiciars who were present enrolled their verdict.

Abbot Samson entered on a dispute with his knights, himself against all, and all against him. He put to them that they ought to do him full service of fifty knights in respect of scutages, aids and the like, since, as he said, they held so many knights' fees; why should ten of those fifty knights do no service, or for what reason and by whose authority should those forty receive the service of ten knights. They all replied with one voice that it had always been the custom for ten of them to help the forty, and they neither would nor ought to be answerable nor to be called into court on this matter. So when

---

[4] This may be regarded as a round number, or alternatively we may assume that at least *duo* has dropped out. The correct number was 52. The statement below that the Abbot's profit will be £12 when £1 per knight is demanded, implies a total of 52 knights. It may be noted that a little later when he deals with the problem of castleward at Norwich, he again speaks of the total as 50.

ergo fuissent summoniti inde responsuri in curia regis,
quidam exoniauerunt se ex industria, quidam appar-
uerunt in dolo, dicentes se non respondere sine paribus
suis. Alia uice se presentauerunt, qui prius se absentauerunt, dicentes similiter se non debere respondere sine
paribus suis, qui in eadem querela fuerunt. Cumque
sic sepius illusissent abbati, et in magnis et in grauibus
expensis uexassent, conquestus est inde abbas H. archiepiscopo tunc iusticiario ; qui respondit in generali
concione quemlibet militem pro se ipso debere loqui et
pro suo proprio tenemento. Et dixit palam abbatem
bene scientem et bene potentem esse ad dirationandum
ius ecclesie sue contra omnes et singulos. Comes ergo
R. Bigot primus sponte confessus est in iure se debere
F.139v abbati domino suo seruicuim trium militum / integre, et
in releuiis [1] et in scutagiis et in auxiliis, set de warda
facienda ad castellum Norwici tacuit. Uenerunt postea
duo ex militibus, postea tres, postea plures, postea sepe [2]
omnes, et ad exemplum comitis idem seruicium recognouerunt ; et quia non sufficiebat recognicio inde facta
in curia Sancti Ædmundi, secum ducebat omnes abbas
Lundonias ad suos sumptus, et uxores et mulieres, que
erant terrarum heredes, ut recognicionem facerent in
curia regis, et singuli singulos cirographos acceperunt.
Albericus de Ver, et Willelmus de Hastinga, et duo alii
fuerunt in seruitio regis ultra mare, quando hec fiebant,
et ideo loquela de eis differri debuit. Albericus de Ver
ultimus erat qui abbati resistebat ; abbas uero aueria
eius cepit et uendidit, unde oportuit eum uenire in
curiam et respondere sicut pares sui. Inito ergo consilio,

---

[1] Sums paid by tenants' heirs to their lord on coming into their inheritance ; see PM i. p. 308
[2] Rokewode suggests *fere*

they had been summoned to answer for this in the King's court, some of them deliberately excused themselves, while others appeared out of guile, saying that they would not answer in the absence of their peers.   On another occasion those presented themselves who had previously been absent, and they likewise said that they ought not to answer in the absence of their peers, who were concerned in the same dispute.   And when they had thus many times baffled the Abbot and had vexed him with great and heavy expenses, he complained to Archbishop Hubert who was then justiciar ;   and he answered in full council that every knight ought to speak for himself and for his own holding.   And he said openly that the Abbot had both the knowledge and the power to make good the claim of his Church against each and all.   Therefore Earl Roger Bigot, first of them all, of his free will acknowledged in court that he owed his lord the Abbot full service of three knights in reliefs, scutages and aids ;   but he was silent about the performance of castleward at Norwich.   After him there came first two knights, and then three, more later, and finally almost all, and following the example of the Earl they acknowledged that they owed the same service ;   and because their acknowledgement of this in the court of St. Edmund was not sufficient, the Abbot took them all to London at his own expense, and their wives as well and such women as were heiresses of lands, that they might make their acknowledgement in the King's court ;   and each of them received separate records of the fine. Aubrey de Vere and William de Hastings and two others were absent on service of the King across the sea, when these things were done, and therefore the plea concerning them had to be postponed.   Aubrey de Vere was the last who resisted the Abbot ; but the Abbot seized and

recognouit tandem Sancto Ædmundo et abbati ius suum.
Superatis ergo omnibus militibus, ex tali uictoria tale
lucrum poterit [1] abbati, nisi abbas uoluerit aliquibus
parcere; quociens xx. solidi ponentur super scutum,
remanebunt abbati xii. libre, et si plus uel minus ponatur,
plus uel minus ei remanebit secundum debitam porcionem. Item solebat abbas et antecessores sui semper
in fine xx. ebdomadarum dare vii. solidos ad wardam [2]
castelli de Norwico de sua bursa pro defectu trium
militum, quos comes R. Bigot tenet de Sancto Ædmundo,
et solebant singuli milites de quatuor constabiliis dare
xxviii. denarios, quando intrabant ad wardas faciendas,
et unum denarium marescaldo, qui illos denarios colli-
gebat, et ideo xxviii. denarios et non amplius dabant, quia
decem milites de quinta constabilia solebant adiuuare
ceteros quadraginta; ita quod ubi debebant dare tres
solidos integre, dederunt tantummodo xxix. denarios, et
qui debebat intrare ad wardam faciendam in fine iiii^{or}
mensium, intrauit in fine xx. ebdomadarum. Modo
autem dant singuli milites plene tres solidos et remanet
abbati superexcrescentia que excrescit ultra xxix. denarios, unde poterit se adquietare de pronominatis vii.
solidis. Ecce patet quam uim optinuerunt commina-
ciones abbatis, quas fecit die prima, quando recepit
homagium de militibus suis, sicut prescriptum est, quando
singuli milites promiserunt ei xx. solidos, et statim se
retraxerunt, nolentes dare ei in summa nisi xl. libras,
dicentes quod decem milites deberent adiuuare ceteros
F.140 qua/draginta in auxiliis et wardis faciendis, et in omnibus
consimilibus.

---

[1] *poterit* must mean ' will be possible for.' But the addition of *accrescere*,
suggested by Rokewode, would be an improvement.
[2] See Appendix P

sold his beasts, so that he was forced to come to the court and answer like his peers ; and so after taking counsel, he at last acknowledged the right of St. Edmund and the Abbot. So by this victory over all his knights the Abbot will be the gainer by the following amount, unless he desire to spare some of them : as often as twenty shillings is placed upon the shield, the Abbot will be left with a surplus of twelve pounds, while if more or less should be exacted, more or less will accrue to him in due proportion. The Abbot and his predecessors used also at the end of twenty weeks to pay seven shillings for castleward at Norwich out of their own purse owing to the default of three knights whom Earl Roger Bigot holds of St. Edmund ; and each knight of the four con-stabularies used to pay twenty-eight pence, when they entered on their turn of castleward, and one penny to the marshal who collected the money ; and they paid twenty-eight pence and no more, because the ten knights of the fifth constabulary used to help the other forty, so that, whereas they ought to pay three shillings in full, they gave only twenty-nine pence, while those who ought to enter on their turn at the end of four months did so at the end of twenty weeks. But now each knight pays his three shillings in full, and there is left to the Abbot the surplus over twenty-nine pence, whence he will be able to reimburse himself for the aforesaid seven shillings. Lo now, you may clearly see the meaning of the Abbot's threats, which he uttered on the first day when he received homage from his knights, as has been set down above, when each knight promised him twenty shillings, and then immediately withdrew, refusing to give him a total sum of more than forty pounds, and saying that ten knights should help the other forty in aids and performance of castleward and all such levies.

Est autem quedam terra in Tiuetteshale de feudo abbatis que reddere solet uigilibus de castello Norwici *Waite fe*, id est, xx. solidos per annum, scilicet quinque solidos in quolibet ieiunio quatuor temporum.[1] Antiqua est hec consuetudo, quam abbas libenter uellet mutare si posset ; set inpotenciam suam considerans in hac parte adhuc tacet et disimulat.

De Henrico de Esexia [2]

Ad beati regis et martiris memoriam diffusius dilatandam, prescriptis non incontinue,[3] ut credimus, istud connectimus, non quod ego tantillus et nullius fere momenti istud memoriali titulo commendauerim,[4] quia dominus Iocelinus, elemosinarius noster, uir religionis eximie, potens in sermone et opere, ad potestatis preces imperiosas, sic tandem exorsus est ; que mea reputo, quia, iuxta preceptum Senece [5] quicquid ab aliquo bene dictum est, mihi inpresumptuose ascribo.

Cum uenisset abbas apud Radingas, et nos cum eo, sicut decuit suscepti sumus a monacis eiusdem loci ; inter quos Henricus de Esexia deuotus occurrit, qui, nacta loquendi oportunitate abbati et omnibus assidentibus, narrauit qualiter uictus fuit in duello, et qualiter Sanctus Ædmundus et ob quam causam confudit eum

---

[1] The four ember-day fasts

[2] *De Henrico de Essexia.* This excellent story is an interpolation, though based upon a narrative by Jocelin. The story begins with the words *cum abbas uenisset*, and Jocelin is the speaker. Henry of Essex held lands in Suffolk : (i) Nayland (Lailand here, and Eiland in DB) in Suffolk (Babergh) on the Essex border, within the liberty of St. Edmund ; hence the Abbot's claim to try the case mentioned below in his court. (ii) The Honour of Haughley in the hundred of Stowe, outside the liberty. This ' Honour ' carried with it the office of Constable and apparently Standard-Bearer. Previously Haughley had heen held by a de Montfort. The fact that Robert de Montfort appealed Henry of treason and defeated him may be

There is, however, a certain land in Tivetshall of the Abbot's fee, which used to pay to the watch of Norwich castle 'waite fee,' that is, twenty shillings, being five shillings on each fast of the four terms. This custom is of ancient date, and the Abbot would gladly change it if he could ; but considering his powerlessness in this matter, he is still silent and conceals his desire.

Concerning Henry of Essex

That I may the more widely spread abroad the memory of the blessed King and Martyr, I attach this story to what has gone before and, as I hope, without any breach of continuity : not that I, being so mean and insignificant, would venture myself to set this on record. For lord Jocelin, our almoner, a man of much piety, powerful in word and work, in answer to a request which brooked no denial, thus at length began the tale. And I regard his words as my own, for following Seneca I claim for myself without presumption whatever has been well said by anyone else :

'When the Abbot had come to Reading and we with him, we were received with due honour by the monks of that place ; and among them Henry of Essex, who had taken the vows of a religious, came to meet us ; and he, when the opportunity arose, related to the Abbot how he was vanquished in duel, and how and why St.

---

regarded as suggesting a grudge on the part of a descendant of the dis-possessed line (J. H. Round, *Geoffry de Mandeville*, p. 326f.).

[3] Perhaps an error for *inconcinne*, 'unfittingly'.

[4] The insertion of *sed* before *quia* suggested by Rokewode would be an improvement, but is not absolutely necessary ; for *non quod . . . commen-dauerim* may be treated as parenthetical.

[5] Cp. Seneca *Epistles*, 12. 11, ' *Epicurus* ' inquis ' *dixit. Quid tibi cum alieno?* ' *quod uerum est, meum est.* No such word as *inpresumptuose* is found in classical Latin.

in ipsa hora pugnandi. Ego uero narracionem eius in scriptum redegi domino abbate precipiente, et scripsi in hec uerba :

Quoniam non potest malum uitari nisi cognitum, actus et excessus Henrici de Estsexia memoriali scripto tradere dignum ducimus, ad cautelam quidem, non ad usum. Utilis et indempnis solet esse castigacio, quam persuadent exemplaria. Predictus itaque Henricus dum floreret in prosperis, inter primates regni uir magni nominis habebatur genere clarus, armis conspicuus, regis signifer, uerendus omnibus priuilegio potestatis. Ceteri conprouinciales [1] ecclesiam beati Ædmundi regis et martiris in rebus et redditibus ampliabant ; ille uero non solum clausis oculis hoc preteribat, uerum etiam ui et iniuriis et per iniuriam annuum redditum quinque solidorum abstraxit, et in proprios usus conuertit. Processu uero temporis, cum in curia Sancti Ædmundi ageretur causa de raptu cuiusdam uirginis, accessit idem H. protestans et asserens, loquelam illam in curia sua debere tractari ratione natiuitatis eiusdem puelle, que in dominio suo de Lailand [2] nata fuerat. Cuius rationis pretextu, curiam

F.140v Sancti Ædmundi in itineribus et / innumerabilibus expensis longo temporis tractu uexare presumsit. In hiis interim et consimilibus arridens ad uotum, prosperitas perpetui subintulit causam doloris, et sub fantasia iocundi principii tristes in eum exitus moliebatur ; ex usu etenim est ei arridere ut seuiat, blandiri ut fallat, extollere ut deprimat. Nec mora, insurrexit in eum Robertus de

---

[1] 'neighbours,' probably also with the implication that they lived outside the Liberty of St. Edmund.

[2] Lailand, now Nayland. The L may be due to the tendency of French scribes to confuse L and N ; *e.g.* the initial L of Lincoln is not infrequently altered to N. Alternatively it may be due to the addition of the French article to the Eiland of DB.

Edmund confounded him in the very hour of battle.
I therefore set down his story in writing at the bidding
of the Lord Abbot and wrote as follows :

' " Since evil cannot be avoided unless it be known, we
deem it fit to set on record the deeds and transgressions
of Henry of Essex as a warning and not for imitation.
For the castigation of error is wont to be profitable and
painless, if it is enforced by moral examples. This same
Henry, then, while he was in the blossom of his fair
fortune, was accounted a man of high renown among
the first in the realm, for he was of illustrious birth, con-
spicuous in feats of arms, the King's standard-bearer,
and feared by all ; for such is the privilege of power.
The rest of his neighbours enriched the church of the
blessed Edmund, King and Martyr, in property and
revenues ; but he not only shut his eyes to this duty and
passed it by, but even by force, injury and wrong robbed
the Saint of a yearly revenue of five shillings and converted it to his own use.   And in course of time, when
a suit concerning the ravishing of a certain maiden was
being heard in the court of St. Edmund, the said Henry
appeared, protesting and asserting that this suit ought
to be tried in his court because of the girl's place of
birth ; for she was born in his domain of Nayland. And
on this pretext he presumed to vex the court of St.
Edmund with journeys and countless expenses over a long
space of time.   But Fortune, who for a while had smiled
on him in these deeds and the like, secretly brought upon
him that which should work him endless woe, and under
the flattering semblance of a joyous beginning contrived
a dismal end for him. For it is her way to smile that she
may rage, to flatter that she may deceive, and uplift that
she may lay low. And right soon did Robert de Montfort, his kinsman and his equal in birth and strength,

Monteforti, ipsius consanguineus, nec genere nec uiribus
impar, in conspectu principum terre dampnans et
accusans eum de proditione regis. Asseruit enim eum
in expedicione belli apud Waliam in difficili transitu de
Coleshelle [1] uexillum domini regis fraudulenter abiecisse,
et mortem eius sublimi uoce proclamasse, et in presidium
eius uenientes in fugam conuertisse. In rei ueritate,
predictus Henricus de Esexia inclitum regem Henricum
secundum, Walensium fraudibus interceptum, diem
clausisse credidit extremum ; quod reuera factum
fuisset, nisi Rogerus comes Clarensis, clarus genere et
militari clarior excercitio, cum suis Clarensibus maturius
occurrisset, et domini regis uexillum eleuasset, ad corro-
boracionem et animacionem tocius excercitus. Henrico
quidem resistente et predicto Roberto in concione, et
obiecta penitus inficiante, euoluto breui temporis spacio,
ad corporale duellum [2] peruentum est. Conuenerunt
autem apud Radingas pugnaturi in insula quadam satis
Abbatie uicina ; conuenit et gentium multitudo, uisura
quem finem res sortiretur. Et factum est, cum Robertus
duris et crebris ictibus uiriliter intonasset, et audax prin-
cipium fructum uictorie promisisset, Henricus parumper
deficiens circumquaque respexit, et ecce in confinio terre
et fluminis uidit gloriosum regem et martirem Ædmundum armatum et quasi in aere uolitantem et cum quadam
uultus austeritate uersus eum crebro capitis motu minas
iracundie et indignacionis plenas pretendentem ; uidit
et alium cum eo militem, Gilbertum de Ceriuilla, non
solum quantum ad apparentiam gradu dignitatis in-

---

[1] Near Hawarden, where owing to Henry's rashness, his forces got into
serious difficulties in thickly wooded country (1157) ; see J. E. Lloyd,
Hist. of Wales, II. p. 498.
[2] In view of the fact that after his defeat in this combat Henry was

rise up against him, condemning him in the sight of the princes of the earth and accusing him of treason against the King. For he alleged that during the war in Wales he had falsely cast away the standard of the King in the difficult passage of Coleshill, and had cried in a loud voice that the King was dead, thereby causing those who were coming to his defence to turn and flee. And in very truth Henry of Essex had believed that the glorious King Henry II had perished, cut off by the wiles of the Welsh ; and this indeed would have come to pass, had not Roger Earl of Clare, a man of famous birth and yet more famous in the field of war, hastened betimes with his men of Clare and raised up the King's standard to rally and hearten the whole host. And though Henry withstood the said Robert in the assembly and utterly denied his accusations, after a brief strife the matter came to trial by battle, and they met at Reading to fight upon an island not far from the Abbey ; and a great multitude of folk gathered together to see what the end should be. And it came to pass after Robert had thundered manfully against him with many a grievous blow, and his bold onslaught already promised victory, that Henry, his strength failing, looked about him, and behold ! where land and river met, he saw the glorious King and Martyr Edmund arrayed in armour and, as it seemed, hovering in air and with stern countenance and frequent nodding of the head, launching threats against him full of anger and indignation ; and he saw yet another knight with him, Gilbert de Cereville, who seemed not only his inferior in rank, but shorter in stature by a head, turning in-

---

deprived of all his lands and honours, it may safely be assumed that R. de Montfort had formally appealed him of treason, and that this fight is a definite example of ordeal by combat.

feriorem, set et ab humeris supra statura minorem, oculos
quasi indignantes et iracundos in eum conuertere. Hic
ad preceptum ipsius Henrici uinculis et tormentis afflictus
diem clausit extremum, intrusus occasione et accusacione
uxoris Henrici, que propriam nequitiam in innocentem
deflectens dicebat se petitiones precarias Gilberti de
illicito amore non posse sustinere. Hos itaque tam
sollicitus quam timidus intuens, Henricus antiquum
F.141 scelus/nouum ferre pudorem recordatur. Et iam totus
desperans, et rationem in impetum conuertens, impug-
nantis non defendentis assumpsit officium. Qui dum
fortiter percussit, fortius percussus est ; et dum uiriliter
inpugnabat, uirilius inpugnabatur. Quid multa ? uictus
occubuit. Cumque mortuus crederetur, ad magnam
peticionem magnatum Anglie, eiusdem Henrici con-
sanguineorum, concessum est monachis eiusdem loci, ut
darent eius corpus sepulture. Postea tamen conualuit,
et, resumpto sanitatis beneficio, sub regulari habitu
superioris eui labem detersit, et, longam dissolute etatis
ebdomadam uno saltem sabbato curans uenustare, studia
uirtutum in frugem felicitatis excoluit.—

Galfridus Ridellus episcopus Eliensis petiit ab abbate
materiem lignorum ad quedam magna edificia facienda
apud Glemesford ; [1] quod et abbas concessit, set inuitus,
non ausus tunc eum offendere. Abbate moram apud
Meleford faciente, uenit quidam clericus episcopi, rogans
ex parte domini sui ut ligna promissa possent capi apud
Ælmeswellam ; et errauit in uerbo dicens Ælmeswellam
ubi dicere deberet Ælmessethe, quod est nomen cuiusdam
nemoris de Meleford. Et mirabatur abbas de mandato,
quia talia ligna non potuerunt inueniri apud Ælmes-

---

[1] A manor of the Bishop of Ely within the Liberty of St. Edmund

dignant, angry eyes upon him. Now this man had at Henry's command been cast into chains and tortured so that he perished, having been brought to this pass by the accusations of Henry's wife, who turning her own wickedness against an innocent man, had said that she could no longer hold out against Gilbert's entreaties that she would lie with him in unlawful love.

' " So when he saw these two, Henry remembered that past sin brings new shame, and now, giving up all hope and turning his mind to attack, he began to play the assailant and not the defender. But though he struck hard, he was yet more hardly stricken, and though he manfully assailed his enemy, he was yet more manfully assailed. In short, he was conquered and fell ; and since he was thought to be dead, at the strong entreaty of great lords of England, his kinsmen, his body was given to the monks of the place that it might receive burial. But afterwards he recovered, and once more enjoying the blessing of health, he took the habit of a regular, wiped away the stains of his previous life and, desiring to adorn the long week of his life with at least one sabbath, he turned to the study of the virtues that so he might receive the fruits of felicity." '

Geoffrey Ridell, Bishop of Ely, asked the Abbot to give him timber for the making of certain great buildings at Glemsford, and this request the Abbot, not wishing to offend him, granted though sore against his will. Now while the Abbot was making a stay at Melford, there came to him a clerk of the Bishop's, who asked on behalf of his lord that the promised timber might be taken from a part of his domain at Elmswell ; and he made a slip of the tongue, saying Elmswell, when he should have said Elmset, which is the name of a certain great wood of

wellam. Quod cum audisset Ricardus forestarius de
eadem uilla, dixit occulte abbati, episcopum misisse
proxima ebdomada preterita carpentarios suos tanquam
exploratores in boscum de Ælmessethe, et eligisse meliora
ligna tocius bosci, et signa sua imposuisse. Quo audito,
subito conperit abbas nuncium episcopi errasse in mandato, respondens ei se facere libenter uoluntatem episcopi.
In crastino recedente nuntio, statim post missam auditam
iuit abbas cum carpentariis suis in boscum prenominatum, et omnes quercus prius signatas cum plusquam
centum aliis suo signo signari fecit ad opus Sancti
Ædmundi, et ad culmen magne turris, [1] precipiens ut
quamtocius succiderentur. Episcopus autem, cum ex
responso sui nuntii intellexit ligna predicta apud Ælmeswellam esse capienda, eundem nuntium multis contumeliis affectum remisit ad abbatem, ut uerbum in quo
errauerat corrigeret, dicendo Ælmesethe non Ælmeswellam ; set antequam uenisset ad abbatem, iam succisa
erant omnia ligna que episcopus desiderauerat, et
carpentarii sui signauerant, unde et eum ligna alia et
alibi capere oporteret si uellet. Ego autem, quando
F.141v hec uidebam, / ridebam et dicebam in corde meo : ' Sic
ars deluditur arte.' [2]

Mortuo Hugone abbate, uoluerunt custodes [3] abbatie
deponere prefectos uille Sancti Ædmundi et nouos
constituere sua auctoritate, dicentes hoc pertinere ad
regem, in cuius manu abbatia fuit. Nos autem inde
conquerentes, misimus nuncios nostros domino Ranulfo
de Glanuilla, tunc iusticiario ; qui respondit se bene

---

[1] The Western tower nearing completion
[2] Cato, *Disticha*, I. 26
[3] The *bailliui regis*

Melford. And the Abbot wondered at his message, since such timber was not to be found at Elmswell. But when Richard, the forester of the same township, heard this, he said in secret to the Abbot that the Bishop had, during the past week, sent his carpenters to explore the wood of Elmset, and that they had chosen the best trees in the whole wood and placed their marks upon them. Hearing this the Abbot suddenly perceived that the messenger of the Bishop had made a mistake in delivering his errand, and said to him in answer that he would gladly do as the Bishop desired. On the next day the messenger set off on his return, and the Abbot, after hearing mass, went at once with his carpenters to the aforesaid wood and caused all the oaks already marked together with more than a hundred others to be marked with his mark for the use of St. Edmund and for the top of the great tower ; and he gave orders that they should be cut down as soon as possible. But the Bishop when he learned from his messenger's reply that the aforesaid timber was to be taken at Elmswell, after roundly abusing that same messenger, sent him back to the Abbot to correct his mistake by saying Elmset, not Elmswell ; but before he reached the Abbot, all the trees that the Bishop had desired and his carpenters had marked were already cut down, and so he would have to find other timber elsewhere, if he wanted any. But I, when I beheld this, laughed and said in my heart, ' Thus guile is tricked by guile.'

On the death of Abbot Hugh the custodians of the Abbey wished to depose the town-reeves of St. Edmund and to appoint others on their own authority, asserting that this right belonged to the King in whose hand the Abbey then was. But we complained of this and sent our messengers to Lord Ranulph de Glanvill, then

scire xl. libras debere reddi de uilla annuatim sacriste [1]
nostre, et nominatim ad luminaria ecclesie ; et dixit
H. abbatem pro uoluntate sua et in talamo suo sine
consensu conuentus prefecturam dedisse quotiens uoluit
et quibus uoluit, saluis xl. libris altari reddendis, et ideo
non esse mirandum si bailiui regis hoc ipsum exigerent
ex parte regis ; et acerbe loquens, nos omnes monachos
stultos nominauit, ex hoc quod passi sumus abbatem
nostrum talia fecisse ; non aduertens quod monachorum
summa religio tacere est, et excessus suorum prelatorum
clausis oculis preterire ; nec attendens quod baratores
dicimur si in aliquo siue iuste siue iniuste contradicimus,
et quandoque rei lese maiestatis uel carceris uel exilii
pena dampnamur ; unde et sanius consilium mihi et
consimilibus meis uidetur, ut confessores quam ut mo-
riamur martires. Redeunte ad nos nuntio nostro, et
narrante que audierat et uiderat, quasi inuiti et coacti
iniuimus consilium, ut communi uoluntate et conuentus
et custodum abbatie deponerentur ueteres prefecti uille,
reluctante Samsone subsacrista nobiscum, quantum
potuimus. Samson autem abbas factus, non immemor
iniurie conuentui illate, in crastino Pasche proxime post
electionem suam fecit conueniri in capitulo nostro milites
et clericos et multitudinem burgensium, et coram omnibus dixit istam uillam pertinere ad conuentum et ad
altare, nominatim ad inuenienda luminaria ecclesie ; et
se uelle renouare antiquam consuetudinem, ut coram
conuentu et cum communi assensu tractaretur de pre-
fectura uille et consimilibus que ad conuentum pertine-

---

[1] Pope Eugenius III (1145–53) and his successor Adrian IV (1154–59)
both granted the revenues derived from the town to the service of the
altar of the Abbey Church and the use of the Sacrist.

Justiciar : and he replied that he was well aware that an annual payment of forty pounds was due to our sacristy from the town for the special purpose of providing lights for the church : and he said that Abbot Hugh had given the reeveship of the town, as he pleased and in his lodgings, without the assent of the Convent, giving it to whom he willed and when he willed, saving always the forty pounds for the altar : therefore it was not surprising if the King's bailiffs demanded this right on the King's behalf. And speaking sharply he called all of us monks fools, because we had suffered our Abbot to do such things—but he did not reflect that the supreme duty of monks is to be silent and shut their eyes to the transgressions of their superiors, nor that we are called barrators, if we gainsay the Abbot in anything, whether justly or unjustly, and sometimes we are condemned for lese-majesty either to imprisonment or exile ; wherefore to me and my like it seems the soundest counsel to die confessors rather than martyrs. When our messenger returned and told us what he had heard and seen, we resolved, as it were against our will and under compulsion, that, if it should be possible, the old town reeves should be removed by the common counsel of the Convent and the custodians of the Abbey, though Samson the sub-sacrist withstood us. But when he was made Abbot, Samson, remembering the wrong that had then been done to the Convent, on the morrow of Easter next after his election, ordered the knights and clerks and a number of the burgesses to be assembled in our chapter-house, and said before them all that this town belonged to the Convent and the altar, more especially for the finding of lights for the church ; and that he wished to revive the ancient custom that questions concerning the reeveship of the town and like matters that belonged to

bant. Et nominati sunt eadem hora duo burgenses,
Godefridus et Nicholaus, ut essent prefecti, habitaque
disputacione de cuius manu cornu acciperent, quod
dicitur *Mothorn*,[1] tandem illud receperunt de manu
prioris, qui post abbatem capud est de rebus conuentus.
Illi autem duo prefecti bailiuam suam pacifice custo-
F.142 dierunt per plures annos, quousque dicerentur / remissi
in iustitia regis custodienda : dictante autem ipso
abbate, ut maior securitas daretur conuentui super
hac re, remotis illis recepit Hugo sacrista uillam in
manu sua, nouos seruientes constituens, qui ei de pre-
fectura responderent ; set processu temporis, nescio
quomodo, postea noui prefecti substituti sunt alibi
quam in capitulo, et sine conuentu : unde uel simile
uel maius timetur periculum post decessum abbatis
Samsonis, quam fuerit post decessum Hugonis abbatis.
Quidam autem ex fratribus nostris de amore et fami-
liaritate abbatis plenius confidens, nacta oportunitate, et
modeste sicut decuit, conuenit inde abbatem, asserens
inde murmur fieri in conuentu. Abbas uero hiis auditis
diu tacuit, ac si aliquantulum inde turbaretur, et tandem
ita dicebatur respondisse : ' Nonne ego, ego sum abbas ?
nonne mea interest disponere de rebus ecclesie mihi
commisse, dummodo sapienter egero et secundum Deum?
Si defectus fuerit regie iustitie in uilla ista, ego calumpniatus ero, ego ero summonitus, mihi incumbet labor

---

[1] The horn, by which the burgesses were summoned to the portman-
moot, was a symbol of office.

the Convent should be settled in the presence of the Convent and by common consent. And in that same hour two burgesses were nominated as reeves, Godfrey and Nicholas by name, and after debating from whose hand the horn, known as ' moot-horn,' should be received, they at length received it from the hand of the Prior, who, after the Abbot, is chief in all the affairs of the Convent. Now these two reeves kept their bailiwick in peace for several years, until they were said to be remiss in their administration of the King's justice ; but by order of the Abbot himself, that greater security might be given to the Convent in the matter, after the removal of these reeves, Hugh the Sacrist took the town into his hands and appointed new sergeants, to answer to him for the reeveship. But in process of time, I know not how, new reeves were appointed in their place elsewhere than in the chapterhouse and without the assent of the Convent : wherefore a like or even greater peril is feared after the decease of Abbot Samson than there was after the death of Abbot Hugh. But one of our brethren, trusting more fully in the love and friendship which the Abbot bore him, when occasion offered, spoke to the Abbot on this matter, saying modestly, as was fitting, that there was some murmuring in the Convent concerning this thing. But the Abbot, when he heard this, for a long time was silent, as though he were somewhat disquieted thereby, but at length was said to have made answer thus : ' Am not I, I the Abbot ? Is it not my duty to dispose of the things of the Church committed to my charge, provided that I act wisely and according to the will of God ? If there be default of the King's justice in this town, it is I that shall be accused, I who shall be summoned ; it is on me that will fall the toil of travel and expense and the defence of the town and all that

itineris et expense, et defensio uille et pertinentium ; ego
stultus habebor, non prior, non sacrista, non conuentus,
set ego, qui caput eorum sum et esse debeo. Per me et
consilium, Domino adiuuante, erit uilla seruata indemp-
niter pro posse meo, et salue erunt quadraginta libre
annuatim reddende altari. Murmurent fratres, detra-
hant, dicant inter se, quod uoluerint : pater eorum sum
et abbas ; quamdiu uixero, honorem meum alteri non
dabo.'[1]   Hiis dictis recessit monachus, qui eadem
responsa referebat. Ego autem de talibus uerbis mirabar,
et contrariis motibus mecum disputaui ; tandem dubitare
coactus, eo quod regula iuris [2] dicit et docet, ut omnia
sint in dispositione abbatis.

Mercatores Lundonienses uoluerunt esse quieti de
theloneo [3] ad nundinas [4] Sancti Ædmundi ; plures
tamen inuiti et coacti dederunt illud ; unde multus
tumultus et comotio magna facta est inter ciues Lundonie
in suo hustengio.[5] Conuenientes ergo inde abbatem
S., dixerunt se quietos esse debere per totam Angliam
auctoritate carte,[6] quam habuerunt de rege Henrico
secundo. Quibus abbas respondit quod, si necesse esset,
bene posset trahere regem in warantum, quod nunquam
aliquam cartam eis fecit in preiudicium ecclesie nostre,
F.142v nec in detrimentum libertatum / Sancti Ædmundi, cui

---

[1] Isa. xlii. 8 ; xlviii. 11
[2] Cp. Gratian, pars 2, caus. 18, quaest. 2, canon 9
[3] Toll was paid for the right to bring goods to market for sale. Persons
living outside the town, even within the Liberty of St. Edmund, were liable
to toll. Even within the town all owners of haggovele tenements in the
town (see p. 76) were compelled to pay toll (*Mem.* III. p. 306 ; L p. 50 *n.*).
[4] The first evidence for this market is a charter of Henry I (1124–29),
granting Abbot Anselm the right to hold an annual fair, lasting ' for seven
days in each year, to wit three days before the feast of St. James the Apostle,
and two days after the feast, and on the feast itself ' (FD p. 73).

pertains to it ; it is I who shall be deemed the fool, not the Prior, not the Sacrist, not the Convent, but I, who am and ought to be their head.   It is by me and by my counsel, God helping me, that the town shall be kept without loss, as far as in me lies, and that the forty pounds due each year to the altar shall be safe.   Let the brethren murmur, let them blame me, let them say among themselves what they will.   I am their father and their Abbot ; as long as I live, I will not give my honour to another.' When he had said this, the monk, who reported his words, withdrew ;   but I marvelled that the Abbot should have spoken thus and debated in my heart this way and that ; but at length I was constrained to remain in doubt, since the legal rule tells us and teaches us that all things are in the disposal of the Abbot.

The merchants of London desired to be quit of toll at the market of St. Edmund ; none the less many of them paid it, though unwillingly and under compulsion ;   and there was great disturbance and commotion concerning this among the citizens of London in the Hustings-court. Therefore they came and spoke to Abbot Samson on the matter, saying that they had the right to be quit of toll throughout all England in virtue of the charter which they had from King Henry II.   To this the Abbot replied that, if it should be necessary, he might well call the King to warrant that he had never given them any charter to the prejudice of our Church nor to the detriment of the liberties of St. Edmund, to whom the holy Edward

---

[5] The Hustings Court, supplementing the folkmoot, which could not be summoned with any great frequency (see Page's *London*, pp. 216ff.).

[6] This charter (not later than 1162) is preserved at the Guildhall and printed in *Liber Custumarum*, ed. Riley (RS), Part i, p. 31.   There was an earlier charter to the same effect given by Henry I ; see W. Stubbs, *Select Charters* (ed. 9), p. 129.

sanctus Ædwardus tollum et themum [1] et omnia iura
regalia [2] concessit et confirmauit, ante conquestum
Anglie ; et quod rex Henricus dedit Lundoniensibus
quietantiam theolonei per dominia sua propria, ubi
poterat dare eam ; quia in uilla Sancti Ædmundi non
poterat, quod suum non erat. Audientes hec Lundonienses, communi consilio decreuerunt, quod nullus ex eis
ueniret ad nundinas Sancti Ædmundi, et duobus annis
absentauerunt se, unde magnum detrimentum habuerunt
nundine nostre, et oblatio sacriste minorata fuit in magna
parte. Tandem, episcopo Lundonensi et aliis pluribus
interloquentibus, ita conuenit inter nos et eos, quod ipsi
uenirent ad nundinas, et aliqui ex eis darent theloneum,
set statim eisdem redderetur, ut sub tali uelamento
utrimque libertas seruaretur. Set processu temporis, cum
fecisset abbas concordiam cum militibus suis, et quasi in
pace dormisset, ecce iterum ' Philistiim super te, Samson ! ' [3] Ecce Lundonienses, una uoce comminantes,
quod domos lapideas, quas abbas eodem anno edifi-
cauerat, ad terram prosternerent, uel contra, namum
de hominibus Sancti Ædmundi in centuplum acciperent,
nisi abbas cicius emendaret iniuriam eis illatam a prefectis uille Sancti Ædmundi, qui xv. denarios acceperant
a carettis ciuium Lundoniensium, que uenientes de
Gernemue allec [4] portantes transitum per nos fecerunt.
Et dicebant ciues Lundonienses [5] fuisse quietos de

---

[1] ' The " team " of the Anglo-Norman charters seems to be the right
to hold a court into which foreigners (persons not resident within the
jurisdiction) may be vouched ' (PM II. p. 157 n.)
[2] This phrase is taken from the Latin charter (Kemble 915) ; for which
see p. 147, Appendix K
[3] Judges, xvi. 9, 12, 14, 20
[4] The ancestors of the Yarmouth ' bloater '

granted and confirmed toll and team and all royal rights
before the Conquest of England ; and that King Henry
gave the citizens of London quittance from toll through
his own dominions, where he could give it, but in the
town of St. Edmund he could not give it, since it was
not his to give.   Hearing this, the citizens of London
decreed by common consent that none of them should
come to the market of St. Edmund, and for two years they
absented themselves ; from which our market suffered
great loss, and the oblations received by the Sacrist
were greatly diminished.   At length, thanks to the
intervention of the Bishop of London and many others,
it was agreed between us and them that they should come
to our market, and that some of them should pay toll,
but that it should immediately be returned to them, in
order that under this disguise the liberty of both parties
should be preserved.   But in process of time, after the
Abbot had come to an agreement with his knights and,
as it were, slept in peace, behold once more the cry arose,
' The Philistines be upon thee, Samson ! '   For behold !
the men of London threatened with one voice that they
would raze to earth the stone houses which the Abbot
had built that year, or else distrain a hundredfold upon
the men of St. Edmund, unless the Abbot should speedily
set right the wrong that had been inflicted upon them
by the reeves of the town, who had taken fifteen pence
from the carts of the citizens of London which had passed
through the town carrying pickled herrings from Yarmouth.   And the citizens of London said that they had
been quit of toll in every market at all times and places

---

[5] These rhetorical claims were characteristic of the age ; cp. Fitz-
Stephen's ' Description of London,' more especially at the beginning and
the end.   Geoffrey of Monmouth (I. 17, 18) had made the foundation of
London (Trinovantum) contemporary with the reign of a son of Aeneas.

theloneo in omni foro et semper et ubique, per totam
Angliam, a tempore quo Roma primo fundata fuit; et
ciuitatem Lundonie eodem tempore fundatam talem
debere habere libertatem per totam Angliam, et ratione
ciuitatis priuilegiate que olim metropolis [1] fuit et caput [2]
regni, et ratione antiquitatis. Abbas uero competentes
indutias quesiuit inde, usque ad reditum domini regis [3]
in Angliam, ut eum super hoc consuleret; et habito
consilio cum iuris discretis, replegiauit calumpniatoribus
illos xv. denarios, reseruata utrique parti questione de
iure suo.

Decimo anno [4] abbatie S. abbatis, de communi consilio capituli nostri, conquesti sumus abbati in curia sua,
dicentes redditus et exitus omnium bonarum uillarum
et burgorum Anglie crescere et augmentari in commodum
possidencium et emendacionem dominorum, preter
uillam istam, que xl. libras dare solet, et nunquam ad
F.143 plus extenditur; et / burgenses [5] uille esse in causa huius
rei, qui tantas et tot purpresturas tenent in foro de sopis
et seldis et stalagiis,[6] sine assensu conuentus et ex solo
dono prefectorum uille, qui annuales firmarii [7] et quasi
seruientes sacriste fuerunt, pro beneplacito eius re-
mouendi. Burgenses uero summoniti responderunt, se

---

[1] Geoffrey of Monmouth in the Prophecy of Merlin (*Hist. Reg. Brit.*
VII. 3) asserts that London was originally the seat of the Archbishopric,
and that it had later been transferred to Canterbury.

[2] The head of the secular power, here contrasted with Winchester's
position at the time ; *i.e.* the capital.

[3] It is is not clear whether this refers to Henry II or Richard, the date
of the dispute being uncertain.

[4] 1192

[5] The exact status of the burgesses is obscure. They may correspond
to the 118 men *ad uictum monachorum,* who could give or sell their land
(DB f. 372). The town had greatly increased since then ; but as late as
1327 there were haggovele tenants who were not exempt from toll and
probably not burgesses (*Mem.* III. p. 306 ; L p. 50), although technically
freeholders.

throughout all England, ever since the day when Rome first was founded ; and that the city of London had been founded at the same time, and ought to have this liberty throughout all England, both because it was a privileged city, which had of old been the metropolitan city and capital of the realm and because it was of such ancient date. But the Abbot asked for a suitable truce on this matter, until our lord the King should return to England, that he might consult him thereon ; and, after taking counsel with men learned in the law, he replevined those fifteen pence to the claimants, the question of the rights of each party being reserved.

In the tenth year of the abbacy of Abbot Samson, by the common counsel of our Chapter, we complained to the Abbot in his court, saying that the revenues and expenditure of all good towns and boroughs in England were growing and increasing to the profit of their possessors and for the good of their lords, save only in this town, which pays us forty pounds and never more ; and that the burgesses of the town were the cause of this ; for they held so many and such great encroachments in the market-place, in respect of shops, booths, and stallage, without the assent of the Convent and at the sole gift of the reeves of the town, who were the annual tenants and, as it were, the sergeants of the Sacrist, removable from office at his good pleasure. But the burgesses on being summoned replied, that they were in the King's assize, and refused to answer a claim which contravened

---

⁶ *stalagia* normally means ' stall rents,' though here it may perhaps mean stalls. The passage suggests the possibility that the shops and stalls had become permanent buildings and that rent was either evaded or inadequate ; see L p. 48.

⁷ *i.e.* they are responsible for paying the fixed rent of £40 mentioned above.

esse in assisa regis,[1] nec de tenementis, qui illi et patres
eorum tenuerunt bene et in pace uno anno et uno die
sine calumpnia, se uelle respondere contra libertatem
uille et cartas suas ; et dixerunt talem fuisse consuetudinem antiquam, ut prefecti darent, inconsulto conuentu, loca soparum et seldarum in foro per aliquem
redditum prefecture annuatim reddendum. Nos autem
reclamantes uolumus, ut abbas dissaisiaret eos de talibus
tenementis, unde warantum nullum habuerunt. Abbas
uero ueniens ad consilium nostrum, tanquam unus ex
nobis, secreto nobis dixit, se uelle nobis rectum tenere
pro posse suo ; set ordine iusticiario se debere procedere,
nec sine iudicio curie posse dissaisiare liberos homines
suos de terris uel redditibus suis, quos per plures annos
tenuerunt siue iuste siue iniuste : quod si faceret, dicebat
se cadere in misericordiam regis per assisam regni.
Burgenses ergo, ineuntes consilium, optulerunt conuentui
redditum c. solidorum pro bono pacis, et ut tenerent
tenementa sua, sicut solebant. Nos uero hoc noluimus
concedere, malentes ponere loquelam in respectum,
sperantes forsitan, tempore alterius abbatis, uel omnia
recuperare uel locum nundinarum mutare ; et ita res
cepit dilacionem per plures annos. Cum autem redisset
abbas de Allemannia, optulerunt ei burgenses lx. marcas,
et pecierunt confirmacionem suam de libertatibus uille,
sub eadem forma uerborum, sicut predecessores eius
Anselmus et Ordingus et Hugo eis confirmauerant ; quod
et abbas S. benigne annuit eis. Nobis autem murmu-
rantibus et grunnientibus, facta est eis carta sicut eis
promiserat ; et quia pudor esset ei et confusio, si non

---

[1] They had charters from previous Abbots and threatened to appeal
to royal justice, if their privileges were questioned. They claim prescrip-
tion as having held their tenements for a year and a day.

their liberties and charters in respect of the holdings which they and their fathers had held in comfort and in peace for a year and a day without any claim upon them ; and they said that it had been the custom from of old that the town-reeves should, without consulting the Convent, grant places for shops and booths in the market-place for a sum to be paid to them every year. But we protested and desired that the Abbot should disseize them of such holdings, for which they had no warrant. The Abbot, however, coming to our council, as if he had been one of us, said to us in secret, that he desired that we should keep our rights in so far as he could secure them ; but that he was bound to proceed in accordance with the law, and that without an order from the court he could not disseize free men of their lands or revenues, which, justly or unjustly, they had held for a number of years ; if he did so disseize them, he would fall under the King's mercy by assize of the realm. The burgesses therefore, taking counsel, offered the Convent a revenue of a hundred shillings for a peaceful settlement, and that they might keep their holdings as they were accustomed to do. But we refused to agree to this, preferring to postpone our suit, in the hope that perchance in the time of some other Abbot we might recover all or change the place of the market ; and so the matter was put off for several years. But when the Abbot had returned from Germany, the burgesses offered him sixty marks and asked that he should confirm the liberties of the town in the same form of words in which his predecessors, Anselm, Ording, and Hugh, had confirmed them ; and the Abbot graciously granted their request. And though we murmured and grumbled, a charter was given to them as he promised, and since it would put him to shame and confusion, if he could not fulfil his promise,

posset implere quod promiserat, nolumus ei contradicere, nec ad iracundiam prouocare. Burgenses autem, ex quo habuerunt cartam [1] abbatis S. et conuentus, confidebant plenius quod nunquam tempore abbatis S. amitterent tenementa sua nec libertates suas ; unde nunquam postea, sicut prius, uoluerunt prenominatum redditum centum solidorum dare nec offerre. Abbas autem, hoc F.143v tandem aduertens, con/uenit burgenses super hoc, dicens quod, nisi facerent pacem cum conuentu, prohiberet seldas eorum edificari ad nundinas Sancti Ædmundi. Illi uero responderunt, se uelle dare singulis annis cappam sericam, uel aliquod aliud ornamentum ad precium centum solidorum, sicut prius promiserunt ; set tamen hoc pacto, ut quieti essent inperpetuum de decimis denariorum,[2] quos sacrista acriter ab eis exigebat. Abbas autem et sacrista hoc contradixerunt, et ideo posita est iterum loquela in respectum. Nos uero illos c. solidos hucusque amisimus, secundum quod uulgariter solet dici : ' Qui non uult capere quando potest, non capiet quando uolet.'

Celerarii celerariis plures pluribus succedebant, et quilibet eorum in fine anni magno debito deprimebatur. Dabantur celerario in auxilium xx. libre de Mildenhal, nec sufficiebant. Assignate sunt postea quinquaginta libre celerario singulis annis de eodem manerio ; et adhuc dicebat celerarius hoc non sufficere. Uolens ergo abbas indemnitati et utilitati tam sue quam nostre prouidere, sciens in omni defectu nostro ad eum, tanquam ad patrem monasterii, esse recurrendum, quendam clericum de mensa sua, magistrum Ranulfum

---

[1] This charter is virtually a repetition of that granted by Anselm. See FD p. 114.
[2] They demand relief from the Sacrist's rigorous exaction of tithing pence at view of frankpledge.

we were unwilling to gainsay him or provoke him to anger. But the burgesses, once they had got the charter of Abbot Samson and the Convent, had even greater confidence that they would never, so long as Samson was Abbot, lose their holdings or their liberties ; and for this reason never again were they willing to give or offer the aforesaid revenue of a hundred shillings. But the Abbot, at last taking note of this, spoke to the burgesses on the matter, saying that, unless they made their peace with the Convent, he would forbid them to build booths at the market of St. Edmund. They, however, replied that they were willing every year to give a silken cope or some other ornament worth the hundred shillings which they had formerly promised ; yet only on this condition, that they should be quit in perpetuity of the tithing pence which the Sacrist exacted with such harshness. But the Abbot and the Sacrist refused, and so the suit was once more postponed ; and even to this day we have lost those hundred shillings, as the proverb says, 'He that will not when he may, When he will he shall have nay.'

Cellarer succeeded Cellarer, one after the other, and at the end of the year everyone of them was burdened with a great load of debt. Twenty pounds from Mildenhall was given to help the Cellarer, but that was not enough. Later fifty pounds were assigned him every year from the same manor, but still the Cellarer said that this was insufficient. The Abbot, therefore, desiring to provide both for our comfort and his own, and to secure that neither we nor he should suffer loss, since he knew that whenever we were in default, we must needs have recourse to him as the father of the monastery, attached a certain clerk from his own table, Master Ranulph by name, to serve the Cellarer both as a witness

nomine, celerario nostro associauit, ut ei tanquam testis
et socius assisteret et in expensis et in receptis. Et ecce
multi multa loquuntur. Densescunt murmuraciones,
fabricantur mendacia, consuuntur detractiones detrac-
tionibus, nec est angulus in domate, qui uenenoso
non resonet sibilo. Dicit aliquis alicui : ' Quid est
quod factum est ? quis uidit talia ? nunquam tale
dedecus factum est conuentui. Ecce abbas constituit
clericum super monachum ; ecce clericum constituit
magistrum et custodem super celerarium, ut nichil boni
possit facere sine eo. Monacos suos uilipendit abbas,
monacos suspectos habet, clericos consulit, clericos diligit.
Quomodo obscuratum est aurum, mutatus est color
optimus.' [1] Dixit item amicus amico : ' Facti sumus in
opprobrium uicinis nostris.[2] Omnes nos monachi uel
infideles uel improuidi reputamur ; clerico creditur, non
monacho ; magis confidit abbas de clerico quam de
monacho. Numquid clericus ille magis fidelis est uel
magis sapiens quam aliquis monachus ? ' Item dixit
socius socio : ' Celerarius et subcelerarius nonne sunt,
uel esse possunt, tam fideles homines ut sacrista uel ut
F.144 camerarius ? / Consequens ergo est, ut iste abbas uel
successor eius clericum ponat cum sacrista, clericum cum
camerario, clericum cum subsacristis ad colligendam
oblacionem ad feretrum, et sic cum singulis officialibus,
unde nos erimus in subsanacionem et derisum [3] omni
populo.' Ego autem talia audiens, solebam respondere :
' Si ego essem celerarius, uellem utique, ut clericus mihi
testis esset in omnibus agendis ; quia si bene facerem,
ipse testimonium perhiberet de bono ; si uero in fine

---

[1] Lament. iv. 1
[2] Ps. lxxviii. 4 (Vulg.) ; lxxix. 4 (AV)
[3] Ps. xliii. 14 (Vulg.) ; xliv. 14 (AV)

and a partner in respect both of income and expenditure. And behold ! many said many things. Murmurings became more and more frequent, lies were fabricated, blame heaped on blame, nor was there a corner in the house that did not resound with venomous hissings. One said to another, ' What is this that has been done ? Did anyone ever see the like ? Never was such dishonour put upon the Convent ! Behold ! the Abbot has set a clerk over a monk ! Behold ! he has set up a clerk to be master and guardian of the Cellarer, so that no good can be done without him. The Abbot holds his monks of no account, he suspects his monks, he goes to clerks for advice, it is clerks he loves. How is the gold become dim ! How is the most fine gold changed ! ' Another also said to his friend, ' We have become a reproach to our neighbours. All we monks are deemed faithless or improvident ; a clerk is trusted, not a monk, the Abbot puts more confidence in a clerk than in a monk. Is that clerk more faithful or more wise than any monk ? ' Again comrade said to comrade, ' Are not our Cellarer and sub-cellarer, or may they not be, as faithful men as the Sacrist or the Chamberlain ? Because of this it follows that this Abbot or the next will place a clerk with the Sacrist, a clerk with the Chamberlain, a clerk with the sub-sacrists to collect the oblations at the feretory, and so on with each official : and we shall be " for a mockery and derision to all the people." ' But I, when I heard such things, used to reply, ' If I were Cellarer, I should be very glad that a clerk should be my witness in all that I did ; for if I did well, he would bear witness concerning the good, and if at the end of the

anni aliquo debito oppressus essem, credi possem et
excusari per clericum illum.' Unum autem ex fratribus
nostris, uirum utique discretum et litteratum, audiui
quiddam dicentem, quod mouit me et plures alios :
' Non est,' inquid, ' mirandum, si dominus abbas de
nostris rebus custodiendis partes suas interponat, qui
porcionem abbatie, que eum contingit, sapienter regit
et domui sue sapienter disponit, cuius interest defectum
nostrum supplere, si [1] ex incuria uel inpotentia nostra
contingat. Set unum,' inquit, ' restat periculum post
mortem S. abbatis futurum quale nunquam nobis contigit diebus uite nostre. Uenient sine dubio bailiui regis
et saisiabunt abbaciam in manu sua, scilicet baroniam
que pertinet ad abbatem, sicut olim factum est post
mortem ceterorum abbatum, et sicut olim post mortem
H. abbatis uoluerunt balliui regis constituere nouos
prefectos in uilla Sancti Ædmundi, auctoritatem alle-
gantes, H. abbatem hoc fecisse : consimili ratione,
processu temporis, balliui regis ponent clericum suum ad
custodiendum cellarium, ut per eum et ad preceptum
eius omnia fiant ; et dicturi sunt se debere hoc facere,
quia abbas Samson sic fecit ; et ita poterunt commisceri
et confundi abbatis res et redditus et conuentus, quos
abbas Robertus [2] bone memorie requisito consilio distinxit et ab inuicem separauit.' Cum hec et consimilia
uerba audirem a uiro magni consilii et prouido, stupui
et tacui, domnum abbatem de tali facto nec uolens
condempnare nec uolens excusare.

Hubertus Walteri archiepiscopus Cantuariensis, et
legatus apostolice sedis et iustitiarius Anglie, cum multas
ecclesias uisitasset et multa mutasset et innouasset iure

---

[1] si] the MS has set
[2] See Introduction xix and p. 90

year I was burdened with a certain amount of debt, I
might find credence and be excused thanks to his testimony.' But I heard one of our brethren, a very wise
and literate man, saying a thing that moved both myself
and many others. ' It is no matter for wonder,' he said,
' if the lord Abbot should intervene to keep watch over
our affairs, seeing that he rules with wisdom that portion
of the Abbey which is his, and with wisdom orders his
own house ; and it is his duty to make good our default,
if it should arise from carelessness or incapacity. But,' he
added, ' a danger awaits us after the death of the Abbot
such as has never befallen us in all the days of our life.
Without doubt the King's bailiffs will come and will
seize the Abbey into their hands, to wit, the barony that
belongs to the Abbot, as has been done in the past after
the death of other Abbots ; and just as after the death
of Abbot Hugh the King's bailiffs desired to appoint
new reeves in the town of St. Edmund, alleging as
authority that Abbot Hugh had done this, even so in
process of time the King's bailiffs will set a clerk of their
own to keep watch over the Cellarer, that all things may
be done through him and at his command ; and they
will say that it is their duty to do this, because Abbot
Samson did so ; and thus the property and revenues of
the Abbot and the Convent which Abbot Robert, of
happy memory, after taking counsel, divided and set
apart one from the other, may well be confused together.'
When I heard these words and their like uttered by a
man of much wisdom and foresight, I was astounded
and struck dumb, neither wishing to condemn or to
excuse the Lord Abbot in this matter.

Hubert Walter, Archbishop of Canterbury, Legate
of the Apostolic See and Justiciar of England, after he
had visited many churches and made many changes and

legatie, rediens de matre sua carnali [1] morante et
moriente apud Derham, transmisit ad nos ii. clericos
suos, portantes literas domini sui signatas, quibus con-
F.144*v*   tinebatur, / ut dictis et factis eorum fidem haberemus.
Illi uero abbati et conuentui proposuerunt interrogando,
utrum uellemus recipere dominum suum legatum ad nos
uenientem, sicut debet recipi legatus, et recipitur ab aliis
ecclesiis. Quod et si concederemus, in breui ueniret ad
nos, una cum consilio abbatis et conuentus de rebus et
negociis ecclesie nostre secundum Deum dispositurus :
quod et si ei hoc nollemus concedere, clerici illi duo
mandatum domini sui nobis plenius exprimerent. Abbate
uero conuocante plures de conuentu, tale consilium
iniuimus, ut clericis ad nos missis benigne responderemus,
dicentes, nos uelle dominum suum recipere, ut legatum,
cum omni honore et reuerentia, et mittere simul cum eis
nuntios nostros, qui hoc domino legato ex parte nostra
dicerent ; et consultum habuimus ut, sicut prius feceramus episcopo Eliensi [2] et aliis legatis, ei omnem honorem
exiberemus cum processione et campanis resonantibus,
et cum ceteris solempnibus eum reciperemus, donec
ueniretur ad scrutinium in capitulo forsitan faciendum :
quod si uellet facere, tunc demum ei omnes unanimiter
resisteremus in facie, Romam appellantes et cartis nostris
innitentes. Dixitque dominus abbas : ‘ Si ad presens
uoluerit legatus ad nos uenire, ita faciemus sicut supra-
dictum est ; si uero aduentum suum ad nos distulerit ad
tempus, interim dominum papam consulemus, querentes
quam uim habere debeant priuilegia ecclesie nostre, ab
eo et antecessoribus suis impetrata, contra archiepisco-

---

[1] Matilda de Valognes, sister-in-law of Ranulph de Glanvill, in whose
house Hubert Walter was brought up.
[2] Longchamp. See pp. 52, 53

innovations in virtue of his legatine authority, as he was
returning from his mother in the flesh, who dwelt at
Dereham and was there dying, sent us two of his clerks
carrying letters of their lord, sealed with his seal, the
purport of which was, that we might trust them in word
and in deed.   They asked the Abbot and the Convent,
whether, if their lord visited us in his capacity as Legate,
we were ready to receive him as a Legate should be
received and is received by other churches ; if we
granted this, he would shortly come to us that he might
in consultation with the Abbot and the Convent settle the
affairs and business of our Church in accordance with
the will of God ; if we refused to grant him this, those
two clerks would set forth the commands of their lord
more fully.   Now when the Abbot had summoned a
number of the Convent, we resolved that we should give
a friendly answer to the clerks whom he had sent to us,
saying that we were ready to receive their lord as Legate
with all honour and reverence, and that we should at
the same time send with them our messengers to tell him
this on our behalf.   And we thought it wise that, as we
had previously done for the Bishop of Ely and other
Legates, we should show him all honour with a procession
and ringing of bells and other solemnities, until such time
as he should attempt to hold a scrutiny in our chapterhouse : but if he should desire to do this, then indeed
we should all with one accord withstand him to his face,
appealing to Rome and relying on our charters.   And
the Lord Abbot said, ' If the Legate desires to come to
us immediately, we will do as has been written above ;
but if he puts off his coming for a time, we will in the
meantime consult the Lord Pope, and ask him what
force the privileges of our Church, which we secured from
his predecessors, should have against the Archbishop,

pum, qui super omnes priuilegiatas ecclesias Anglie a
sede apostolica potestatem impetrauit.' Tale fuit consilium nostrum. Cum autem audisset archiepiscopus,
quod uellemus recipere eum ut legatum, nuntios nostros
gratanter recepit et cum gratiarum actione, et factus est
domino abbati in omnibus negociis suis benignus et
propicius, et aduentum suum ad nos quibusdam causis
emergentibus distulit ad tempus. Omni ergo dilacione
postposita, misit abbas domino pape [1] easdem literas,
quas legatus miserat ei et conuentui, in quibus continebatur quod ipse uenturus esset ad nos auctoritate
legacie sue, et auctoritate domini pape, in quibus
scribebatur, quod et ei data fuit potestas super omnes
exemptas ecclesias Anglie, non obstantibus litteris Eboracensi ecclesie uel alicui impetratis. Instante autem nuntio abbatis, scripsit dominus papa [2] domino Cantuariensi
asserens ecclesiam nostram spiritualem filiam suam nulli
F.145   legato respondere, nisi legato a latere domini / pape misso,
et prohibuit ne in nos manum extenderet ; et adiecit
dominus papa de suo, prohibens etiam ne in aliquam
aliam ecclesiam exemptam potestatem excerceret. Rediit
ad nos nuntius noster et absconditum fuit hoc aliquot
diebus. Significatum tamen hoc fuit domino Cantuariensi a familiaribus suis de curia domini pape. Cum
autem in fine anni uisitacionem suam faceret legatus per
Norfolchiam et Suthfolchiam, et uenisset primo apud
Colecestriam, misit legatus ad abbatem nuntium occulte,
mandans ei, quod bene audiuit dici, quod abbas im-
petrauerat literas contra legatiam suam, et petens ut

---

[1] Innocent III, newly elected 1198
[2] Innocent confirmed the privileges of the Abbey in general terms, but
there is no record of any letter to the Abbot on this special point. But the
Registers of Innocent III do record a letter being sent to the Archbishop
on December 1, 1198, to this effect.

who has obtained from the apostolic see full power over all privileged churches in England.' Such was our counsel. Now when the Archbishop heard that we were willing to receive him as Legate, he received our messengers with gratitude and giving of thanks, and became kindly and well-disposed to the Lord Abbot in all his affairs, and for certain causes which had arisen he for a time postponed his visit to us. Therefore without a moment's delay the Abbot despatched to the Lord Pope the letters sent by the Archbishop to himself and the Convent, in which he said that he intended to come to us in virtue of his authority as Legate and by authorisation of the Lord Pope, giving him authority over all the exempt churches of England, notwithstanding the letters obtained by the Church of York or any other. Now, at the instance of the Abbot's messenger, the Lord Pope wrote to the Lord Archbishop of Canterbury, asserting that our Church, being his spiritual daughter, was not answerable to any Legate save he were sent by the Pope himself as Legate *a latere*, and he forbade him to stretch forth his hand over us. And in addition the Lord Pope of his own accord prohibited him from exercising his power over any exempted church. Our messenger returned to us, and the news was concealed for several days. Yet it was none the less made known to the Lord Archbishop by his friends at the Lord Pope's Court. But when at the end of the year the Legate carried out his visitation through Norfolk and Suffolk and came first of all to Colchester, he secretly sent a messenger to the Abbot, telling him that he had clearly heard it alleged that the Abbot had obtained letters against his legatine

mitteret ei amicabiliter literas illas. Et ita factum est ;
habuit enim abbas duo paria literarum[1] sub eadem
forma. Abbas uero nec uisitauit legatum, nec per se
nec per interpositam personam, quamdiu fuit in episco-
patu Norwicensi, ne putaretur uelle facere finem cum
legato de hospicio ei faciendo, sicut ceteri monachi et
canonici fecerunt. Legatus autem turbatus et iratus, et
timens excludi si ad nos ueniret, per Norwicum, per
Acram, per Derham, transiuit in Heli, Lundoniam
tendens. Abbate autem apparente infra mensem[2]
coram legato inter Waltham et Lundoniam in uia regia,
conuenit eum quod noluit ei occurrere utpote iustitiario
domini regis quando fuit in regione ista. Abbas autem
respondit, eum non isse ut iustitiarium, set ut legatum,
facientem scrutinium in singulis ecclesiis, et allegauit
racionem temporis, et quod passio Domini instabat[3] et
oportebat eum interesse diuinis obsequiis et claustralibus
obseruantiis. Cum autem uerba uerbis, obiectiones
obiectionibus opposuisset abbas, nec posset minis terreri
nec flecti, respondit legatus cum indignacione se bene
scire quod disputator bonus esset, et illum esse meliorem
clericum[4] quam legatus esset. Abbas ergo, nec tacenda
timide preteriens, nec dicenda tumide loquens, in audientia plurium respondit se talem esse, quod nunquam
sustinebit ecclesie sue libertatem quassari, nec propter
defectum scientie nec pecunie, etiamsi oporteret eum
mori uel perpetuo exilio dampnari. Finitis autem hiis
et huiusmodi altercacionibus, incepit legatus erubescere,

---

[1] This phrase means no more than two letters.
[2] Early in 1199. Cp. *in fine anni* (above).
[3] Holy week 1199. The Pope had already forced Hubert to resign the
Justiciarship in 1198. Either Samson did not know this or J. is wrong.
[4] Hubert Walter knew that he was a poor scholar. Cp. Giraldus
Cambrensis for a diverting account of his ' howlers ' (*Invect.* I. 5).

authority and begging him in all friendship to send him those letters. And this was done ; for the Abbot had two copies of the letters in the same form. But the Abbot did not even visit the Archbishop, neither in person nor by any intermediary, as long as he was within the diocese of Norwich, lest it might be thought that he wished to come to an agreement with the Legate concerning his reception as our guest, as other monks and canons actually did. But the Legate was troubled and angry, and fearing to be shut out if he came to us, he passed through Norwich, Acre, and Dereham to Ely, on his way to London. But when the Abbot, within a month's time, appeared before the Legate between Waltham and London on the King's highway, the Archbishop spoke to him, saying that he had refused to meet him as the King's Justiciar when he was in this part of the country. The Abbot, however, replied that the Archbishop had not journeyed as Justiciar, but as Legate, holding a scrutiny in every church, and he put forward the season of the year by way of excuse, saying that the Passion of Our Lord was drawing near, and that it behoved him to take part in divine services and monastic observances. But when the Abbot had answered him word for word, and objection for objection, and could not be terrified or moved by threats, the Legate indignantly replied that he knew he was a good logician and a better clerk than the Legate himself. The Abbot, therefore, neither timidly passed over the things that ought not to be said, nor used arrogance in saying what ought to be said, but replied in the hearing of many that he was one who would never, either through lack of knowledge or of money, suffer the liberty of his Church to be overthrown, even although he must die or be condemned to perpetual exile. When these altercations and

abbate parcius loquente et rogante, ut mitius ageret cum
ecclesia Sancti Ædmundi, racione natalis soli, quia
quasi natiuus Sancti Ædmundi et eius nutritus [1] fuit.
Erubuit quidem quia uirus, quod intus conceperat, inconsulte effuderat. In crastino nuntiatum est archiepiscopo
Cantuariensi, quod dominus Eboracensis [2] ueniret legatus
in Angliam, et quod ipse suggesserat multa mala domino
F.145v pape de eo, dicens quod ipse grauauerat ecclesias / Anglie
causa uisitacionis sue de triginta millibus marcis argenti
acceptis. Misit ergo legatus ad abbatem clericos suos,
rogans ut scriberet cum ceteris abbatibus domino pape,
et excusaret eum. Quod concessit abbas, et testimonium
perhibuit quod dominus Cantuariensis nec ad nostram
ecclesiam uenit, nec illam nec aliam grauauit ecclesiam,
loquens secundum conscientiam suam. Et cum abbas
tradidisset literas illas nunciis archiepiscopi, dixit coram
omnibus, se non timere etiamsi uoluerit archiepiscopus
in hiis literis malignari ; et responderunt clerici in periculo anime sue dominum suum nichil doli uelle machi-
nari, set tantum uelle excusari, et ita facti sunt amici
archiepiscopus at abbas.

Precepit rex Ricardus [3] omnibus episcopis et abbatibus Anglie, ut de suis baroniis nouem milites facerent
decimum, et sine dilacione uenirent ad eum in Nor-
manniam, cum equis et armis, in auxilium contra regem
Francie. Unde et abbatem oportuit respondere de iiii^{or}
militibus mittendis. Cumque summoneri fecisset omnes
milites suos, et eos inde conuenisset, responderunt feudos

---

[1] The past part. passive is here used as a noun, ' nurseling.'
[2] Geoffrey, Archbishop of York, visited Innocent III soon after the
latter's election in 1198. He was never appointed legate. The story was
probably a mere rumour, to which Hubert gave undue importance, since
he knew he was out of favour with the Pope (see *n.* 3, p. 84), who had lent
continual support to Geoffrey.
[3] See Appendix Q

the like had come to an end, the Legate began to blush ; for the Abbot spoke with greater moderation and asked him to deal more gently with the Church of St. Edmund, reminding him of the land where he was born and saying that he was almost a native and nursling of St. Edmund. Now the Archbishop blushed because he had indiscreetly vomited forth the poison that he had conceived within him. On the next day news reached the Archbishop that the Lord Archbishop of York was coming as Legate to England, and that he had hinted much ill to the Lord Pope concerning himself, saying that he had oppressed the churches of England and had made thirty thousand marks out of his visitation. The Legate therefore sent his clerks to the Abbot, asking him with other Abbots to write to the Lord Pope and exonerate him. This the Abbot said he would do and, speaking according to his conscience, he testified that the Lord Archbishop of Canterbury did not come to our Church nor oppress it or any other. And when the Abbot had given these letters to the Archbishop's messengers, he said before all present that he was not afraid, even though the Archbishop should wish to make an evil use of them. And the clerks replied on peril of their souls that their lord designed no guile, but only desired to be exonerated ; and thus the Archbishop and the Abbot became friends again.

King Richard gave orders to all the Bishops and Abbots of England that out of every ten knights one should be chosen, and that those thus chosen should forthwith come to him in Normandy, with horses and arms, to help him against the King of France. The Abbot therefore was answerable for sending four knights. And when he had summoned all his knights and spoken to them, they replied that the fiefs, which they held of

suos, quos de Sancto Ædmundo tenuerunt, hoc non debere, nec se nec patres eorum unquam Angliam exisse,
set scutagium aliquando ad preceptum regis dedisse.
Abbas uero in arto positus, hinc uidens libertatem suorum
militum periclitari, illinc timens ne amitteret saisinam
baronie sue pro defectu seruicii regis, sicut contigerat
Episcopo Lundoniensi et multis baronibus Anglie, statim
transfretauit ; et fatigatus multis laboribus et expensis et
exeniis quamplurimis que regi dedit, in primis nullum
potuit facere finem cum rege per denarios. Dicenti ergo,
se non indigere auro nec argento, set iiii^{or} milites instanter
exigenti, quatuor milites stipendiarios optulit abbas ;
quos cum rex recipisset, apud castellum de Hou [1] misit.
Abbas autem in instanti eis xxxvi. marcas dedit ad expensas xl. dierum. In crastino autem uenerunt quidam
familiares regis, consulentes abbati ut sibi caute prouideret, dicentes werram posse durare per annum integrum
uel amplius, et expensas militum excrescere et multi-
plicari in perpetuum dampnum ei et ecclesie sue. Et
ideo consulebant, ut antequam recederet de curia finem
faceret cum rege, unde posset quietus esse de militibus
predictis post xl. dies. Abbas autem, sano usus consilio,
centum libras regi dedit pro tali quietantia, et ita cum
gratia domini rediit in Angliam, breue regis portans
secum, ut milites sui distringerentur per feudos suos ad /
F.146 reddendum ei seruicium regis, quod ipse fecerat pro eis.
Milites uero summoniti allegabant paupertatem suam
et multa genera grauaminum, et optulerunt domino suo
duas marcas [2] de quolibet scuto. Abbas autem, non

---

[1] The castle of Eu, seized by Philip of France during Richard's captivity, and restored in 1195–96 by the treaty of Issoudun (Rymer, I. p. 29).
[2] If it be assumed that this sum was levied only on the 40 knights whose
service was owed to the king, we have a total of 80 marks (£53, 6s. 8d.) ;
if all the extra knights contributed, making a total of 52¾, we get the sum
of 105½ marks. In either case the Abbot was considerably out of pocket.

St. Edmund, did not owe such service, and that neither
they nor their fathers had ever served outside England,
though they had sometimes paid scutage at the King's
command. But the Abbot, being in hard case, since on
the one hand he saw that the liberty of his knights was
in peril, and on the other hand he feared that he might
lose seizin of his barony for default of the King's service,
as had happened to the Bishop of London and many
barons of England, crossed the sea forthwith, and after
being vexed by much toil and expense and the many
gifts that he made to our lord the King, he failed to
come to any agreement with the King by means of
money. Therefore, when the King told him that he
wanted neither gold nor silver, but that he must have
four knights on the spot, the Abbot offered him four
stipendiary knights, and the King accepting them, they
were sent to the castle of Eu. The Abbot at once gave
them thirty-six marks for forty days' expenses. But on
the morrow certain of the King's friends came and
advised the Abbot to make careful provision for himself, since the war might well last a whole year or more,
and the expenses of these knights might increase and
multiply to the perpetual loss of himself and his Church :
and therefore they counselled him, before he left court,
to come to an agreement with the King, whereby he
might be quit of those four knights at the end of forty
days. The Abbot therefore wisely gave the King a
hundred pounds for such quittance, and so returned to
England with the King's favour, carrying with him a
royal writ empowering him to distrain upon his knights'
fees and thus to recover from them the service which he
had rendered to the King in their stead. But the knights,
when they were summoned, alleged their poverty and
manifold burdens, and offered to pay their lord two

immemor quod ipse eos grauauerat eodem anno, et
inplacitauerat de scutagio integre reddendo, uolens
eos conciliare in gratiam, gratanter accepit quod illi
gratanter optulerunt. Tunc temporis, licet multas expensas fecisset abbas ultra mare, non rediit uacua manu
ad ecclesiam suam, ferens crucem auream et textum
preciosum ad precium quateruiginti marcarum. Alia
quoque uice cum redisset de ultra mare, sedens in
capitulo dixit, quod si esset celerarius uel camerarius,
aliquem questum faceret, qui sue administracioni com-
peteret ; et cum esset abbas, aliquid adquirere deberet
quod abbatem deceret. Hoc cum dixit, optulit conuentui
casulam preciosam et mitram auro intextam, et sandalia
cum caligis sericis, et cambucam uirge pastoralis
argenteam et bene operatam. Simili modo, quociens
de ultra mare rediit, aliquod ornamentum secum
portauit.

Anno gratie Mº.C. nonagesimo septimo facte sunt
quedam innouaciones et immutaciones in ecclesia nostra,
que sub silentio preteriri non debent. Cum non suffice-
rent celerario nostro antiqui redditus sui, iussit abbas S.
ut quinquaginta libre de Mildenhala darentur de incre-
mento annuatim celerario per manum prioris ; non
simul, set particulatim per menses, ut singulis mensibus
aliquid haberetur ad expendendum, et non totum simul
effunderetur in una parte anni ; et ita factum est uno
anno. Celerarius autem cum conplicibus suis inde conquestus est, dicens quod si illam pecuniam haberet pre
manibus, sibi prouideret et se instauraret. Abbas uero
peticioni sue cessit, licet inuitus. Intrante mense Augusti,
iam expenderat celerarius totum, et insuper xx. sex libras

marks for each shield. And the Abbot, not forgetting
how he had burdened them that selfsame year and had
impleaded them that he might compel them to pay
scutage in full, now desired to win their favour and
freely accepted what they had freely offered. At that
time, though the Abbot had incurred much expense
overseas, he did not return empty-handed to his Church,
but brought with him a cross of gold and a precious
Gospel valued at eighty marks. On another occasion
also, when he returned from overseas and was seated in
the chapterhouse, he said that, if he were Cellarer or
Chamberlain, he would make some profit that might be
of value to his office, and that, being Abbot, it was right
that he should acquire something befitting an Abbot.
And having said this, he offered the Convent a costly
chasuble, a mitre embroidered with gold, sandals and
silken boots, and a crosier-head of silver, finely wrought.
Likewise, as often as he returned from across the sea, he
brought some ornament with him.

In the year of grace 1197 certain innovations and
changes were made in our Church which must not be
passed over in silence. Since his former revenues did not
suffice the Cellarer, Abbot Samson ordered that a yearly
increment of fifty pounds from Mildenhall should be
given to the Cellarer by the hand of the Prior, not however all at once, but by monthly instalments, so that
every month he might have something to spend, and
that the whole sum should not be squandered all at once
in one portion of the year : and this was done for one
year. But the Cellarer and his accomplices complained
of this, saying that, if he had the whole sum, he would
make provision for the future and stock himself. The
Abbot, though unwillingly, granted his request ; and
by the beginning of August the Cellarer had spent all,

debebat, et quinquaginta debiturus erat ante festum
sancti Michaelis. Audiens hoc abbas moleste tulit, et ita
locutus est in capitulo : ' Sepius conminatus sum, quod
ego capiam celerariam nostram in manu mea propter
defectum et inprouidentiam uestram, qui singulis [1]
debito magno uos obligatis. Clericum meum [2] cum
celerario uestro posui in testimonium, ut res consultius
F.146v ageretur ; sed non est clericus uel monacus / qui audeat
mihi dicere causam debiti. Dicitur tamen, quod in-
moderata conuiuia in hospicio prioris per assensum prioris
et celerarii, et superflue expense in domo hospitum per
incuriam hospitiarii, sint in causa. Uidetis,' inquit,
' magnum debitum quod instat ; dicite mihi consilium,
quomodo res emendari debeat.' Multi claustrales hec
audientes, et quasi subridentes, gratum habebant quod
dicebatur, dicentes occulte quia hoc uerum est quod
abbas dixerat. Retorquebat prior culpam in celerarium;
celerarius uero in hospitiarium : quilibet seipsum excusa-
bat. Ueritatem quidem sciebamus ; set tacebamus,
quia timebamus. In crastino uenit abbas, iterum dicens
conuentui : ' Dicite mihi consilium uestrum, quomodo
celeraria uestra consultius et melius regi possit.' Nec erat
qui aliquid respondebat preter unum, qui dixit nullam
omnino superfluitatem esse in refectorio, unde debitum
uel grauamen deberet oriri. Tertio die dixit abbas eadem
uerba ; et respondit unus : ' Consilium istud a uobis debet emanare, tanquam a capite nostro.' Et dixit abbas :
' Cum nec consilium uultis dicere, nec domum uestram
scitis per uos regere, mihi incumbit tamquam patri et
summo custodi disposicio monasterii. Accipio,' inquid,

---

[1] As the text stands *singulis* must be regarded as dependent on *debito*
or *obligatis*, and must mean ' to individuals.' This is so pointless that it
seems almost certain that *annis* has dropped out.
[2] See p. 79

and in addition already owed twenty-six pounds and was like to owe fifty before Michaelmas. Hearing this, the Abbot took it very ill and said in Chapter, ' I have often threatened that I would take our cellary into my own hands on account of your default and improvidence, for you encumber yourselves with a great load of debt every year. I placed my clerk with your Cellarer as a witness, that the business might be carried on with greater wisdom. But there is neither clerk nor monk that dare tell me the cause of the debt. It is said nevertheless that the cause is to be found in the immoderate feasting that takes place in the Prior's lodging with the assent of the Prior and the Cellarer, and in superfluous extravagance in the guest-house owing to the carelessness of the Guest-master. You see,' he said, ' the great debt that weighs upon us. Tell me how the matter may be set right.' Many cloister monks almost smiled at this, and were pleased with what had been said, saying that the Abbot's words were true. The Prior put the blame on the Cellarer, the Cellarer on the Guest-master. Everybody excused himself. We did indeed know the truth, but we were silent because we were afraid. On the morrow the Abbot came and spoke again to the Convent. ' Give your advice as to how your cellary may be better managed.' Nobody replied save one, who said that there was certainly no superfluity in the Refectory that could account for that debt or burden. On the third day the Abbot said the same ; and one replied, ' This advice should proceed from you as being our head.' And the Abbot made answer, ' Since you will not give your advice, and do not know how to govern your house, the management of the monastery falls upon me as your father and supreme guardian. I take into my hand your cellary and all expenses in respect of guests, and the management of all

' in manu mea celerariam uestram et expensam hospitum,
et procuracionem interius et exterius.' Hiis dictis, deposuit celerarium et hospitiarium, et alios duos monachos
substituit habentes nomina subcelerarii et hospitiarii,[1]
clericum suum de mensa sua, magistrum G. eis associans,
sine cuius assensu nichil in cibo uel potu, nec in expensis
nec in receptis ageretur. Antiqui emptores [2] remoue-
bantur ab empcione in foro, et per clericum abbatis
cibaria emebantur ; et de bursa abbatis defectus nostri
supplebantur.   Hospites suscipiendi suscipiebantur et
honorandi honorabantur ; officiales et claustrales omnes
pariter in refectorio reficiebantur, et undique superflue
expense resecabantur.   Dixerunt autem quidam claustrales intra se : ' Septem, utique septem, fuerunt qui
bona nostra comederunt, de quorum comestionibus si
quis loquebatur, quasi reus lese maiestatis habebatur.'
Dicebat alius, tendens ad sidera palmas : [3] ' Benedictus
Deus qui dedit talem uoluntatem abbati, ut talia
corrigat.' Et dicebant plerique, quia bene est. Alii
dicebant non, talem emendacionem honoris depres-
sionem estimantes, et discrecionem abbatis feritatem lupi
appellantes ; reuocabant enim ad memoriam antiqua
somnia, scilicet quod futurus abbas seuiret ut lupus.
F.147 Mirabantur milites, mirabatur/populus super hiis que
fiebant, et dicebat aliquis in plebe : ' Mirum est quod
monachi, tot et literati uiri, sustinent res et redditus
confundi et commisceri cum rebus abbatis, que semper
solebant distingui et ab inuicem separari.   Mirum est
quod sibi non cauent de periculo futuro post mortem

---

[1] This clearly implies that in point of fact the Abbot's clerk was to
perform the duties of Cellarer and Guestmaster.   But this arrangement
did not last long, for within two months the Sub-Cellarer was made Cellarer,
and a new Sub-Cellarer appointed.   The clerk, however, was still in fact
supreme.
[2] Lay buyers employed by the Cellarer
[3] Virgil, *Aeneid*, I. 93

things both within and without.' This said, he deposed
the Cellarer and Guest-master, and set in their places
two other monks, entitled sub-cellarer and guest-master,
associating with them a clerk from his own table,
Master G., without whose assent nothing might be done
in respect of food or drink, expenditure and receipts.
The old buyers were removed from buying in the market,
and food was bought by the Abbot's clerk, and our
deficits were made good from the Abbot's purse. Guests
who had a claim to be received were received, and those
who deserved honour were given it ; officials and cloister
monks all alike fed in the refectory, and superfluous
expenses were everywhere cut down. But some cloister
monks said among themselves, ' There were seven, aye
seven, who devoured our goods, and if anyone spoke of
those devourings he was held guilty of lese-majesty.'
Another said, holding up his hands to heaven, ' Blessed
be God, who has inspired the Abbot with such desire
to set these things right.' And many said that it was
well done. But others said, ' No ! ' thinking such a
reform to be degrading to the honour of their Church,
and styling the Abbot's prudence the ravening of a
wolf ; for they called to mind the ancient dream that
the Abbot would raven like a wolf. The knights wondered
and the people wondered at the things that were done ;
and one of the common folk said, ' It is a wonder that
the monks, being so many and with such knowledge of
letters, suffer their property and revenues to be confounded and mingled with the property of the Abbot ;
for these things used always to be distinguished and kept
apart. It is a wonder that they do not beware of the
danger that will arise after the Abbot's death, if our

abbatis, si dominus rex inuenerit eos in tali statu.' Dixit
quidam alius, abbatem solum sapientem esse in rebus
exterioribus regendis, et eum debere regere totum, qui
scit regere totum. Et erat qui dicebat : ' Si saltem unus
sapiens monachus esset in tanto conuentu, qui domum
sciret regere, abbas talia non fecisset.' Et ita facti sumus
subsanatio et illusio his qui in circuitu nostro sunt.[1]

In tali tempestate contigit diem anniuersarium
Roberti[2] abbatis recitari in capitulo, et decretum fuit ut
Placebo et Dirige[3] cantarentur sollempnius solito, scilicet
cum magnis campanis pulsatis, sicut in anniuersariis
Ordingi et H.[4] abbatum, propter nobile factum predicti
R. abbatis, qui distinxit res et redditus nostros a rebus et
redditibus abbatis. Fiebat autem ista sollemnitas quorundam consilio, ut saltem sic moueretur cor domini
abbatis, scilicet ad bene faciendum. Erat autem aliquis
qui putabat hoc fieri in confusionem abbatis, qui dicebatur uelle confundere et commiscere res et redditus
nostros et suos, eo quod saisiauerat celerariam nostram
in manu sua. Abbas uero audiens insolitum sonitum
campanarum, et bene sciens et aduertens hoc contra
consuetudinem fieri, causam facti sapienter dissimulauit
et missam sollemniter cantauit. Die uero sequente
Sancti Michaelis, uolens in parte conpescere murmuraciones quorundam, illum qui prius fuit subcelerarius
constituit celerarium, et quendam alium iussit nominari
subcelerarium, remanente tamen predicto clerico cum
eis, et procurante omnia sicut prius. Cum autem clericus
ille metas temperantie excederet, dicens : ' Ego sum

---

[1] Ps. lxxviii. 4 (Vulg.) ; lxxix. 4 (AV)
[2] 16th September
[3] Responses from the Office for the dead : *Placebo Domino in regione
uiuorum*, and *Dirige Domine Deus meus in conspectu tuo uiam meam*
[4] 31st January and 16th November respectively

lord the King finds matters in such a state.' Another
said that the Abbot alone was wise in matters outside
the monastery, and that he who knew how to govern
the whole, should rule the whole. And there was one
that said, ' If there were at least one wise monk in so
large a Convent who knew how to rule the house, the
Abbot would not have done such things.' And so we
were made ' a mockery and a laughing-stock to those
that dwell round about us.'

Such being the state of affairs, it chanced that the
service for the anniversary of Abbot Robert was being
read in the Chapter, and orders were given that the
Placebo and Dirige should be sung with greater solemnity than usual, that is, to the ringing of the great bells,
as is done on the anniversaries of Abbot Ording and
Abbot Hugh, because of the great deed of the said
Abbot Robert, who separated our property and revenues
from those of the Abbot. Now this solemn celebration
was due to the design of a few, that thus at least the
Lord Abbot's heart might be moved to do good. But
there were those who thought that this was done for
the confusion of the Abbot who, because he had seized
our cellary into his own hand, was said to desire to
confound and mingle our property and revenues with
his. But the Abbot on hearing the unwonted sound of
bells and knowing well and noting that this was done
contrary to custom, wisely ignored the reason for the
deed and sang mass solemnly. On the following Michaelmas day, wishing in part to silence the murmurings of
certain persons, he gave the office of Cellarer to him
who before was sub-cellarer, and ordered another monk
to be nominated as sub-cellarer, the aforesaid clerk being
still associated with them and managing everything as
before. But when that clerk exceeded the bounds of

Bu.' (id est, celerarius cum metas temperantie in bibendo
excessisset) [1] et, inconsulto abbate, curiam celerarii
teneret et uadia et plegios caperet, et redditus annuos
reciperet et per manum suam expenderet, summus
celerarius publice dicebatur a populo. Cumque sepius
per curiam uagaretur et eum tanquam magistrum et
summum procuratorem multi sequerentur pauperes et
diuites debitores et calumniatores, diuersi diuerse condicionis / et pro diuersis negociis, stetit forte aliquis ex
obedientiariis nostris in curia, et hec uidens pre con-
fusione et pudore lacrimatus est, cogitans hoc esse
dedecus ecclesie nostre, cogitans consequens periculum,
cogitans clericum monacho preferri in preiudicium
tocius conuentus. Procurauit ergo, quisquis fuit ille,
per mediam personam, ut hec domino abbati congrue
et rationabiliter insinuarentur, factumque est ei intelligere quod huiusmodi arrogantia in clerico, que fiebat
in dedecus et turpitudinem uniuersitatis, posset esse
causa magne turbacionis et discordie in conuentu.
Abbas uero, cum hec audisset, statim fecit mandari celerarium et predictum clericum, iussitque ut celerarius
de cetero se haberet ut celerarium in recipiendo denarios,
in tenendo placita, et in omnibus aliis rebus, saluo
tamen hoc, ut predictus clericus ei assisteret, non a pari,
set ut testis et consiliarius.

Hamo Blundus, unus ex ditioribus hominibus istius
uille, agens in extremis, uix aliquid testamentum [2]

F.147v

---

[1] The statement is obscured by the parenthesis, since the clerk was
not cellarer, but usurped the cellarer's duty. If the text is correct, we
must assume that the parenthesis is a clumsy anticipation of *celerarius
publice dicebatur*. Alternatively we may reject the parenthesis as an interpolation of a marginal note, and shall then get a clear statement.

[2] The will was not a proper will. Intestacy was regarded with horror,
for in his last will and testament a man was expected to make his peace
with God by gifts to the Church and to the poor. In cases of intestacy,
it was at this time the custom that the Bishop of the diocese should make

temperance, saying, ' I am Bu ' (that is to say, when the Cellarer had exceeded the bounds of temperance in drinking) and, without consulting the Abbot, held the Cellarer's court and took gage and pledge, and received the yearly revenues and himself expended the moneys, he was openly called the Chief Cellarer by the people. And since he often strolled about the court and as being master and chief manager was followed by many debtors rich and poor, and by claimants, all of different quality and bent on different business, one of our obedientiaries chanced to be standing by in the court and, seeing this, he wept for confusion and shame, thinking it a disgrace to our Church, and thinking too of the peril that would ensue, and that a clerk was preferred over a monk to the prejudice of the whole Convent. He therefore, whoever he may have been, took steps through a third person that these things should be suitably and reasonably brought to the notice of the Abbot, who was thus led to understand that such arrogance in a clerk, displayed to the disgrace and abasement of the whole community, might be a cause of great disturbance and discord in the Convent. The Abbot, therefore, when he heard of it, at once sent for the Cellarer and the aforesaid clerk, and gave orders that for the future the Cellarer should act as Cellarer in respect of receiving money, holding pleas, and all else, saving always this, that the aforesaid clerk should assist him not as his equal, but only as a witness and an adviser.

---

a suitable disposal of the property of the deceased. So here the Abbot, treating the case as one of virtual intestacy, proclaims that he was the dead man's Bishop, and redresses the wrong. Within the *bannaleuca* of St. Edmund the Bishop of Norwich had no jurisdiction. See PM II, pp. 354 sqq.

uoluit facere ; tandem fecit testamentum ad precium
trium marcarum, nullo audiente nisi fratre suo et uxore
sua et capellano. Quod cum abbas recognouisset post
mortem eius, illos tres conuenit, et acriter corripuit super
hoc quod frater eius, qui heres erat, et uxor eius non
sustinuerunt aliquem alium accedere ad infirmum, cu-
pientes omnia capere : dixitque abbas in audientia :
' Ego fui episcopus eius, et curam habui anime eius ;
ne mihi uertatur in periculum sacerdotis et confessoris
eius inscitia, quia infirmo uiuenti consulere non potui
absens, quod mea interest faciam saltem tarde. Precipio, ut omnia debita eius et katalla mobilia que ualent
cc. marcas, sicut dicitur, reducantur in scriptum, et
una porcio detur heredi, et alia uxori, et tercia pauperibus consanguineis suis et aliis pauperibus.   Equum
autem, qui ductus est ante feretrum defuncti et oblatus
est Sancto Ædmundo, iubeo remitti et reddi :   non
debet enim ecclesia nostra coinquinari munere eius, qui
decessit intestatus, et quem fama accusat quod ex
consuetudine solebat pecuniam suam ad usuram dare.
Per os Dei, si alicui de cetero tale quid contigerit diebus
meis, non sepelietur in cimiterio.'   Hiis dictis, recesserunt
ceteri confusi./

F.147*   In crastino Natalis Domini fiebant in cimiterio conuenticula,[1] colluctaciones et concertationes inter seruientes
abbatis et burgenses de uilla ; peruentumque fuit a

---

[1] The words might mean no more than ' there were gatherings and
brawls.' But since the Abbot prohibited *spectacula* as a result of this scandal,
and since there are no words to define the *spectacula* save *colluctaciones et
concertaciones*, it is reasonable to suppose that the words mean, ' gatherings,
wrestling-matches and contests.'   In any case the *spectaculum* or its sequels
were inappropriate in a cemetery. Football of a rude type cannot be
excluded. It is most improbable that these *spectacula* were, as has sometimes
been held, Miracle Plays. The 26th of December is not a suitable time
for such shows, nor would they be likely to cause brawls.

Hamo Blunt, one of the richer men of this town, being on the verge of death, scarce consented to make any kind of will : but at length he did make a will covering the sum of three marks, no one hearing him save his brother, his wife, and a chaplain. When after his death the Abbot came to know of this, he spoke to those three and sharply rebuked them, because his brother, the heir, and his wife did not allow anyone else to approach the sick man, since they desired to seize his whole fortune. And the Abbot said in public, ' I was his bishop and had the care of his soul. That the ignorance of his priest and confessor may not be turned to my peril, I will do my duty, late though it be, because being absent I was not able to advise the sick man while he still lived. I order that all debts owing to him and all his movable possessions, worth, it is said, two hundred marks, be set down in writing ; and that one portion be given to his heir, another to his wife, and a third to his poor kindred and other poor. As for his horse, which was led before the bier of the dead man and offered to St. Edmund, I order that it should be sent back and restored : for our Church ought not to be defiled by the gift of a man, who died intestate and who is accused by rumour of having been accustomed to lend his money on usury. By God's face, if this happens to any man in my day from this time forth, he shall not be buried in the cemetery.' This said, those others retired in confusion.

On the day after Christmas there were gatherings in the cemetery, wrestling bouts and matches between the Abbot's servants and the burgesses of the town ; and from words they came to blows, and from buffets to

uerbis ad uerbera, a colafis ad uulnera et ad effusionem
sanguinis. Abbas uero, hec audiens, conuocatis clanculo
quibusdam, qui ad spectaculum conuenerant set a
longe steterant, nomina malefactorum iussit in scriptum
redigi, quos omnes summoneri fecit, ut starent coram eo
in crastino Sancti Thome archiepiscopi in capella Sancti
Dionisii [1] responsuri ; nec interim aliquem de burgensibus uocauit ad mensam suam, sicut prius solebat facere,
primis quinque diebus in Natali. Die ergo statuto, acceptis iuramentis a sexdecim legalibus hominibus, et
auditis eorum attestacionibus, dixit abbas : ' Constat
quod isti malefactores inciderunt in canonem date [2]
sententie ; set quia laici sunt hinc et inde, et non intel-
ligunt quantum facinus sit tale sacrilegium facere, ut
ceteri magis timeant, istos nominatim et publice excom-
municabo, et, ne in aliqua parte derogetur iustitie, a
domesticis et seruientibus meis incipiam.' Sicque factum
est, acceptis stolis et accensis candelis. Exierunt ergo
omnes ab ecclesia, et, accepto consilio, omnes se ex-
spoliauerunt, et omnino nudi preter femoralia pros-
strauerunt se ante hostium ecclesie. Cumque uenissent
assessores abbatis, monachi et clerici, et dicerent lacri-
mabiliter, quod plusquam centum homines nudi ita
iacerent, lacrimatus est et abbas. Rigorem tamen iuris
in uerbo et uultu preferens, et pietatem animi dissimulans, a consiliariis suis uoluit cogi, ut penitentes absol-
uerentur, sciens quod misericordia superexaltanda est
iudicio, et quod ecclesia omnes penitentes recipit.
Uerberati ergo omnes acriter et absoluti, iurauerunt

---

[1] The Chapel of St. Denys was the lower of the two chapels in the
north-west octagonal tower.
[2] *date* should probably be *late*. Cp. Gratian, Pt. II, 294 caus. 17 quaest. 3 :
*tum dicerem quod statim excommunicatus est sacrilegus, non ratione sacrilegii, sed
ratione sentencie late.*

wounds and bloodshed.   But the Abbot when he heard
of it, after calling to him in private certain persons who
had gathered to watch the show, but had stood afar off,
ordered the names of the evil-doers to be written down,
and caused all of them to be brought before him in the
chapel of St. Denys on the day after the feast of St.
Thomas ; and in the meantime he abstained from in-
viting a single burgess to his table, as he used formerly
to do during the first five days of Christmas.   So on the
appointed day, having sworn sixteen law-worthy men
and heard their testimony, the Abbot said, ' It is clear
that these evil-doers fall under the canon *sententiae latae*.
But because they are laymen and do not understand
how great a crime it is to commit such sacrilege, I will,
that others may be the more afraid, excommunicate
these by name and in public, and that there may be no
failure of justice in any respect, I will begin with my own
household and servants.'   And so it was done, when we
had put on stoles and lighted candles.   Then all of
them went out of the church and, after taking counsel,
they stripped themselves and, naked save for their
drawers, they prostrated themselves before the door of
the church.   And when the Abbot's assessors, both monks
and clerks, came and told him with tears that more than
a hundred men were lying thus naked, the Abbot also
wept.   Yet displaying all the rigour of the law in his
words and countenance, and concealing the pity that
filled his heart, he desired to be compelled by his coun-
sellors to absolve the penitents, knowing well that mercy
must be exalted over judgment and that the Church
receives all that are penitent.   Therefore after they had
all been smartly scourged and then absolved, they all

omnes, quod starent iudicio ecclesie de sacrilegio perpe-
trato. In crastino uero data est eis penitentia secundum
instituta canonum, et sic omnes ad unitatem concordie
reuocauit abbas, minas terribiles omnibus proponens
qui in dicto uel in facto materiam discordie preberent.
Conuenticula autem et spectacula prohibuit publice fieri
in cimiterio; et sic, omnibus ad bonum pacis reductis,
burgenses cum domino suo abbate diebus sequentibus
comederunt cum gaudio magno.

Facta est commissio domini pape [1] H. Cantuariensi
F.147*v archiepiscopo, et domino / Lincolniensi, et S. abbati
Sancti Ædmundi, de reformacione Conuentrensis ecclesie
et de monachis restituendis, sine cause recognicione.
Conuocatis ergo partibus apud Oxneford, receperunt
iudices literas precatorias a domino rege, ut negocium
illud poneretur in respectum. Archiepiscopo et episcopo
dissimulantibus et tacentibus et quasi clericorum fauorem
uenantibus, solus abbas aperte loquebatur, monachus
pro monachis de Conuentria, eorum causam publice
fouens et defendens. Et eo procurante eotenus proces-
sum est illa die, quod quedam simplex saisina facta fuit
uni ex monachis de Conuentria cum uno libro.[2] Set
dilata fuit corporalis institutio ad tempus, ut sic saltem
petitioni domini regis satisfacerent; abbas uero illo
tempore quatuordecim monachos de Conuentria, qui
ibi conuenerant, recepit in hospicio suo, ut sedentibus
monachis ad mensam ex una parte domus, et ex alia
parte magistris scolarum, qui summoniti fuerant, lauda-
batur abbas magnanimus et magnificus in expensis, nec

---

[1] Cp. p. 33. See Appendix R
[2] In theory the giving of seizin was accompanied by the transfer of a
symbolic portion of the thing transferred (*e.g.* from a clod of the land in
question). But in practice the giving of an irrelevant symbol was allowed.

swore that they would stand by the judgment of the
Church concerning the commission of sacrilege. And
on the morrow they were given penance according to
the rule laid down by the canons, and thus the Abbot
recalled them all to unity and concord, uttering terrible
threats against all those who by word or deed should
give cause for dissension. But he publicly forbade all
gatherings and shows in the cemetery. So all having
been brought back to the blessing of peace, the burgesses
feasted with their lord during the days that followed
with much rejoicing.

A commission was given by the Lord Pope to Hubert,
Archbishop of Canterbury, the Lord Bishop of Lincoln
and Samson, Abbot of St. Edmund for the re-establishment of the Church of Coventry and the restoration of
the monks, without further inquiry into the case. The
parties having therefore been called together at Oxford,
the judges received letters from our Lord the King,
asking that the matter should be postponed. The
Archbishop and the Bishop dissembled and were silent,
as though they were courting the favour of the clerks ;
but the Abbot spoke out alone, a monk championing
the monks of Coventry, openly supporting and defend-
ing their cause. And at his suggestion the matter was
carried so far that day that simple seizin was given with
a book to one of the monks of Coventry. But the personal
institution of the monks was postponed for a time, that
thus far at least they might satisfy the request of the
King : none the less the Abbot there and then received
into his lodgings fourteen monks of Coventry who had
assembled there : the monks sat at a table on one side
of the house and on the other sat the masters of the
schools who had been invited thither ; and the Abbot
was praised for his magnanimity and his generous

unquam uidebatur in uita sua magis letus quam tunc
temporis fuit, pro reuerentia monastici ordinis refor-
mandi. Instante festo sancti Hilarii,[1] perrexit abbas cum
magna hilaritate Conuentreiam, nec uictus labore nec
expensis, et dicebat quod si oporteret eum feretro equi-
tatorio portari, non remaneret. Ueniente eo Conuentreiam, et quinque [2] diebus expectante archiepiscopum,
omnes monachos prenominatos cum seruientibus eorum
honorifice secum tenuit, donec creatus fuit nouus prior,
et monachi sollemniter introducti.

' Qui habet aures audiendi, audiat ' [3] factum me-
moriale.   Postquam conuenit [4] inter abbatem S. et
R. de Scalis super medietate aduocacionis ecclesie de
Wertherdene, et idem R. recognouisset Sancto Ædmundo
et abbati ius suum, abbas, nulla conuentione prius habita,
nullo prius facto promisso, dedit illam ecclesie medietatem que eum contingebat magistro R. de Scalis fratri
eiusdem militis, hac condicione, ut annuam pensionem
trium marcarum per manum nostri sacriste redderet
magistro scolarum, quicunque legeret in uilla Sancti
Ædmundi.   Hoc autem fecit abbas memorande pietatis
ductus affectu, et sicut prius emerat domos lapideas ad
scolas regendas, ut pauperes clerici quieti essent a con-
ductione domus, ita de cetero essent quieti ab omni
F.148 exactione denariorum, quos / magister scolarum ex consuetudine exigebat pro erudicione sua ; Domino autem
Deo uolente, et abbate uiuente, tota medietas predicte
ecclesie, que ualet, sicut dicitur, centum solidos, ad tales
usus conuerteretur.

Cum abbas in uillis suis per abbatiam multa et uaria

---

[1] January 13, 1198
[2] 18th January
[3] Matt. xi. 15
[4] April 21, 1198

expenditure, nor did he at any time of his life seem happier than then, such was his zeal for the re-establishment of the monastic order.   When the feast of St. Hilary drew near, the Abbot went with much joy to Coventry, unsubdued either by his labours or his expenses, and saying that, even if he had to be carried in a horse-litter, he would not stay behind.   On his arrival at Coventry he waited five days for the coming of the Archbishop and gave honourable entertainment in his house to all the aforesaid monks and their servants, until a new prior had been appointed, and the monks formally inducted.

' He that hath ears to hear, let him hear ' this memorable deed.   After Abbot Samson and Robert de Scales had come to an agreement about half the advowson of the church of Wetherden, and the said Robert had recognized the right of St. Edmund and the Abbot, the latter, though no compact or promise had previously been made, gave that part of the church which belonged to him to Master Roger de Scales, the brother of the said knight on this condition, that he should through the Sacrist pay a yearly pension of three marks to the master of the schools, whoever he might be, that was teaching in the town of St. Edmund.   Now this the Abbot did, being moved by a spirit of memorable piety that, just as he had formerly bought stone houses for the school that the poor clerks might be quit of hiring houses, so now for the future they might be quit of all the fees, which the master of schools used according to the custom to exact for his teaching.   But if God will, and if the Abbot lives, the whole half of the said church, which is said to be worth a hundred shillings, should be turned to such use.

When the Abbot had built many buildings of divers kinds in his townships throughout the Abbot's domain,

edificia construxisset, et perhendinasset ad maneria sua
sepius et frequencius quam nobiscum domi, tandem quasi
in se rediens, et quasi bonum in melius commutans, dixit
se magis solito domi commoraturum, et edificia infra
curiam [1] ad usus necessarios facturum, respectum habens
ad interiora et exteriora, et sciens quia ' presentia domini
prouectus est agri.' [2] Stabula ergo et officinas in curia
circum circa, que cooperte erant arundine prius, nouis
tectis appositis, lateribus cooperiri iussit, procurante H.
sacrista, ut sic omnis timor excluderetur et periculum
ignis. Et ecce tempus acceptabile, dies [3] desideratus !
quod non sine gaudio scribo, qui curam hospitum habeo.
Ecce, iubente abbate, resonat curia ligonibus et machinis
cementariis ad subuertendam domum hospitum, et iam
fere tota est prostrata : de reedificacione cogitet Altissimus ! [4] Lardearium nouum sibi construxit abbas in
curia, et uetus lardearium conuentui ad opus camerarii
dedit, quod indecenter sub dormitorio fuerat. Capelle
sancti Andree et sancte Katerine et sancte Fidis nouiter
plumbo cooperte sunt.[5] Multe quoque emendaciones
infra ecclesiam et extra facte sunt. Si non credis, aperi
oculos tuos et uide. Tempore quoque suo facta est
elemosinaria nostra lapidea, que prius erat debilis et
lignea, ubi quidam frater noster Walterus medicus, tunc
temporis elemosinarius, multum apposuit, quod arte
medicinali adquisiuit. Item uidens abbas quod tabula

---

[1] The great courtyard in front of the Abbot's lodgings. It was 420
feet in length ; see MRJ pp. 124.

[2] Palladius, I. i, 6

[3] 2 Cor. vi. 2

[4] Clearly the rebuilding did not proceed as quickly as he wished.
Probably this passage was written in 1198 ; for the *crista* of the shrine, of
which he speaks below, was half finished at the time of the fire of October 17,
1198. See p. 109

[5] The Chapel of St. Andrew was probably connected with the Infirmary.
The Chapel of St. Faith was above that of St. Denys, at north-west corner
of west front. The chapel of St. Katherine was above that of St. John
the Baptist at south-west corner of west front.

and had stayed more often at his manors than with us at home, at length, as if he were returning to himself and changing the good into the better, he said that he would live at home more than was his wont, and that he would construct buildings within the court to meet the needs of the Abbey, taking into consideration what was required at home as well as without, and knowing that 'the presence of the master brings profit to his fields.' Therefore he gave orders that the stables and workshops round about the court, which were previously thatched with reeds, should be roofed afresh with tiles under the direction of Hugh the Sacrist, that thus all fear and peril of fire might be removed. And behold ! the acceptable time, the long-desired day is come, of which I write not without joy, seeing that I have charge of our guests. Behold ! at the Abbot's command, the court resounds with the noise of picks and mason's tools for the demolition of the guest-house, and it is now almost all pulled down. As for its rebuilding, may the Most High provide ! The Abbot built a new larder for himself in the court, and gave the old larder to the Convent for the use of the Chamberlain, because its position beneath the dormitory was unsuitable. The Chapels of St. Andrew, St. Catherine and St. Faith were new-covered with lead. Many repairs also were carried out both within and without the church. If thou believe it not, ' open thine eyes and see.' Our new stone almonry was also built ; and it was high time, since before it was of wood and insecure ; and for this purpose our brother, Walter, the physician, who was at that time Almoner, contributed a large sum of money which he had acquired by his practice of the art of medicine. Also the Abbot, seeing that the silver retable of the high altar and many other precious ornaments

argentea magni altaris et multa alia preciosa ornamenta
alienata fuerant propter recuperacionem de Mildenhala
et redempcionem regis Ricardi, tabulam illam noluit
reformare nec alia consimilia, que consimili casu possent
euelli et distrahi ; set ad cristam faciendam pretiosissi-
mam super feretrum gloriosi martiris Ædmundi studium
suum conuertit, ut ibi ornamentum suum poneretur unde
nullo casu posset abstrahi, nec aliquis hominum manus
auderet apponere. Quippe captiuato rege Ricardo in
F.148v Alemannia, non erat thesaurus in Anglia, / qui non
daretur uel redimeretur, set feretrum Sancti Ædmundi
remansit intactum. Uenit tamen in questionem coram
iustitiariis ad scaccarium utrum feretrum Sancti Ædmundi saltem in parte excrustaretur [1] ad redempcionem
regis Ricardi, et abbas se erigens respondit : ' Scitote
pro uero, quod nunquam hoc fiet per me, nec est homo
qui me ad hoc posset cogere, ut consentiam. Set aperiam
hostia ecclesie ; intret qui uelit, accedat qui audeat.'
Responderunt singuli iustitiarii cum iuramentis : ' Nec
ego accedam, nec ego accedam. In remotos et absentes
seuit Sanctus Ædmundus ; multo magis in presentes
seuiet, qui tunicam suam ei aufferre uoluerint.' Hiis
dictis, nec feretrum fuit excrustatum, nec inde precium
datum. Ceteris ergo omissis, conuersus est animus abbatis satis consulte et prouide ad cristam feretri fabrican-
dam. Et iam resonant lamine auree et argentee inter
malleum et incudem, et ' tractant fabrilia fabri.' [2]
Adam [3] de Cokefeld moriens filiam trium mensium

---

[1] MS *incrustaretur*   [2] Horace, *Epistles*, II. i. 116
[3] Adam succeeded his father in 1191, and was still alive in 1200, as
his name is included in the list of knights made in that year ; see p. 121.
The litigation over his lands which occurred after his death took place
in 1201. The wardship of his infant daughter fell to the Abbot as being
her father's feudal lord. Wardships were lucrative and marketable ; the
guardian took the revenues and profits of the tenement for his own use,
subject to providing duly for his ward's maintenance (see PM I. p. 319).
For the sequel see p. 123.

had been alienated for the recovery of Mildenhall and the ransom of King Richard, was unwilling to restore the retable and other like ornaments, which in a like emergency might be torn away and dispersed, but set all his desire on making a very precious crest for the feretory of the glorious Martyr St. Edmund, in order that his ornament might be set there in a place from which it could not under any circumstance be taken, nor would any man dare to lay his hand upon it. For when King Richard was taken captive in Germany, there was no treasure in all England that was not given or redeemed, but the feretory of St. Edmund remained untouched. None the less the question was raised before the judges of the Exchequer, whether the feretory of St. Edmund should be stripped at least in part for the ransoming of King Richard ; and the Abbot arose and said, ' Know this for the truth that it shall never be done if I can prevent it, nor is there any man that can force me to consent thereto. But I will open the doors of the church. Let him enter who will, let him approach who dare ! ' And each of the judges replied with an oath, ' I will not approach, nor will I. For the fury of St. Edmund can reach those who are absent and far away ; much more will it strike those who are present and desire to strip his shirt from off him.' This said, neither was the feretory stripped nor was anything taken therefrom. Then the Abbot, abandoning all other plans, very wisely and providently turned his mind to making a crest for the feretory, and now plates of gold and silver are ringing between the hammer and the anvil and ' craftsmen ply the craft that craftsmen use.'

Adam de Cockfield died and left a daughter three

reliquit heredem ; wardamque dedit abbas de feudo suo,
ubi uolebat. Rex uero Ricardus, sollicitatus a quibusdam
familiaribus suis, peciit anxie wardam et puellam ad
opus cuiusdam seruientis sui, quandoque per literas,
quandoque per nuntios. Abbas uero respondit se wardam dedisse, et carta sua confirmasse ; mittensque
nuntium suum regi temptauit prece et precio, si quo
modo posset iram eius mitigare. Et respondit rex cum
magna indignacione, quod se uindicaret de superbo
abbate, qui ei contradixit, nisi desisteret pro reuerentia
Sancti Ædmundi quem timuit. Redeunte ergo nuntio,
abbas minas regis sapienter dissimulauit, et dixit :
' Mittat rex si uult, et saisiet wardam ; uim et potestatem habet faciendi uoluntatem suam, et aufe-
rendi totam abbatiam. Ego nunquam flectar, ut hoc
uelim quod petit, nec per me hoc unquam fiet. Timendum enim est ne talia trahantur ad consequentiam in
preiudicium successorum meorum : pro negocio isto
nunquam regi pecuniam dabo. Uideat Altissimus. Ego
F.149 quicquid contigerit patienter sustinebo.' / Cum ergo
multi dicerent et crederent regem esse commotum uersus
abbatem, ecce rex amicabiliter scripsit abbati, et mandauit ut de canibus suis aliquos ei daret. Abbas uero
non inmemor illius dicti sapientis : [1]

> munera (crede mihi) capiunt hominesque deosque :
>   placatur donis Iupiter ipse datis,

canes, sicut rex mandauerat, insuper et equos et alia
munera preciosa, ei transmisit. Que cum rex gratanter
suscepisset, probitatem abbatis et fidelitatem eius publice

---

[1] Ovid, *Ars Amatoria*, iii. 653–4. Both the Harley and Cotton MSS
have *Iubiter*.

months old as his heir ; and the Abbot bestowed the
wardship of her fief, as pleased him. But King Richard
on the petition of certain of his friends urgently requested
the wardship on behalf of a certain servant of his, sometimes by letters, sometimes by messengers. The Abbot,
however, replied that he had given the wardship and
had confirmed his gift by charter ; and sending his
messenger to the King, he tried by gifts and entreaties
to assuage his anger. And the King replied in great
indignation that he would be avenged on this proud
Abbot who said him nay, save that he refrained out
of reverence for St. Edmund whom he feared. So when
the messenger returned, the Abbot wisely ignored the
King's threats and said, ' Let the King send, if he will,
and seize the wardship ; he has the strength and power
to do what he wills, and of taking away the whole abbey
from me. Nothing shall move me to grant his request,
nor shall this ever be done, if I can help it. For I fear
lest such actions should prejudice the position of those
that shall come after me ; and I will never give the
King money to settle this matter. Let the Most High
see to it ! I will patiently endure whatever may befall.'
And then, though many said that the King was very
angry with the Abbot, lo and behold ! the King wrote
a friendly letter to the Abbot and demanded that he
should give him some of his hounds. Whereupon the
Abbot, not forgetting the wise saying,

> Believe me, presents win both gods and men,
> And Jove himself is oft appeased with gifts,

sent hounds, as the King had demanded, and horses also
and other rich gifts, which the King received with
gratitude, and in the presence of his earls and barons

coram comitibus et baronibus suis magnifice commendauit, et anulum preciosum, quem dominus papa
Innocentius tercius per magnam caritatem ei donauerat,
primum scilicet donum quod ei post consecracionem
suam oblatum fuerat, abbati per nuntios suos misit in
signum familiaritatis et amoris, et per breue suum de
xeniis sibi transmissis gratias multiplices egit.

Multi mirabantur de consuetudinibus que immuta-
bantur, domino S. abbate uel iubente uel permittente.
A tempore quo uilla Sancti Ædmundi nomen et libertatem burgi [1] accepit, solebant homines de singulis domibus dare celerario unum denarium in principio Augusti,
ad metendum segetes nostras, qui census dicebatur
repseluer ; [2] et antequam uilla fuit libera, solebant omnes
metere ut serui ; sola hospicia militum et capellanorum et
seruientium curie quieta erant a tali censu. Processu
temporis, pepercit celerarius quibusdam ditioribus uille,
nichil exigens ab eis ; alii burgenses hoc uidentes publice
dicebant, quod nemo, qui haberet messuagium proprium, deberet dare illum denarium, set illi qui alienas
domos conducebant. Postea omnes communiter hanc
libertatem petebant, conuenientes inde dominum abbatem, et annuum redditum pro tali exactione offerentes ;
abbas uero attendens qualiter celerarius turpiter ibat
per uillam ad colligendum *repseluer*, et qualiter faciebat
capi uadia in domibus pauperum, quandoque tripodes,
quandoque hostia, quandoque alia utensilia, et qualiter
uetule exibant cum colis suis, minantes et exprobantes
F.149*v* celerario et suis, decreuit ut uiginti/solidi darentur
singulis annis celerario ad portmanemot proximum ante

---

[1] The town is first styled Eadmundes byri in a charter of Edward the
Confessor (Kemble, 883 ; EHR xliii, p. 382), while the charter granted
to the burgesses (FD p. 114) indicates that their rights dated from that reign.
[2] ' Reaping silver,' a due paid in lieu of reaping service

publicly praised the courage and loyalty of the Abbot
in high terms, and as a token of his friendship and love
sent him by his messengers a valuable ring, which the
Lord Pope, Innocent III, had given to him out of his
great affection, it being the first gift offered him after
his coronation as king ; and further wrote to the Abbot
warmly acknowledging the presents sent to him.

Many wondered at the changes in ancient customs
that were made by order of the Abbot or with his permission. From the time when the town of St. Edmund
received the name and liberty of a borough, men used
at the beginning of August to give the Cellarer one penny
for each house towards the cutting of our corn, which
due was called ' repselver.' And before the town received
its liberty, all of them used to reap as though they had
been serfs : only the dwellings of knights, chaplains, and
servants of the court were exempt from such a due. But
in process of time the Cellarer spared some of the richer
men of the town, demanding nought of them ; wherefore
the other burgesses seeing this said openly that no man,
who had a messuage of his own, should pay that penny,
but only those who hired houses that belonged to others.
And afterwards they all in common demanded this
liberty, speaking to the Lord Abbot on the matter and
offering him a yearly payment in lieu of this exaction.
And noting how the Cellarer went through the town to
collect the repselver without any regard to his dignity,
and how he caused security for payment to be taken in
the houses of the poor, sometimes three-legged stools,
sometimes doors and sometimes other utensils, and how
old women came out with their distaffs, threatening and
abusing the Cellarer and his men, the Abbot ordered
that twenty shillings should be given to the Cellarer
every year at the next portmanmoot before August, this

Augustum,[1] per manum prefecti, a burgensibus qui attornauerunt redditum ad hoc soluendum. Sicque factum est, et carta nostra confirmatum ; data eis alia quietantia cuiusdam consuetudinis que dicitur *sorpeni*,[2] pro iiii. solidis ad eundem terminum reddendis. Solebat enim celerarius accipere unum denarium per annum de qualibet uacca hominum uille pro exitu et pastura, nisi forte essent uel uacce capellanorum uel seruientium curie ; quas uaccas solebat inparcare,[3] et circa hoc multum laborare. Primo autem, cum abbas de hoc loqueretur in capitulo, indignabatur conuentus et moleste tulit, unde et Benedictus supprior in capitulo respondens pro omnibus dixit : ' Ille, ille abbas Ordingus, qui illic iacet,[4] non faceret tale quid pro quingentis marcis argenti.' Abbas uero inde iratus rem distulit ad tempus. Item facta est contencio magna inter R. celerarium et H. sacristam de pertinentiis officiorum suorum, ita quod sacrista nolebat accommodare celerario ergastulum uille ad includendum latrones qui capiebantur in feudo celerarii. Unde celerarius sepius uexabatur et, latronibus euadentibus, uituperabatur pro defectu iusticie. Contigit autem, quod quidam libere tenens de celerario, extra portam manens, Ketel nomine, latrocinio calumniatus et duello uictus. suspensus erat. Dolebat autem conuentus propter opprobria burgensium, dicentium quod, si esset homo ille manens infra burgum, non

---

[1] So the Harleian MS in its copy of this passage on f. 123 ; in the main text of the Chronicle, *ante Augustum* follows *prefecti*. See p. xii.

[2] ' Herd money,' a due paid for pasturage in the town fields. F. 123 of our MS spells it *schorenpeny* ; it is elsewhere spelt ' scharpeni,' ' scarpeni,' etc. The payment of a lump sum for both this and the repselver is described in Samson's charter (see L pp. 171, 172). The *prefectus* is to pay 20 shillings before August 1. To secure the payment of this sum the burgesses bought land in the market belonging to Frodo the tanner, on which they erected stone buildings, which they assigned in perpetuity to the *prefecti*.

sum to be paid through the town reeve by burgesses who assigned a revenue for the payment of this due. This was done and confirmed by our charter. And they were also granted exemption from another custom, called ' sorpenny,' in return for four shillings to be paid at the same date. For the Cellarer used to receive one penny each year in respect of every cow belonging to a townsman, for the privilege of turning it out to graze, unless the cows happened to belong to chaplains or servants of the Abbot : and he used to place the cows in an enclosed field, and was at much trouble about the business. At first, when the Abbot spoke about this in Chapter, the Convent was angry and took it ill ; wherefore Benedict the sub-prior, answered him in Chapter on behalf of them all, saying, ' Ording, aye Ording, who lies yonder would not have done such a thing for five hundred marks of silver.' But the Abbot was angry and put off the matter for the time being. Also there was a great dispute between Roger the Cellarer and Hugh the Sacrist concerning the appurtenances of their offices, in that the Sacrist refused to lend the Cellarer the use of the town prison for the safe custody of thieves who were taken in the Cellarer's fee. Consequently the Cellarer was often in trouble and, when thieves escaped, was abused for default of justice. Now it happened that a free tenant of the Cellarer, Ketel by name, who dwelt without the gate, was accused of robbery and, being vanquished in the duel, was hung. And the Convent was grieved because of the reproaches of the burgesses who said that,

---

³ It is not clear which class of cows (*i.e.* exempt or liable to *sorpeni*) were to be placed in an enclosure.

⁴ In the chapterhouse. Ording was the first Abbot to be buried there. See MRJ p. 180.

peruenisset ad duellum, set iuramentis uicinorum suorum
se adquietasset, sicut libertas est eorum qui manent infra
burgum.¹   Uidentes ergo hoc abbas et sanior pars conuentus, et attendentes quod homines, tam extra burgum
quam infra, nostri sunt, et omnes debent eadem libertate
frui infra bannam leucam, preter lancettos ² de Herdewic
et pares eorum, consulte prouiderunt quomodo posset
hoc fieri.   Uolens itaque abbas officia sacristie et celerarii
certis articulis determinare et contenciones sedare, quasi
fouendo partem sacriste, precepit ut seruientes prefecti
uille et seruientes celerarii intrarent simul feudum
celerarii ad capiendos latrones et malefactores, et pre-
F.150 fectus dimidium lucri / haberet pro incarceracione et
custodia et labore suo, et curia celerarii ueniret ad
portmannemot, et ibi comuni consilio iudicarentur iudi-
candi.   Statutum est eciam, ut homines celerarii uenirent
ad domum thelonei cum aliis, et ibi renouarent pleggios
suos,³ et scriberentur in rolla prefecti, et ibi darent
prefecto denarium, qui dicitur *borthseluer*, et celerarius
haberet dimidiam partem.   Set nunc nichil omnino inde
capit celerarius :   hoc autem totum fuit factum, ut omnes
equali libertate gauderent.   Dicunt tamen adhuc burgenses, quod suburbani non deberent esse quieti de
theloneo in foro, nisi fuerint in gilda mercatorum.⁴

¹ As in other boroughs (*e.g.* London, Winchester, Lincoln), the burgesses had the privilege of not submitting themselves to trial by battle ;
see Bigelow, *History of Procedure*, p. 307.
² A Latinization of A.S. *landsetta* ('tenant') ; like *villanus* the word
suffered degradation and came to imply servile tenure.   The name is rarely
found outside East Anglia.   These *lancetti* were ascript to the soil, and held
their land by various services.
³ At the View of Frankpledge, which was normally conducted by the
Sheriff.   Within the Liberty of St. Edmund his place is taken by the Abbot,
who appoints a deputy to carry out the duties ; the plegii are the men
who stand as sureties for their tithing (a group of 10–12 men).
⁴ This guild was clearly of some importance, but nothing is known
of its constitution.   See L pp. 72 and 75.

if the man had dwelt within the borough, he would not have been forced to do battle, but would have acquitted himself by the oaths of his neighbours according to the liberty belonging to those who dwell within the borough. Therefore when the Abbot and the sounder portion of the Convent saw this and recognised that, whether they live within the borough or without, the men are equally our men and ought all of them to enjoy the same liberty within the bounds of the four crosses, excepting always the *lancetti* of Hardwick and their like, they wisely took steps to put this into effect. And so the Abbot desiring strictly to define the offices of the Sacrist and the Cellarer and to end their disputes, gave his support to the Sacrist, as it seemed, and ordered that the servants of the reeve and the servants of the Cellarer should enter the Cellarer's fee together for the purpose of taking thieves and evil-doers, and that the reeve should have half the profit derived from their imprisonment and custody and for his own labour, and that the court of the Cellarer should come to the portmanmoot, and that those to be tried should be tried there by the two courts in common counsel. It was also decreed that the Cellarer's men should come to the toll-house with the rest, renew their pledges there, and be set down on the reeve's roll, and there pay him the penny known as ' borth-selver,' and that the Cellarer should have half of this sum. But now the Cellarer receives nothing at all from this payment, though this was all of it done that everyone might enjoy equal liberties. But the burgesses still assert that those living in the suburbs should not be exempt from toll in the market, unless they belong to the guild of merchants ;

Prefectus autem, abbate dissimulante, placita et foris-
facturas sibi uendicat de feudo celerarii hiis diebus.

Antique consuetudines celerarii, quas uidimus, tales
fuerunt : celerarius habebat mesuagium et horrea[1] sua
iuxta fontem Scuruni, ubi sollemniter curiam suam solebat tenere de latronibus et omnibus placitis et querelis,
et ibi solebat ponere homines suos in plegios et inrollare,
et renouare singulis annis, et inde lucrum capere sicut
prefectus capiebat ad portmanmot. Quod mesuagium,
cum orto adiacente quem nunc infirmarius tenet, fuit
mansio Beodrici,[2] qui fuit antiquitus dominus istius uille,
unde et uilla dicta fuit Beodrichesworh, cuius campi
dominici nunc sunt in dominico celerarii. Quod autem
nunc uocatur *auerland*,[3] fuit terra rusticorum eius. Erat
autem summa tenementi eius et suorum tricesies triginta
acre terre, que adhuc sunt campi istius uille, quorum
seruicium, cum uilla fuit facta libera, diuidebatur in
duas partes, ut sacrista siue prefectus acciperet liberum
censum,[4] scilicet de qualibet acra duos denarios ; celerarius haberet araturas et alia seruitia, scilicet araturam
unius rode pro qualibet acra sine cibo, que consuetudo
adhuc obseruatur ; haberet et faldas ubi omnes homines
uille, preter senescaldum qui propriam faldam habet,
tenentur ponere oues suas, que consuetudo adhuc obseruatur ; haberet et *auerpeni*,[5] scilicet pro singulis triginta
acris ii. denarios ; que consuetudo mutata fuit ante
mortem H. abbatis, Gilberto de Aluedena existente
celerario. Solebant autem homines uille, iubente / celerario, ire apud Laginghehe et reportare auragium[6] de

---

[1] Known as the Grange of St. Edmund, or Eastgate Barns (see L pp.
18, 19) ; Scurun's Well was probably on this land.
[2] See p. xxvi
[3] Land held by the service of beasts of burden (*aueria*)
[4] Free tax or rent ; known as *landmol* (see L p. 56)
[5] The due paid in lieu of service by *aueria*
[6] Service with pack or cart horses

while the reeve, with the connivance of the Abbot, nowadays claims for himself all the pleas and forfeitures of the Cellarer's fee.

The ancient customs of the Cellarer, which we have seen in our day, were as follows : the Cellarer had a messuage and barns near Scurun's Well, where he used in all due state to hold his court for the trial of robbers and the hearing all pleas and disputes, and there also he used to place his men in frankpledge, to enroll them and re-enter them every year, and to make profit thereby such as the reeve made at the portmanmoot. This messuage, with the adjoining garden now held by the Infirmarer, was once the abode of Bederic, who was of old the lord of this town, wherefore it was called Bedericsworth, and his domain fields are now in the Cellarer's domain. But that part, which is now called ' averland,' was the land of his peasants ; and the sum of his holding and that of his men was nine hundred acres of land, which are still the fields of this town, service of which, when the town was made free, was divided into two parts, so that the Sacrist or the reeve received a free tax, to wit, two pence per acre ; while the Cellarer had plough and other services, to wit, the ploughing of one rood per acre without food (which custom is still observed), he had also folds, where all the men of the town are bound to keep their sheep, except the seneschal, who has his own fold (which custom likewise is still observed) ; and also had ' averpenny,' to wit, two pence for every thirty acres, which custom was changed before the death of Abbot Hugh, Gilbert of Elveden being then Cellarer. Now the men of the town used at the bidding of the Cellarer to go to Lakenheath and perform cartage-

anguillis de Surteia,[1] et sepe uacui redire et ita uexari
sine aliquo emolimento celerarii ; unde conuenit inter
eos, ut singule triginta acre de cetero darent unum
denarium per annum, et homines remanerent domi.
Terre autem ille, nunc tempore, in tot partes diuise
sunt, quod uix scitur a quo ille census dari debet ; ita
quod uidi celerarium in uno anno capere xxvii. denarios,
set uix nunc potest habere x. denarios et obolum. Item
celerarius solebat habere potestatem in uiis extra uillam,
ita quod nulli licuit fodere cretam uel argillam sine licentia eius. Solebat etiam summonere fullones uille, ut ei
accomodarent pannos ad sal suum ducendum. Alioquin
ipse prohiberet eis usum aquarum, et caperet telas quas
ibi inueniret ; que consuetudines adhuc obseruantur.
Item quicumque emit a celerario bladum uel aliud,
solebat esse quietus de theloneo ad portam uille quando
exiret, unde celerarius rem suam carius uendebat, quod
adhuc obseruatur. Item celerarius solet accipere theloneum de lino, tempore rotacionis, scilicet unam bottam
de qualibet cerna. Item solus celerarius debet uel solebat
habere liberum taurum [2] in campis huius uille ; nunc
habent plures. Item quando aliquis delegabat terram
burgagii [3] in elemosinam conuentui, et hoc assignabatur
celerario uel alio officiali, terra illa solebat de cetero esse
quieta de haggouele,[4] et maxime celerario propter
dignitatem officii, quia secundus pater est in monasterio,

---

[1] Aelfgifu the wife of Canute gave the monks of St. Edmund 4,000 eels
per annum from the fisheries at Southrey. The situation was modified
by Samson's successor, who substituted a due of half a mark for a thousand eels.
[2] A ' free bull ' and ' free boar ' were normal privileges of a manor.
Cp. Appendix T.
[3] Burgage is a term for a form of tenancy in a borough, closely corresponding with socage in country districts. Tenure is not military and
involves no service, but does involve rent.

service, bringing eels from Southrey ; and often they would return empty and thus be put to trouble without any profit to the Cellarer ; wherefore it was agreed between them that for the future a penny a year should be paid for every thirty acres, and the men should remain at home. But nowadays those lands are divided into so many parts, that it is scarce known who should pay those dues ; so that I have seen the Cellarer receive as much as twenty-seven pence in one year, but now he is scarce able to get tenpence halfpenny. Also the Cellarer used to have power to prevent anyone from digging chalk or clay on the roads outside the town without his licence. He used also to summon the fullers of the town to provide him with cloth for carriage of his salt. If they refused, he would forbid them use of the water and would seize the cloths which he found there ; which customs are still observed. Also anyone who bought corn or anything else from the Cellarer used to be exempt from toll at the town gate when he went out, wherefore the Cellarer sold his goods at a higher price ; this practice is still observed. Also the Cellarer is wont to take toll of flax at the time of carting, to wit, one truss for each load. Also the Cellarer alone ought or used to have a free bull on the fields of this town ; now a number of persons have them. Again when anyone assigned burgage land as alms to the Convent, and this land was assigned to the Cellarer or another official, that land used for the future to be quit of hawgable, more especially when the Cellarer was concerned, because of the dignity of his office, seeing that he is second father in the monastery, or else out of respect for the Convent, since the

---

Haggovele (hadgovel, haugable) is in the nature of a land tax. For 'govel gavel gable' cp. Ger. *Gabel* and Fr. *gabelle*. See L p. 54.

uel propter reuerentiam conuentus, quia fauorabilis
debet esse condicio eorum qui uictum nostrum pro-
curant ; set talem consuetudinem dicit abbas esse inius-
tam, ubi sacrista amittit seruicium suum.¹ Item celerarius
solebat warentizare seruientibus curie, ut essent a scotto
et tailagio quieti ; set nunc non est ita, quia burgenses
dicunt, quod seruientes curie debent esse quieti in eo
quod sunt seruientes, set non in hoc quod tenent burga-
gium in uilla, et quia ipsi uel uxores eorum faciunt
publicas emtiones et uendiciones in foro.   Item cele-

F.151 rarius libere solebat / capere omnia sterquilinia ad opus
suum, in omni uico, nisi ante hostia eorum qui habebant
auerland ; illis enim solis licebat fimum colligere et
habere.   Ista consuetudo paulatim defecit tempore
Hugonis abbatis, usque quo Dionisius et Rogerus de
Hehingheham fuerunt celerarii, qui, uolentes antiquam
consuetudinem reuocare, ceperunt redas burgensium
fimo honeratas, et eas exhonerari fecerant ; set reclamante multitudine burgensium et preualente, quilibet
in tenemento suo fimum colligit, et pauperes suum
uendunt, quando et cui uoluerint.   Item celerarius in
foro istius uille tale priuilegium solet habere, quod ipse
uel emptores sui primam emtionem habebunt de omni
cibo ad opus conuentus, si abbas domi non fuerit.
Emtores abbatis uel celerarii, qui prius uenient in foro,
prius ement, siue isti sine illis, siue illi sine istis.   Si autem
hinc et inde presentes fuerint, deferendum est emtoribus
abbatis. Item tempore quo uenditur allec, ement emtores
semper abbatis centenarium de allec minus quam ceteri,
uno obolo ; similiter celerarius et sui emptores.   Item si
summa de pisce uel alio cibo uenerit in curiam primo uel

¹ *i.e.* the haggovele which would naturally have gone to the Sacrist

condition of those who procure us our food should receive special favour ; but the Abbot says that this custom is unjust, since the Sacrist loses the revenue that is his due. Again the Cellarer was wont to warrant the servants of the court that they should be exempt from all scot or tallage ; but this is no longer observed, since the burgesses say that the servants should be exempt because they are our servants, and not because they hold burgage land in the town, and themselves or their wives buy or sell publicly in the market. Also the Cellarer used to take all the dung for his own purposes in every street, save from before the doors of those that hold averland ; for to them alone it is permitted to collect and keep such dung. This custom gradually decayed during the time of Abbot Hugh until Denys and Roger of Hingham were Cellarers, who, wishing to restore the ancient custom, took the carts of the burgesses that were laden with dung, and caused them to be unloaded ; but since many of the burgesses protested and prevailed, everyone now collects dung on his own holding, and the poor sell theirs when and to whom they will. Again the Cellarer is wont to hold this privilege in the market of the town, to wit, that he or his buyers should have the right of first purchase in respect of all food required for the Convent, if the Abbot be not in residence. The buyers employed by the Abbot or the Cellarer shall buy first, whichever come first to market, the former in the absence of the latter or the latter in the absence of the former. But if they are both present, precedence shall be given to the Abbot's buyers. Again, when pickled herring is sold, the buyers of the Abbot shall always buy a hundred herring at a half-penny less than the others, so too shall the Cellarer and his buyers. Again if a load of fish or other food comes

in forum uenerit, et summa illa non fuerit discargiata de equo uel de carecta, celerarius uel emtores sui summam integram ement et secum ducent sine theloneo. Abbas autem S. precepit emtoribus suis, ut cederent celerario et suis, quia, sicut ipse dixit, maluit ut ipse esset in defectu quam suus conuentus. Emtores ergo, honore se inuicem preuenientes,[1] si aliquid emendum inuenerint quod non sufficiat ambabus partibus, rem pariter emunt et a pari diuidunt, et sic capitis ad menbra, patris ad filios, remanet discordia concors.[2]

Poeta dixit, ' summa petit liuor ; '[3] hec icirco repeto quia cum aliquis presens scriptum inspiceret, et tot bene acta legeret, adulatorem abbatis me nominauit, et uenatorem fauoris et gratie, dicens quod quedam suppressi tacitus, que tacenda non essent. Cumque interrogarem F.151v que et qualia, respondit : ' Nonne uides, quod abbas / dat eschaetas [4] terrarum de dominicis terris conuentus, et puellas heredes terrarum,[5] et uiduas,[6] tam in uilla Sancti Ædmundi quam extra, pro beneplacito suo ? Nonne uides, qualiter abbas abstrahit sibi loquelas et placita calumpniantium, per breue regis, terras que sunt de feudo conuentus, et maxime illas loquelas unde lucrum surgit ; et illas unde lucrum non sequitur, illas remittit celerario uel sacriste aut aliis officialibus ? ' Quibus respondi, ut sciui, forte bene forte male, dicens quod quilibet dominus

---

[1] Rom. xii, 10
[2] Cp. Lucan I. 98, *temporis angusti mansit concordia discors*
[3] Ovid, *Remedia Amoris*, 369
[4] Land escheats to the lord, when the tenant commits a felony or dies heirless
[5] Cp. the case of Adam of Cockfield's daughter, p. 123
[6] The widow of a military tenant is allowed at most only a third of her husband's land as a dower ; if she has children, they and the rest of the land are held in ward by the feudal lord. Her marriage may be sold by the lord, just as may her children's. Cp. PM I. p. 325

into the court or the market, and if that load has not been unloaded from horse or cart, the Cellarer or his buyers may buy the load in its entirety and take it with them without toll. But Abbot Samson ordered his buyers to give way to the Cellarer and his buyers because, as he said, he preferred that he rather than the Convent should go short. Therefore the buyers, in mutual deference to each other, if they find something to be bought which is not sufficient for both, buy it jointly and divide it equally ; and so betwixt head and limbs and between father and sons

Concord that is no concord still abides.

The Poet has said, 'Envy assails earth's highest' ; I repeat these words, because when a certain person looked at this writing of mine and read of so many great achievements, he called me a flatterer of the Abbot and a hunter after favour and popularity, saying that I had suppressed certain things and passed them over in silence, where silence was wrong. And when I asked him what things I had suppressed and of what kind they were, he replied, ' Do you not see that the Abbot gives away escheats from the domain-land of the Convent and bestows girls and widows who are heiresses of lands, both in the town of St. Edmund and without, according to his good pleasure ? Do you not see how the Abbot appropriates to himself suits and pleas of persons who claim by the King's writ lands which are of the Convent's fee, and above all those suits which are productive of profit, whereas he assigns those which bring in no such profit to the Cellarer, the Sacrist or other officials ? ' To this I replied according to my knowledge, perhaps well, perhaps ill, that every lord of a fief owing homage ought of right to have an escheat, when it occurs in a

feudi, cui sit homagium, debet de iure habere eschaetam,
cum euenerit in feudo, unde ipse accepit homagium ; et
consimili racione, generale auxilium burgensium et wardas
puerorum et donaciones uiduarum et puellarum in illis
feudis unde accepit homagium, que omnia soli abbati
conuenire uidentur, nisi forte uacauerit abbatia.   In
uilla tamen Sancti Ædmundi consuetudo extitit ratione
burgi, ut proximus consanguineus habeat wardam pueri
cum hereditate, usque ad annos discrecionis.   Item de
loquelis et placitis respondi, me nunquam uidisse abbatem
sibi usurpasse placita nostra, nisi pro defectu iustitie
nostre ; set tamen pecuniam aliquando accepisse ut, sua
auctoritate interueniente, loquele et placita debitum
sortirentur finem.   Uidi etiam aliquando placita, que ad
nos spectant, tractari in curia abbatis ; quia non erat
aliquis, qui in principio litis ex parte conuentus forum
allegaret.

Anno gracie Mº.C. nonagesimo viiiº. uoluit gloriosus
martir Ædmundus terrere conuentum nostrum et docere,
ut corpus eius reuerentius et diligentius custodiretur.
Erat quidam ligneus tabulatus inter feretrum et magnum
altare, super quem duo cerei, quos solebant custodes
feretri reclutare et cereum cereo superponere et indecenter conjungere.   Erant sub tabulato illo multa reposita indecenter, linum et filum et cera et utensilia uaria,
immo quicquid ueniebat in manus custodum, ibi re-
ponebatur hostio et parietibus ferreis existentibus. Cum
ergo dormirent custodes nocte sancte Aleldrethe,[1] cecidit,
F.152 ut credimus, pars cerei reclutati / iam conbusti super

---

[1] June 23, 1198

fief from which he himself has received homage ; and likewise he is entitled to a general aid from the burgesses and to wardships of boys and bestowal of widows and girls in those fiefs whence he has received homage—all of which privileges seem to belong to the Abbot alone, unless the abbacy should chance to be vacant. But in the town of St. Edmund a custom has arisen in virtue of its being a borough, that the next of kin should have wardship of a boy together with his inheritance until he has reached years of discretion. Again with regard to suits and pleas I answered that I had never seen the Abbot usurp our pleas, save when there was default of justice on our part ; but that I had seen the Abbot take money, that by the intervention of his authority suits and pleas might be settled as they ought to be. I have also at times seen pleas, which were our concern, dealt with in the Abbot's court, because there was not anyone to claim jurisdiction for the Convent at the opening of the suit.

In the year of grace 1198 the glorious Martyr Edmund desired to terrify our Convent and to teach it that his body should be guarded with greater reverence and care. There was a wooden platform between the feretory and the High Altar, on which there were two candles, which the guardians of the shrine used to stick and join together in a most unseemly manner by placing one candle on the top of another. And under this platform many things were stored without regard to seemliness, such as flax, thread, wax, and divers utensils ; in fact, anything that came into the hands of the guardians was placed there, since the platform had a door and iron walls. So, while the guardians were asleep on the night of the Feast of St. Ethelreda, part of a candle (as is believed) which had been stuck together and had

predictum tabulatum pannis opertum, et cepit omnia
proxima que supra et subtus erant accendere, ita quod
parietes ferrei omnino igne candescerent. Et ecce furor
Domini,[1] set non sine misericordia, juxta illud, ' cum
iratus fueris, misericordie recordaberis.' [2] Eadem enim
hora cecidit horologium ante horas matutinas, sur-
gensque magister [3] uestiarii, hec percipiens et intuens,
cucurrit quamtocius et, percussa tabula tanquam pro
mortuo, sublimi uoce clamauit dicens feretrum esse
conbustum. Nos autem omnes accurrentes flammam
inuenimus incredibiliter seuientem, et totum feretrum
amplectentem, et non longe a trabibus ecclesie ascen-
dentem. Iuuenes ergo nostri propter aquam currentes,
quidam ad puteum, quidam ad horologium,[4] quidam
cucullis suis impetum ignis cum magna difficultate ex-
tinxerunt, et sanctuaria [5] quedam prius diripuerunt.
Cumque frigida aqua super frontem feretri [6] fun-
deretur, ceciderunt lapides et quasi in puluerem redacti
sunt. Claui autem, quibus lamine argentee configge-
bantur feretro, exiliebant a ligno subtus conbusto ad
spissitudinem digiti mei, et pendebant lamine sine clauis
una ex altera. Aurea quidem maiestas in fronte feretri
cum quibusdam lapidibus remansit firma et intacta, et
pulcrior post ignem quam ante, quia tota aurea fuit.

---

[1] Num. xi. 33
[2] Hab. iii. 2
[3] A subordinate of the Sacrist
[4] Clearly a water-clock with a large tank. As it could strike, it must
have been a mechanical water-clock ;   cp. the elaborate clock described
in Du Cange, s.v. *horologium* ; at the end of the description there is a reference to the clocks described by Vitruvius. The clock of Ctesibius described
by Vitruvius is simple to construct—a working model can be easily con-
structed at the cost of a few pence. In the more elaborate of these clocks
gearing was used, and they could easily be made to actuate a striking
mechanism.
[5] The word has a large range. It might mean ' reliquaries,' but as it
seems to be distinguished from *philateria cum reliquiis*, it probably means
pyxes containing the Holy Sacrament, which were often suspended from
beams.

burned down, fell on the aforesaid platform which was covered with cloth, and began to set fire to everything near it both above and below, so that the iron walls were white hot with the heat. ' And behold the anger of the Lord was kindled,' yet not without mercy, as it is written, ' In wrath thou wilt remember mercy.' For in the same hour the clock struck before Matins, and the master of the vestry, when he arose, perceived and saw the fire, and running with all speed beat upon the board as though to announce a death, and cried with a loud voice that the feretory was burned. And we all of us ran together, and found the flames raging beyond belief and embracing the whole feretory and reaching up nearly to the beams of the Church. So the young men among us ran to get water, some to the well, and others to the clock, while yet others with the utmost difficulty succeeded in extinguishing the fire with their cowls and carried off certain small pyxes, before harm could happen to them. And when cold water was poured upon the front of the feretory, the stones fell and were reduced almost to powder. But the nails, by which the plates of silver were fastened to the feretory fell from the wood, which was burnt beneath them to the thickness of my finger, and the plates hung one from another without any nails to support them. But the golden Majesty on the front of the feretory, together with certain stones, remained firm and intact, and seemed fairer after the fire than it was before, because it was all of gold.

---

6 The *feretrum* (lit. ' bier ') is technically called a ' feretory.' Strictly speaking it should be a box, which could be lifted from its base and carried about. But it is clear from the description which follows that it was casing without a bottom, since the coffin rested upon the stone base of the shrine. See p. 112. Both the Bodleian MSS which contain this story read *ceciderunt praeciosi lapides*.

Contigit etiam, uolente Altissimo, tunc temporis
magnam trabem,[1] que solebat esse ultra altare, sublatam
esse, ut noua sculptura repararetur. Contigit et crucem
et Mariolam et Iohannem,[2] et loculum cum camisia [3]
sancti Ædmundi, et philateria cum reliquiis, que ab
eadem trabe pendere solebant, et alia sanctuaria que
super trabem steterant, omnia prius sublata esse ;
alioquin omnia conbusta essent, ut credimus, sicut pannus
depictus conbustus fuit, qui in loco trabis pendebat.
Set quid fieret si cortinata esset ecclesia ? Cum ergo
securi essemus quod ignis in nullo loco perforasset feretrum, rimas et foramina, si qua essent, attentissime
investigantes, et omnia frigida esse percipientes, miti-
F.152v gatus est in parte dolor noster : et ecce clama/uerunt
quidam ex fratribus nostris cum magno eiulatu ciphum
sancti Ædmundi esse combustum. Cumque plures hinc
et inde quererent lapides et laminas inter carbones et
cineres, extraxerunt ciphum omnino inuiolatum, iacente[4]
in medio magnorum carbonum, qui iam extincti erant,
et inuenerunt eundem inuolutum panno lineo, set
semiusto. Pixis uero quercina, in qua ciphus de more
ponebatur, conbusta erat in puluerem, et sole ligature
ferree et sera ferrea inuenta sunt. Uiso itaque miraculo,
omnes lacrimati sumus pre gaudio. Maiorem ergo
partem frontis feretri excrustatam uidentes et turpitudinem combustionis abhorrentes, de communi consilio,
acersito clam aurifabro, laminas coniungi fecimus et

---

[1] A cross-beam above and behind the High Altar
[2] Presumably placed on either side of the cross
[3] The garments of the saint had been removed by Abbot Leofstan,
and the shirt was preserved in a case.
[4] Both Oxford excerpts correctly written *iacentem*, but the Harley and
Cotton MSS agree in *iacente*.

It happened also, by the will of the most High, that
at that time the great beam, that used to be behind the
High Altar, had been removed, that it might be adorned
with new carving. It happened also that the cross and
the little statue of the Virgin and the statue of St. John,
and the case containing the shirt of St. Edmund and the
other reliquaries which used to hang from the said beam,
together with other small pyxes which had stood upon
the beam, had all been previously removed ; otherwise
it is thought that they would all have been burned, as
was the painted cloth which hung in place of the beam.
But what would have happened, if the church had been
hung with curtains ? When therefore we were sure that
the fire had nowhere found its way into the feretory, and
after a careful examination of such cracks and holes as
were visible we perceived that everything was cold, our
grief was somewhat allayed : when lo and behold !
some of our brethren cried out in loud lamentation that
the cup of St. Edmund was burned. But when a number
of them were searching for stones and silver plates among
the embers and ashes, they pulled out the cup, which was
lying quite unscathed in the midst of great embers that
were by now extinguished ; and they found it wrapped
in a linen cloth, which was half-burned. But the oaken
casket in which the cup used to be kept, was burned to
dust, and only the iron bands and lock were to be found.
And seeing the miracle, we all of us wept for joy. So,
seeing that the greater part of the front was stripped of
its plating, and dismayed at the hideous appearance
presented by the burning, we took counsel together, and
secretly sent for the goldsmith, and to avoid scandal had
the plates joined together and placed upon the feretory
without delay, while we had the traces of the burning

feretro apponi, sine omni dilacione, propter scandalum;
uestigia quoque conbustionis uel cera uel alio modo cooperiri fecimus. Set teste ewangelista, ' Nichil opertum
quod non reuelabitur.' ¹ Uenientes summo mane pere-
grini oblaturi nichil tale quid perceperunt : quidam
tamen circumcirca intuentes querebant, ubi fuit ignis
quem circa feretrum fuisse iam audierant. Cumque ergo
omnino celari non potuit, responsum est querentibus,
candelam cecidisse et manutergia tria conbusta esse, et
ad ignis calorem lapides quosdam in fronte feretri
deperisse. Fingebat tamen fama mendax caput sancti
esse conbustum : quidam dicebant capillos tantum esse
conbustos ; set cognita postmodum ueritate, obstructum
est os loquentium iniqua.² Hec omnia facta sunt, proui-
dente Domino, ut loca circa feretrum sancti sui honestius
custodirentur, et ut propositum domini abbatis ³ cicius
et sine dilacione debitum finem sortiretur ; scilicet, ut
ipsum feretrum cum corpore sancti martiris securius et
gloriosius in loco eminentiore poneretur ; quia antequam
hoc predictum infortunium accidit, iam crista feretri
usque ad medietatem facta fuit, et lapides marmorei ad
eleuandum et sustinendum feretrum ex parte magna
parati et politi fuerant.

Ualde dolebat dominus abbas qui absens erat, auditis
hiis rumoribus ; qui domum rediens et in capitulum
F.153 ueniens, hec et consimilia / et etiam maiora pericula dixit
posse euenire propter peccata nostra, et maxime propter
murmuraciones ⁴ nostras de cibo et potu ; culpam
quodammmodo in uniuersitatem conuentus retorquens,
pocius quam in auariciam et negligenciam custodum

¹ Luke xii. 2
² Ps. lxii. 12 (Vulg.) ; lxiii. 11 (AV)
³ See p. 97
⁴ See p. 88

covered by wax or in other ways. But, as the Evangelist bears witness, ' Nothing is hidden that shall not be revealed.' For pilgrims coming early in the morning to make their oblations, although they saw no damage, yet some of them, looking round about them, asked where the fire was, which they heard had broken out in the neighbourhood of the feretory. So, since it was impossible altogether to conceal the truth, they were told in answer to their inquiries, that a candle had fallen and that three towels had been burned, and that the heat of the fire had caused damage to some of the stones on the front of the feretory. None the less lying rumour alleged that the head of the saint had been burned, while some said that only his hair had been burned ; but when later the truth was known, ' the mouth of them that speak lies was stopped.' All these things were done that by God's providence the places round the saint's feretory might be more honourably guarded, and that the desire of the Lord Abbot might the sooner find its fulfilment without further delay : to wit, that the feretory itself with the body of the holy Martyr might be placed with more security and to his greater glory upon a loftier base. For before this mis- fortune occurred, the crest of the feretory had been half completed, and the marble stones for raising and support- ing the feretory had for the most part been prepared and polished.

The Abbot, who was absent at the time, was much grieved when he heard these rumours, and when he returned home and came into Chapter, he said that like and even greater dangers might arise on account of our sins, above all because of our murmurs concerning our food and drink, thus turning the blame against the whole Convent rather than against the avarice and negligence

feretri. Ut ergo nos prudenter induceret ad hoc, ut
abstinenciam faceremus de pitantiis nostris saltem uno
anno, et ad frontem feretri reparandam de puro auro
redditus de pitanceria apponeremus, ipse primus dedit
exemplum largitatis, et totum tesaurum suum quem habebat de auro, scilicet xv. anulos aureos, ualentes, ut creditur, sexaginta marcas, coram nobis ad reparacionem
feretri dedit. Nos autem pitanceriam nostram esse dan-
dam ad tale opus omnes concessimus ; set mutatum est
consilium per sacristam dicentem, sanctum Ædmundum
bene posse reparare feretrum suum sine tali auxilio.

Tunc temporis uenit aliquis magni nominis, nescio
quis, qui uisionem suam narrauit abbati, unde ipse
multum mouebatur, et eam in pleno capitulo asperima
narrauit prolacione ; et exposuit hoc modo : 'Uerum
est,' inquid, 'quod quidam uir magnus per uisionem
uidit, scilicet quod sanctus martir Ædmundus uidebatur
extra feretrum suum iacere, et gemendo dicere se pannis
suis expoliatum et macilentum esse fame et siti, et
suum cimiterium et atria [1] ecclesie sue negigenter
custodiri.' Et hoc somnium exposuit abbas coram omnibus, retorquens culpam in nos hoc modo : 'Sanctus
Ædmundus nudum se asserit, quia pannos uestros ueteres
subtraitis nudis pauperibus, et inuiti datis quod dare
debetis, et de cibo et de potu similiter ; desidia, etiam
negligencia sacriste et sociorum eius, patens ex recenti
infortunio combustionis que fuit inter feretrum et altare.'
Hiis dictis contristabatur conuentus, et post capitulum
conueniebant plures fratres in unum et interpretabantur
somnium hoc modo : 'Nos,' inquiunt, 'sumus nuda

---

[1] The word is used in Med. Lat. in the sense of 'cemetery' and 'porch.'
It might mean 'porches' here, but it may equally well be used more
generally to include church and cloisters.

of the guardians of the feretory. And so, that he might discreetly induce us to forego our pittances for at least one year and contribute the revenues of the pittancery for the restoration of the front of the feretory in pure gold, he himself first set us an example of generosity and, in our presence, gave all the treasure that he had in gold, to wit, fifteen gold rings, worth, it is believed, some sixty marks, to be employed for the restoration of the feretory. We all agreed that our pittancery should be assigned for this purpose ; but this design was abandoned, since the Sacrist said that St. Edmund could easily restore his own feretory without any such assistance.

At that time a person of some repute came to the Abbey—I do not know his name—who told the Abbot of a vision that had appeared to him ; whereat the Abbot was much moved and told the story in full Chapter, with some sharp comments. ' The thing,' he said, ' which a certain great man saw in vision is true ; for the holy Martyr St. Edmund seemed to him to be lying outside the feretory and to say with groaning that he had been stripped of his clothing and was lean with hunger and thirst, and that his cemetery and the porches of his church were negligently guarded.' This vision the Abbot expounded before us all, turning the blame on us, after this fashion : ' St. Edmund declares that he is naked, because you withhold your old garments from the naked poor and give them, what you must give, most unwillingly ; so too is it in respect of your food and drink. And the sloth, or rather the negligence, of the Sacrist and his associates is revealed by our late misfortune, the fire which broke out between the feretory and the altar.' The convent was grieved by these words, and after Chapter a number of the brethren gathered together and interpreted the dream after this wise :

menbra sancti Ædmundi, et conuentus est nudum corpus
eius, quia nos spoliati sumus antiquis consuetudinibus et
libertatibus nostris.   Abbas omnia habet, cameriam,[1]
sacristiam, cellariam ; et nos perimus fame et siti, qui
F.153v uictum nostrum non habemus, nisi per / clericum abbatis
et per eius administracionem. Si custodes feretri negg-
ligentes sint, abbas sibi imputet, quia tales ipse constituit.' Hoc modo multi loquebantur in conuentu.
Cum autem hec interpretacio ostensa esset abbati in
foresta de Herlaua, in redeundo de Lundoniis, ualde
iratus est et comotus, et respondens ait : ' Uolunt ipsi
retorquere somnium illud in me ?   Per os Dei ! quam
cito domum rediero, reddam eis consuetudines quas suas
dicunt, et remouebo clericum meum a celerario, et eos
eis relinquam ; et uidebo sapientiam eorum in fine anni.
Hoc anno residebam domi, et feci cellariam eorum
seruari sine debito ; et tales michi reddunt graciarum
actiones ! '   Rediens ergo domum abbas, habens in
proposito transferre sanctum martirem, humiliauit se
coram Deo et hominibus, cogitans ut se in omnibus
emendaret, et pacem cum omnibus et maxime cum
conuentu suo reformaret.   Sedens ergo in capitulo,
celerarium et subcelerarium per communem assensum
nostrum eligi precepit, et clericum suum remouit, dicens
quod quicquid fecerat, propter commodum nostrum id
fecerat, teste Deo et sanctis eius, et se multis modis
excusauit.

Audite, celi,[2] que loquar, audiat terra factum Samsonis abbatis.   Igitur, apropinquante festo [3] sancti
Ædmundi, politi sunt lapides marmorei, et parata sunt

---

[1] There is no reference elsewhere to any appropriation of the chamberlain's department by the Abbot.
[2] Isa. i. 2, and xxxiv. 1
[3] November 20, 1198, a Friday (cp. *sexta feria*)

' We,' they said, ' we are the naked limbs of St. Edmund, and the Convent is his naked body, because we are despoiled of our ancient customs and liberties. The Abbot holds everything—the chamberlainship, the sacristy, the cellary ; and we are perishing of hunger and thirst, and have not the maintenance that is our due, save at the hands of the Abbot's clerk and by his administration. If the guardians of the feretory are negligent, let the Abbot take the blame for it, since it was he that appointed such persons.' Thus many spoke in the Convent. But when this interpretation was told the Abbot in the forest of Harlow, as he was returning from London, he was very angry and much troubled, and replied, ' Do they wish to turn the dream against me ? By God's face, as soon as I come home, I will restore to them those customs which they claim to be their own, and will remove my clerk from the cellary, and leave them to themselves ; and I will see what their wisdom comes to at the end of the year. This year I stayed at home, and kept their cellary free of debt ; and is this the thanks they show me in return ? ' So on his return the Abbot, desiring to translate the holy Martyr, humbled himself before God and man, resolving to amend himself and to make peace with all men and above all with his own Convent. So taking his seat in Chapter he ordered that our Cellarer and sub-cellarer should be elected by our common consent and removed his own clerk, saying that whatever he had done, was done for our good, and he called God and His Saints to bear witness thereto, and excused himself in many ways.

' Hear, O heavens, and give ear, O earth ' to the deed that was done by Abbot Samson ! When the feast of St. Edmund was drawing nigh, the marble stones were

omnia ad eleuacionem feretri. Celebrato igitur die festi sexta feria, sequente die dominica indictum est triduanum ieiunium populo, et ostensa est eis publice causa ieiunii. Abbas autem predixit conuentui, ut se prepararent ad transferendum corpus [1] nocte proxima post feriam secundam, et ad transferendum feretrum et consistendum super magnum altare, donec machina cementaria perficeretur ; et tempus et modum prefixit ad tale opus. Cum ergo uenissemus illa nocte ad horas matutinas,[2] stetit magnum feretrum super altare, uacuum, intus ornatum coriis albis ceruinis sursum et deorsum et circumcirca, que affigebantur ligno clauis argenteis, et panellus unus stetit deorsum iuxta columnam ecclesie, et sanctum corpus adhuc iacebat, ubi iacere solebat.

F.154 Percan/tatis laudibus, omnes accessimus ad disciplinas suscipiendas. Quo facto, uestiti sunt in albis dominus abbas et quidam cum eo, et accedentes reuerenter, sicut decebat, festinabant detegere loculum. Erat autem pannus lineus exterius, qui loculum et omnia cetera includebat, qui quibusdam ligamentis suis desuper ligatus inuentus fuit ; postea quidam pannus sericus, et postea alter lineus pannus, et postea tertius, et ita tandem discoopertus est loculus stans super ligneum alueolum, ne ipse loculus possit ledi a lapide marmareo. Iacuit super pectus martiris affixus loculo exterius angelus aureus ad longitudinem pedis humani, habens ensem aureum in una manu, et uexillum in altera ; et subtus erat foramen in operculo, ubi antiqui custodes martiris solebant manus inponere ad tangendum sanctum corpus. Et erat uersus superscriptus imagini :

---

[1] The words *corpus . . . transferendum* are omitted by mistake in our MS, but preserved in MSS Bodley 297 and 240.
[2] About 6 a.m. in winter

polished, and all was ready for the raising of the feretory. So after the celebration of the feast, which fell upon the sixth day of the week, upon the Sunday following a three days' fast was proclaimed to all the people, and the cause thereof was publicly declared. And the Abbot told the Convent betimes to make themselves ready to transfer the body in the night following the second day of the week, and to transfer the feretory and place it on the High Altar, until the masons' work was done ; and he appointed the time for so doing, and the manner of its accomplishment. When therefore we came that night to Matins, we found the feretory on the altar ; it was empty, and adorned within with white deer skins above and below and round about, all fixed to the wood with silver nails, and one panel stood below against a pillar of the church, while the sacred body still lay where it was wont to lie. And when we had sung Lauds, we all went to receive discipline. This done the Abbot and some others with him were robed in albs and, approaching the coffin with all due reverence, they made haste to uncover it. Now there was a linen cloth without, which enclosed the coffin and all else that was within, and was tied by cords which were fastened above it : after that there was a silken cloth, and after that another of linen and then yet a third ; and thus at last the coffin was revealed standing in a wooden trough, that the coffin itself might not suffer damage from the stone. Over the Martyr's breast, fixed to the outside of the coffin, was an angel of gold, about the length of a man's foot, having a sword of gold in one hand and a banner in the other ; and beneath it there was a hole in the coffin-lid through which the guardians of the feretory used of old to thrust their hands that they might touch the holy body. And above the angel was written this verse :

Martiris ecce zoma [1] seruat Michaelis agalma.

Erantque anuli ferrei ad duo capita loculi, sicut solebat
fieri in cista Norensi.[2] Subleuantes ergo loculum cum
corpore, portabant usque ad altare, et apposui manum
meam peccatricem in auxilium ad portandum, licet
abbas precepisset, ne aliquis accederet nisi uocatus ;
et inclusus est loculus in feretro, panello apposito et
coniuncto. Putabamus omnes, quod abbas uellet loculum ostendere populo in octauis festi et reportare sanctum corpus coram omnibus ; set male seducti sumus,
sicut sequentia docebunt. Feria quarta,[3] canente conuentu conpletorium, locutus est abbas cum sacrista et
Waltero medico, et initum est consilium, ut duodecim
fratres uocarentur, qui fortes essent ad portandos panellos
feretri, et prudentes essent ad coniungendos eos et dis-
iungendos. Dixitque abbas se habere in uotis uidere
patronum suum, et se uelle sibi associari sacristam et
Walterum medicum ad inspectionem ; et nominati sunt
duo capellani abbatis, et duo custodes feretri, et duo
magistri de uestiario ; et alii sex, sacrista Hugo, Walterus
medicus, Augustinus, Willelmus de Dice, Robertus,
F.154v Ricardus. Dormiente ergo conuentu, uestiti/sunt illi
duodecim albis, et extrahentes loculum de feretro por-
tauerunt illum, et ponentes super tabulam iuxta antiquum locum feretri, parauerunt se ad disiungendum
operculum, quod coniunctum et confixum erat loculo
sexdecim clauis ferreis longissimis. Quod cum difficul-

---

[1] A corruption of the Greek σῶμα. (Both Bodleian MSS read
Michaelis seruat.)
[2] Possibly presented by the Archbishop of Trondjem, when he was
the Abbey's guest ; see p. 15. (The two Bodleian MSS read *solet* for
solebat, with *ad portandum* after *loculi*.)
[3] The Wednesday following 25th November

Lo ! Michael's image guards the holy corse.

And at the ends of the coffin were iron rings, after the fashion of a Norse chest. Then lifting the coffin with the body, they bore it as far as the altar, and I placed my sinful hand upon it to aid them, though the Abbot had commanded that no-one should approach it un-called ; and the coffin was enclosed in the feretory, the panel being set in its place and refixed. We all thought that it was the Abbot's purpose to display the coffin to the people during the octave of the feast, and to carry back the holy body in the presence of them all ; but we were sorely deceived, as the sequel will declare. On the fourth day of the week, while the Convent was singing Compline, the Abbot spoke with the Sacrist and Walter the physician, and it was resolved that twelve brothers should be called, who were strong enough to carry the panels of the feretory, and skilled to fit them together and to take them apart. And the Abbot said that it was his great desire to behold his patron and that he wished that the Sacrist and Walter the physician should go with him to look upon the body ; and there were nominated two chaplains of the Abbot and two guardians of the feretory and two masters of the vestry, and another six : Hugh the Sacrist, Walter the physician, Augustine, William of Diss, Robert and Richard. So, while the Convent slept, these twelve put on albs and, drawing forth the coffin from the feretory, they carried it and, setting it on a table near the ancient place of the feretory, they made ready to remove the lid, which was attached and fastened to the coffin by sixteen very long iron nails. And when they had done this with difficulty, they were all bidden to retire to a distance saving the Abbot's two associates whom I named above. And the coffin was so

tate fecissent, iussi sunt omnes longius abire, preter duos
socios prenominatos. Eratque loculus ita repletus sancto
corpore, et in longitudine et in latitudine, quod uix
posset acus interponi inter caput et lignum, uel inter
pedes et lignum : et iacebat caput unitum corpori,[1]
aliquantum leuatum paruo ceruicali. Abbas ergo intuens cominus, inuenit prius pannum sericum uelantem
totum corpus, et postea pannum lineum miri candoris ;
et super caput pannum paruum lineum, et postea alium
paruum pannum sericum et subtilem, tanquam hoc esset
uelum alicuius sanctimonialis femine. Et postea inuenerunt corpus inuolutum lineo panno ; et tunc demum
patuerunt omnia lineamenta sancti corporis. Hic res-
titit abbas, dicens se non esse ausum ultra procedere, ut
sanctam carnem nudam uideret. Accipiens ergo caput
inter manus suas, gemendo ait : ' Gloriose martir, sancte
Ædmunde, benedicta sit illa hora qua natus fuisti.
Gloriose martir, ne uertas michi in perdicionem auda-
ciam meam, quod te tango, peccator et miser ; tu scis
deuocionem et intencionem meam.' Et procedens
tetigit oculos et nasum ualde grossum et ualde eminentem, et postea tetigit pectus et brachia, et subleuans
manum sinistram digitos tetigit et digitos suos posuit
inter digitos sanctos. Et procedens inuenit pedes rigide
erectos tanquam hominis hodie mortui, et digitos pedum
tetigit, et tangendo numerauit. Datumque est consilium,
ut ceteri fratres uocarentur et miracula uiderent, et
uenerunt sex uocati et sex alii fratres cum illis qui se
intruserunt sine assensu abbatis, et uidebant sanctum
corpus ; scilicet, Walterus de Sancto Albano, et Hugo
infirmarius, et Gilbertus frater prioris, et Ricardus de
Hehingham, et Iocellus celerarius, et Turstanus Paruus,

---

[1] See Introduction p. xviii

filled with the holy body, both lengthwise and across, that a needle could scarce be placed between the Saint's head or feet and the wood ; and the head lay united to the body, and raised a little on a small pillow.   The Abbot, therefore, standing close by, looked within and found first a silken cloth veiling the whole body, and after that a linen cloth of wondrous whiteness : and over the head was a small linen cloth and beneath it a small cloth of silk, finely woven, like a nun's veil. And afterwards they found the body wrapped in a linen cloth, and then at last the lineaments of the holy body were revealed.   Here the Abbot stopped, saying that he did not dare go further, to see the sacred flesh unclothed. Therefore taking the head between his hands, he said groaning, ' Glorious Martyr, Saint Edmund, blessed be the hour when thou was born !   Glorious Martyr, turn not to my perdition this my boldness, that I, a miserable sinner, now touch thee ;   thou knowest my devotion, thou knowest my intent.'   And he proceeded to touch the eyes and the nose, which was very large and prominent, and afterwards he touched the breast and arms and, raising the left hand, he touched the fingers and placed his fingers between the fingers of the saint ;   and going further he found the feet turned stiffly upwards as of a man dead that self-same day, and he touched the toes of the feet and counted them as he touched them. And this counsel was given that the other brethren should come and see these marvels ;   and there came six who were called and six others who thrust themselves in without the Abbot's leave, and they saw the holy body—to wit, Walter of St. Albans, Hugh the Infirmarer, Gilbert the Prior's brother, Richard of Hingham, Jocellus the Cellarer, and Turstan the little, who alone put forth his hand and touched the feet and knees of the Saint.

qui solus manum apposuit et pedes sancti tetigit et
F.155 genua./Et, ut esset copia testium, disponente Altissimo,
unus ex nostris fratribus Iohannes de Dice sedens supra
testitudinem[1] ecclesie, cum seruientibus de uestiario,
omnia ista euidenter uidebat.   His factis, affigebatur
operculum loculo eisdem clauis et totidem, et simili modo,
ut prius, cooperto martire eisdem pannis et eodem ordine,
sicut prius inuentus fuit.   Et postea collocatus est loculus
in solito loco, et positus est super loculum, iuxta angelum,
furulus quidam sericus, in quo reposita fuit scedula
Anglice scripta, continens quasdam salutaciones Ailwini
monachi,[2] ut creditur, que scedula prius fuit inuenta
iuxta angelum aureum quando loculus detegebatur.
Et iubente abbate, statim scriptum fuit et aliud breue,
et in eodem furulo reconditum, sub hac forma uerborum : 'Anno ab incarnatione domini M°.C. nonagesimo octauo, abbas Samson, tractus deuotione, corpus
sancti Ædmundi uidit et tetigit, nocte proxima post
festum sancte Katerine,[3] his testibus—' et subscripta
sunt nomina decem et octo monachorum.   Inuoluerunt
autem fratres totum loculum panno lineo satis apto, et
posuerunt desuper pannum sericum preciosum et nouum,
quem Hubertus archiepiscopus Cantuariensis eodem
anno optulerat, et quendam pannum lineum dupplica-
tum ad longitudinem loculi posuerunt proximum lapidi,
ne loculus uel alueolus eius posset ledi a lapide.   Et
postea portati sunt panelli et decenter coniuncti in feretro.
Cum autem ueniret conuentus ad matutinas cantandas,
et ista perciperet, doluerunt omnes qui hec non uiderant,
intra se dicentes quod 'male seducti sumus.'   Cantatis

---

[1] The word bears its normal architectural meaning : an open roof of
wood ; cp. p. 107, where the flames are said to have almost reached the
beams of the roof.   (All our three MSS give this spelling for *testudinem*.)

[2] See Introduction, p. xvi

[3] 25th November

And that there might be abundance of witness, by the disposition of the Most High, one of our brethren, John of Diss, sitting above in the roof of the church with the servants of the vestry, saw all these things clearly.   This done the lid was fastened to the coffin with the self-same sixteen nails, in the same manner as it had been before, after the Martyr had been wrapped in the same clothes and in the same order, as when he had been first found. Then the coffin was set in its accustomed place and on it, near the angel there was laid a small silken bag in which there was put a little sheet of parchment with words thereon written in the English tongue, containing, as is believed, the salutations of Ailwin the monk, the said sheet having been found near the golden angel when the coffin was being uncovered.   And at the Abbot's bidding, another writing was made and put away in the same bag ; and it ran as follows : ' In the eleven hundred and ninety-eighth year after the Incarnation of our Lord, Abbot Samson, drawn thereto by devotion, saw and touched the body of St. Edmund, on the night before the feast of St. Katharine, with these for witnesses,'— and thereafter were written the names of eighteen monks. The brethren then wrapped the whole coffin in a linen cloth very meet for the purpose, and above it they placed a silken cloth, costly and new, which Archbishop Hubert had offered that same year, and they placed a linen cloth, doubled to match the coffin's length, next to the stone that neither the coffin nor the trough might be injured by the stone.   And then the panels were brought and fitted together on the feretory in seemly fashion. But when the Convent came to sing Matins and saw it, all those who had not seen these things were grieved, saying among themselves, ' We have all been sorely deceived.'   But when Matins had been sung, the Abbot

autem horis matutinis, conuocauit abbas conuentum ante
magnum altare, et ostendens eis breuiter rem gestam,
allegabat quod non debuit nec potuit omnes uocare ad
talia. Quibus auditis, cum lacrimis ' Te Deum laudamus'
cantauimus, et ad campanas in choro resonandas prope-
rauimus.

Quarto die sequente, custodes feretri et custodem
sancti Botulfi [1] deposuit abbas, nouos substituens et leges
eis proponens, ut sanctuaria honestius et diligentius/
F.155v custodirent. Magnumque altare, quod prius concauum
erat, ubi sepius quedam indecenter reponebantur, et
spacium illud quod erat inter feretrum et altare, solidari
fecit lapide et cemento, ne aliquod ignis periculum fieri
possit per neggligenciam custodum, sicut prius, iuxta
dictum sapientis dicentis :

Felix, quem faciunt aliena pericula cautum.[2]

Cum abbas emisset fauorem et graciam regis Ricardi
donis et denariis, ita quod omnia negocia sua crederet
posse perficere pro suo desiderio, mortuus est rex R.,
et abbas perdidit opera et impensam. Rex autem
Iohannes post coronacionem suam, omissis omnibus
aliis negociis suis, statim uenit ad sanctum Ædmundum
uoto et deuocione tractus. Nos uero credebamus quod
oblaturus esset aliquid magnum ; pannum quidem
sericum unum optulit, quem seruientes eius a nostro
sacrista mutuo acceperant, nec adhuc precium reddi-
derunt. Hospicium uero sancti Ædmundi suscepit,
magnis celebratum expensis, et recedens nichil omnino

---

[1] When Abbot Baldwin built his church, not only the body of St.
Edmund but those of St. Botolph and St. Jurnin were translated thither
and placed near the shrine of the patron saint ; see *mem.* I. Appendix,
p. 352.
[2] This quotation occurs not infrequently in medieval writers. Its
source is unknown. Its nearest parallel is Tibullus, III. vi. 43, *felix quicunque
dolore alterius disces posse cauere tuo.*

called the Convent together before the High Altar, and briefly set forth what had been done, saying that it was neither right nor possible to summon all to see such things. And when we heard this, we sang the ' Te Deum ' weeping and hastened to ring the bells in the choir.

On the fourth day after this the Abbot deposed the guardians of the feretory and the guardian of St. Botolph, appointing new guardians in their stead and making rules for them, that they might guard the shrines more honourably and with greater diligence. And he caused the High Altar, which had formerly been hollow and wherein certain things had been stored in unseemly fashion, and also the space between the feretory and the altar, to be filled in with stone and mortar, that there might be no more danger of fire owing to the negligence of the custodians, as there had been before ; for a wise man says,

Blest he whom others' perils do forewarn.

When the Abbot had purchased the favour and grace of King Richard by gifts and money, so that he thought he could carry out all his affairs in accordance with his desire, King Richard died, and the Abbot lost his money and his labour. But King John after his coronation, postponing all other business, came straightway to St. Edmund, led thither by devotion and a vow that he had made. We indeed believed that he would make some great oblation ; but he offered nothing save a single silken cloth which his servants had borrowed from our Sacrist—and they have not yet paid the price. And yet he received the hospitality of St. Edmund at great cost to the Abbey, and when he departed he gave nothing

honoris uel beneficii sancto contulit, preter xiii. ster-
lingos, quos ad missam suam optulit, die qua recessit a
nobis.

Eo tempore conquesti sunt quidam obedientiarii
nostri, dicentes in capitulo, Radulfum ianitorem, seruien-
tem nostrum, stare in causis et querelis contra eos in
damnum ecclesie et in preiudicium conuentus. Pre-
ceptumque fuit a priore de communi assensu, ut casti-
garetur secundum consuetudinem nostram, qua solent
castigari seruientes nostri, scilicet per subtractionem sti-
pendiorum suorum. Preceptum est ergo, ut celerarius
substraheret ei non conredium [1] quod de iure pertinebat
ad officium suum, secundum attestationem carte sue,
set quasdam adiectiones et gratias quas celerarii et
subcelerarii ei fecerant, inconsulto conuentu. R. uero
predictus, assumtis secum quibusdam de mensa abbatis,
conquestus est abbati redeunti de Lundoniis, quod prior
et conuentus dissaisiauerant eum de conredio suo, quo
saisiatus fuit quando abbas uenit primo ad abbatiam.
Dixerunt etiam abbati, quod hoc factum fuit sine eo et
ad dedecus suum et irrationabiliter, eo inconsulto et
causa incognita. Abbas uero credidit, et aliter quam
decebat uel solebat motus est, Radulfum constanter
F.156 excusans et innocentem / esse protestans, ueniensque in
capitulum, et inde conquerens, dixit tale quid factum
esse in preiudicio, eo inconsulto. Responsumque est ab
uno, ceteris omnibus conclamantibus, hoc esse factum
per priorem et assensum tocius capituli. Abbas uero
inde confusus, et dicens, ' filios enutriui et exaltaui, ipsi
uero spreuerunt me,' [2] nichil dissimulans, sicut deceret

---

[1] ' Grant of maintenance.' The word ' corody ' still survives in connection with certain ancient charities.
[2] Isa. i. 2

at all to the honour or advantage of the Saint save twelve
pence sterling, which he offered at his mass on the day
when he left us.

At that time some of our obedientiaries complained
in the Chapter, that Ralph the gatekeeper, our servant,
was appearing in causes and suits against them to the
loss of the Church and to the prejudice of the Convent :
and with our common consent orders were given by the
Prior that he should receive the customary punishment
inflicted on our servants, namely the withdrawal of his
pay. It was ordered therefore that the Cellarer should
take from him, not the corody which of right belonged
to his office, as was testified in his charter, but certain
additions and grants, which the Cellarer and sub-cellarer
had made to him without consulting the Convent. But
the aforesaid Ralph, taking with him some of those that
sat at the Abbot's table, complained to the Abbot, as
he was on his way home from London, that the Prior
and the Convent had deprived him of his corody, of
which he was seized when the Abbot first entered on
his abbacy. Moreover, they told the Abbot that this was
done without his knowledge, unreasonably and to his
dishonour, since he was not consulted and the case was
decided without inquiry being made. And the Abbot
believed them and was moved thereby more than was
seemly or than was his wont, continually making excuses
for Ralph and protesting his innocence ; and when he
came to the Chapter and complained of it, he said that
this had been done to his prejudice and without consulting him. And one of us made answer, the whole Convent
acclaiming his words, that this was done by the Prior
and with the consent of the whole Chapter. At this the
Abbot was confounded and said, ' I have nourished and
brought up children and they have despised me,' and

propter pacem multitudinis, set pocius potentiam suam
ostendens, nec uinci se sustinens, publice precepit celerario, ut omnia sublata Radulfo plene et integre redderet, nec biberet aliquid nisi aquam, donec omnia
redderet. Iocellus uero celerarius, hoc audiens, elegit
magis illa die bibere aquam, quam reddere conredium
Radulfo contra uoluntatem conuentus ; quod cum abbas
sciuisset, in crastino prohibuit celerario et esum et potum
donec omnia redderet. His dictis, statim recessit abbas
de uilla, et absentauit se octo diebus. Eo die, quo
recesserat abbas, surrexit celerarius in capitulo et preceptum abbatis ostendens, tenensque claves suas in
manu, et dixit se malle deponi de bailia sua, quam
aliquid facere contra conuentum. Factusque est tumultus magnus in conuentu, qualem nunquam prius uidi ;
dixeruntque preceptum abbatis non esse tenendum.
Seniores uero et sapientiores de conuentu, discrete
tacentes, tandem pronuntiauerunt obediendum esse
abbati in omnibus, nisi in manifestis contra Deum, et
assensum prebuerunt, ut hanc turpitudinem ad tempus
sustineremus propter bonum pacis, ne deterius contin-
geret. Cumque prior incepisset cantare ' Uerba mea ' [1]
pro defunctis, sicut consuetudo est, restiterunt nouitii
et cum eis fere media pars conuentus, et sublimi uoce
reclamauerunt et contradixerunt. Et preualuit tamen
senior pars conuentus, licet pauci essent numero in
respectu cetere multitudinis. Abbas uero absens per

[1] The opening words of Ps. v, regularly sung at the close of Chapter,
and here sung by the Prior to closure the debate

instead of shutting his eyes to what had been done, as
would have been seemly for the sake of our peace, he
openly displayed his power and, refusing to own defeat,
ordered the Cellarer in the presence of us all to restore
to Ralph everything that had been taken from him ; and
he forbade him to drink anything save water until all
had been given back. But Jocellus the Cellarer, on
hearing this, chose to drink water for that day sooner
than to restore Ralph his corody against the will of
the Convent. And when the Abbot knew of this, on
the morrow he forbade the Cellarer both meat and
drink, until he should return all. Having said this the
Abbot left the town and absented himself for eight days.
And on the day of the Abbot's departure, the Cellarer
rose in the Chapter and, setting forth the Abbot's commands and holding his keys in his hands, said that he
had rather be deprived of his office than do anything
against the will of the Convent. And there was a great
uproar in the Convent, such as I never beheld before,
and they said that the Abbot's order ought not to be
obeyed. But the older and more prudent members of
the Convent, after keeping a discreet silence, at length
pronounced that the Abbot should be obeyed in all
things, save in such as were manifestly against the will
of God ; and they agreed that we should for the time
being endure this disgrace for the sake of peace, lest
worse should follow. And when the Prior had sung,
' Verba mea ' from the office for the dead, as the custom
is, the novices withstood him, with the support of nearly
half the Convent, protesting loudly and crying out against
him. None the less the older members of the Convent
prevailed, though they were few in number compared
with the rest who were many. But the Abbot from a distance by his messengers terrified some and cajoled others

internuntios quosdam minis terruit, quosdam blandiciis
attraxit, et maiores de conuentu, tanquam timerent
tunice sue, a consilio uniuersitatis separauit, ut adim-
pleretur illud ewangelium, ' omne regnum in se diuisum
desolabitur.'¹ Et dixit abbas, se nequaquam uenturum
inter nos propter conspiraciones et iuramenta que, ut
aiebat, feceramus in eum, cnipulis nostris occidendum./
F.156v Rediens ergo domum sedensque in talamo suo, uni ex
fratribus nostris, qui ei magis suspectus erat, mandauit
ut ad eum ueniret, et quia ad eum uenire noluit, timens
capi et ligari, excommunicatus est, et postea tota die
conpeditus, residens usque mane in domo infirmorum.
Tres uero alios innodauit abbas leuiori sententia, ut
ceteri timerent. In crastino initum est consilium, ut
mandaretur abbas, et humiliaremur coram eo, uerbo et
gestu, quo animus eius mitigari posset ; factumque est
ita. Ipse uero satis humiliter respondens, semper tamen
iustitiam suam allegans, et in nos culpam retorquens,
cum uidit nos uelle uinci, ipse uictus est. Et perfusus
lacrimis iurauit se nunquam doluisse aliqua de causa,
sicut in hoc casu, tum propter se, tum propter nos, et
maxime propter notam infamie, que iam publicauerat
dissencionem nostram, dicendo monachos sancti Ædmundi uelle interficere suum abbatem. Cumque nar-
rasset abbas, qualiter absentasset se ex industria, donec
ira sua deferbuisset, repetens dictum philosophi, ' In te
uindicassem nisi iratus fuissem,' ² lacrimans surrexit, et

---

¹ Matt. xii. 25
² Probably suggested by Cicero, *Tusculan Disputations*, IV. xxxvi, 78.
Archytas of Tarentum is the philosopher to whom the words are there
attributed. See also Seneca *de Ira*, I. 15 ; *Valerius Maximus*, IV. i. ext. 1 ;
and Cicero *de Republica*, I. 38 ; the last of these works was unknown in
the Middle Ages.

detaching the more important members of the Convent
(who seemed to fear for their shirts) from the counsels
of the body as a whole, that the words of the Gospel
might be fulfilled, ' Every kingdom that is divided
against itself shall be brought to desolation.' And the
Abbot said that he would not come among us because
of the conspiracies and oaths, which he said we had
made against him, to slay him with our knives. So when
he was come home and was sitting in his lodgings, he
commanded one of our brethren, whom he most sus-
pected, to come to him ; and because he did not come,
since he feared to be seized and bound, he was excommunicated, and afterwards put in chains for a whole
day, and remained till morning in the infirmary. On
three others the Abbot imposed a lighter sentence that
the rest might be afraid. On the morrow it was determined that the Abbot should be sent for, and that we
should humble ourselves before him in word and bearing, that his anger might be assuaged. And so it was
done. And he himself answered quite humbly, while
still asserting the justice of his conduct and throwing the
blame upon us ; yet seeing that we were ready to be
vanquished, he was vanquished himself ; and with tears
streaming from his eyes, he swore that he had never
grieved for anything so much as for this trouble, both
on his own account and ours, and above all for the shame
brought upon us by evil rumour, which had already
spread the tale of our dissensions abroad, saying that the
monks of St. Edmund desired to kill their Abbot. And
when the Abbot told us how he had absented himself
of set purpose, until his anger had cooled down, and he
repeated the saying of the philosopher, ' I would have
revenged myself upon you, had I not been angry,' he
arose all in tears and received us all with the kiss of

omnes et singulos recepit in osculo pacis. Plorauit ille :
plorauimus et nos. Absoluti sunt illico fratres qui ex-
comunicati fuerant, et sic ' cessauit tempestas, et facta
est tranquillitas magna.' [1] Occulte tamen precepit
abbas, ut solitum conredium integre daretur Radulfo
ianitori, sicut prius ; quam rem dissimulauimus, tandem
comperientes, quod non est dominus qui dominari non
uelit, et periculosa est pugna que contra fortiorem initur
et contra potentiorem arripitur.

Anno gracie M°.CC^mo. facta est descripcio [2] de militibus sancti Ædmundi et de feudis eorum, unde antecess-
sores eorum fuerunt feffati.

Albericus de Ver tenet quinque milites et dimidium ;
scilicet, in Lodenes, et in Brom, unum militem ; in
Mendham et Prestun, i. militem ; in Rede, i. militem ;
et in Cokefeld, dimidium ; et in Liuermere, duos milites.

Willelmus de Hastinges tenet v. milites ; scilicet, in
Lidgate et in Blunham et in Herlinghe, tres milites ; et
in Tibebeham et in Gersinghe, duos.

F.157   Comes Rogerus tenet tres / milites, in Nortune et
Brisingeham.

Robertus filius Rogeri tenet i mil, in Marlesford.

Allexander de Kirkebi tenet i mil. in Kirkebi.

Rogerus de Hou tenet duos milites, in Michlesfela et
in Topescroft.

Arnaldus de Charneles et parcenarii eius i militem,
in Acle et in Quidenham, et in Turstune et Tutestun.

Osebertus de Wachesham i militem, in Marlingeford
et in Wrtham.

Willelmus de Totestoche i militem, in Randestune.

Gilbertus filius Radulfi tres milites ; scilicet, in
Teueltham et in Hepeword, i militem ; in Reidun et in
Gersinge, i militem ; et in Saxham i militem.

---

[1] Mark iv, 39 ; Luke viii. 24   [2] See Appendix S

peace. He wept and we wept also. Those brothers who had been excommunicated, were at once absolved, and thus ' the storm ceased and there was a great calm.' None the less the Abbot secretly gave orders that Ralph the gatekeeper should have back his wonted corody in its entirety as of old. To this we shut our eyes, since we had at last learned that there is no master that does not desire to have the mastery, that it is perilous to fight with one who is braver than oneself, and that to take up arms against one who is stronger is full of hazard.

In the year of grace 1200 a list was made of the knights of St. Edmund and of the fieffs of which their ancestors were enfieffed.

Aubrey de Vere holds five knights and a half : to wit, in Loddon and Broome, one knight ; in Mendham and Preston, one knight ; in Rede, one knight ; and in Cockfield, a half ; and in Livermere, two knights.

William de Hastings holds five knights : to wit, in Lidgate and Blunham and Harling, three knights ; and in Tibenham and Gissing, two.

Earl Roger holds three knights, in Norton and Bressingham.

Robert FitzRoger holds one knight in Marlesford.

Alexander de Kirby holds one knight in Kirby.

Roger de Hou holds two knights, in Mickfield and Topcroft.

Arnold de Chernelles and his partners, one knight in Oakley and in Quidenham, and in Thurston and Stuston.

Osbert de Wattisham, one knight, in Marlingford and in Wortham.

William de Tostock, one knight in Thrandeston.

Gilbert FitzRalph, three knights : to wit, in Thelnetham and in Hepworth, one knight ; in Reydon and in Gissing, one knight ; and in Saxham, one knight.

Radulfus de Bucheham dimidium militem, in antiquum Bucheham.

Willelmus de Berdewella duos milites, in Berningham, et in Berdewelle, et in Hunterestune et in Stantun.

Robertus de Langetot tenet tres milites, in Stowe, et in Asfeld, et in Trostune, et in paruo Waltham in Estsexia.

Adam de Kokefeld duos milites ; scilicet, in Lautnei et in Honus i militem, et Lelesaeia.

Robertus filius Walteri i militem, in magno Facheham, et in Sapestun.

Will. Blundus i militem, in Torp.

Gilbertus Peccatum duos milites ; scilicet, in Waude et in Geddinge, i mil. ; in Falesham, et Eustuna, et in Grotena, i militem.

Gilbertus de sancto Claro duos milites, in Bradefelda et in Watlesfelda.

Galfridus de Welfetham et Gilbertus de Manetuna i mil., in Wefetham et in Manetuna.

Hubertus de Hanesti dimidium militem, in Brighingeham.

Geruasius de Roinghe i mil., in Clipeleie et in Roinghe

Robertus de Halstede i militem in Halsted, et dimidium in Broclei.

Reinaldus de Brocleie unum militem, in Brocleie.

Simon de Pateshala dimidium militem, in Whatefelda.

Petrus filius Alani dimidium militem, in Brocleie.

Radulfus de Presseni dimidium militem, in Stanesfelda.

Ricardus de Ikeworda duos milites, in Ikeworda et in Wanforda.

Robertus de Horningis dimidium mil., in Horningis.

F.157v   Walterus de Saxham i militem, in Asfelde / et in Saxham.

Ralph de Buckenham, half a knight in Old Buckenham.

William de Bardwell, two knights, in Barningham, and in Bardwell, and in Hunston, and in Stanton.

Robert de Longtoft holds three knights, in Stowe and in Ashfield Magna and in Troston, and in Little Waltham in Essex.

Adam de Cockfield, two knights : to wit, in Lavenham and in Onehouse, one knight ; and in Lindsey.

Robert FitzWalter, one knight, in Fakenham Magna and in Sapiston.

William Blunt, one knight in Thorp.

Gilbert de Peche, two knights : to wit, in Weald and in Gedding, one knight ; and in Felsham and Euston and in Groton, one knight.

Gilbert de St. Clare, two knights, in Bradfield and Wattisfield.

Geoffrey de Whelnetham and Gilbert de Manston, one knight in Whelnetham and in Manston.

Hubert de Ansty, half a knight in Briddinghoe.

Gervase de Roding, one knight in Chipley and in Roding.

Robert de Hawstead, one knight in Hawstead and half a knight in Brockley.

Reginald de Brockley, one knight in Brockley.

Simon de Patteshall, half a knight in Whatfield.

Peter FitzAlan, half a knight in Brockley.

Ralph de Presseni, half a knight in Stanningfield.

Richard de Ickworth, two knights in Ickworth and in Wangford.

Robert de Horningsheath, half a knight in Horningsheath Parva.

Walter de Saxham, one knight in Ashfield Parva and in Saxham.

Willelmus de Wridewella dimidium militem, in Whelfetham.

Normannus de Risebi dimidium militem, in Risebi.

Petrus de Liueremere et Alanus de Flemetun i militem, in Liueremere et in Ametuna.[1]

Rogerus de Muriaus i militem, in Torp.

Hugo de Illeghe, in Illeghe, et in Prestuna, et in Bradefelda, ii milites.

Stephanus de Brochedis unum quater, in Brochedis.

Adam de Bernigham i quater, in Berningham.

Willelmus de Wridewella, in paruo Liueremere, et in Wridewella, i quater.

Galfridus Ruffus monachus noster, licet se nimis seculariter se gereret, utilis fuit nobis in custodia iiii^{or} maneriorum, Bertuna, Pakeham, Rucham, Bradefeld, ubi prius defectus sepe solebat esse de firmis. Audiens abbas infamiam continentie eius, diu dissimulauit, forte quia G. utilis uidebatur uniuersitati. Tandem, cognita ueritate, subito fecit capi cistas eius, positas in uestiario, et omnia instauramenta maneriorum districte custodiri, et eundem G. posuit in claustrum. Inuenta fuit uis magna auri et argenti, ad ualentiam cc. marcarum, quod totum dixit abbas esse apponendum ad fabricandum frontem feretri sancti Ædmundi. Instante festo sancti Michaelis, decretum est in capitulo, ut duo fratres, non unus solus, succederent ad custodiendum maneria, quorum unus erat R. de Hehingham, qui publice promisit se uelle et se bene posse custodire simul maneria et cellariam, et assensum prebuit abbas, set conuentu inuito : et depositus est Iocellus de cellaria, qui bene et prouide instaurauerat officium suum, et duobus annis

---

[1] The MS has *Amenina*

William de Wordwell, half a knight in Whelnetham.

Norman de Risby, half a knight in Risby.

Peter de Livermere and Alan de Flempton, one knight, in Livermere and in Ampton.

Roger de Morieux, one knight in Thorp.

Hugh de Eleigh, in Eleigh and in Preston and in Bradfield, two knights.

Stephen de Brockdish, one quarter in Brockdish.

Adam de Barningham, one quarter in Barningham.

William de Wordwell, in Little Livermere and in Wordwell, one quarter.

Geoffrey Ruff, a monk of ours, though he conducted himself in too worldly a fashion, was useful to us in his custody of four manors, Barton, Pakenham, Rougham, and Bradfield, where in the past the rents had often been in default. But the Abbot, though he heard evil reports of his behaviour, for a long time ignored it, perhaps because Geoffrey seemed useful to our house. At length learning the truth, he suddenly caused his chests to be seized and placed in the vestry and, ordering that all the stock of the manors should be close-guarded, he placed the said Geoffrey in prison. A great quantity of gold and silver was found, to the value of two hundred marks, all of which the Abbot said should be applied to making the front of the feretory of St. Edmund. And when Michaelmas drew near, it was decreed in Chapter that two of our brothers, not one alone, should succeed to the custody of the manors, of whom one was Roger of Hingham, who promised us in public that he was ready and able to look after both the manors and the cellary ; and to this the Abbot gave his assent, though against the will of the Convent ; and Jocellus who had carried out his duties with skill and foresight and, unlike other cellarers, had managed the cellary for two years

rexerat cellariam sine debito, contra consuetudinem
aliorum celerariorum, et factus est subcelerarius. In
fine autem anni, reddens R. celerarius rationem de
receptis et expensis, protestatus est se accepisse lx.
marcas de instauramentis maneriorum ad supplendum
defectum celerarii. Inito ergo consilio, substitutus est
predictus Iocellus ad cellariam, et concessa sunt ei
Mildenhala et Chebenhala et Sutwalda, et conmissa sunt
cetera maneria Rogero et Albino, et diuisa sunt a cellaria,
F.158 ne uel maneria distruerentur per / cellariam, uel cellaria
destrueretur per maneria.

Mortuo Adam de Cokefeld, potuit abbas accepisse
ccc. marcas pro warda unice filie eiusdem Ade ; set quia
auus puelle tulerat eam furtim, nec abbas potuit habere
saisinam puelle, nisi per auxilium archiepiscopi, abbas
concessit wardam illam H. archiepiscopo Cantuariensi,
acceptis c. libris. Archiepiscopus, acceptis quingentis
marcis, concessit Thome de Burgo, fratri camerarii Regis,[1]
wardam illam, et data fuit ei puella cum iure suo per
manum abbatis. Thomas ergo statim petiit saisinam
trium maneriorum que in manu nostra habuimus post
mortem Ade, Kokefeld, Semere et Grotona : credentes,
quod omnia possemus retinere in dominico nostro uel
saltem duo, Semere et Grotona ; tum quia Robertus de
Cokefeld, in extremis agens, dixerat publice, se nichil
in illis ii. maneriis iure hereditario posse uendicare, tum
quia Adam filius eius in plena curia reconsignauerat
nobis illa duo maneria, et cartam suam inde fecit, qua
continetur, quod ille tenet illa ii. maneria per graciam
conuentus solummodo in uita sua. Thomas ergo querens
inde breue de recognicione, fecit summoneri milites, ut

---

[1] Hubert de Burgh

without debt, was deposed and made sub-cellarer. But at the end of the year Roger the Cellarer, when he gave account of his receipts and expenditure, acknowledged that he had taken sixty marks from the stock of the manors to make good the Cellarer's deficit. Then, after consideration, the said Jocellus was made Cellarer in his place and was given Mildenhall, Chippenhall, and Southwold, while the other manors were entrusted to Roger and Albin, and were separated from the cellary, lest the manors should be impoverished by the cellary or the cellary by the manors.

When Adam de Cockfield died, the Abbot might have received three hundred marks for the wardship of his only daughter, but since the girl's grandfather had taken her away by stealth, and the Abbot could not have seizin of her, save with the aid of the Archbishop, he granted the wardship of the girl to Hubert, Archbishop of Canterbury for the sum of one hundred pounds. And the Archbishop for the sum of five hundred marks granted the wardship to Thomas de Burgh, the brother of the King's chamberlain ; and the girl was given him with all her rights by the hand of the Abbot. Thomas therefore demanded seizin of three manors which we held in our hands after Adam's death, namely, Cockfield, Semer, and Groton ; for we believed that we could keep all three in our hands, or at least Semer and Groton, both because Robert de Cockfield on his death-bed had publicly declared that he could claim no hereditary right in those two manors, and because Adam his son had in full court reconsigned those two manors to us and had given us a charter for them, in which it was written that he held these two manors by grace of the Convent for his lifetime only. Thomas therefore demanded a writ of recognition in this matter and caused knights to be summoned

uenirent apud Theochesberie, coram Rege iuraturi.
Carta nostra lecta in publico nullam uim habuit, quia
tota curia erat contra nos.[1] Iuramento facto, dixerunt
milites se nescire de cartis nostris, nec de priuatis con-
uencionibus ; set se credere dixerunt, quod Adam et
pater eius et auus a centum annis retro tenuerant maneria
in feudum firmum, unusquisque post alium, diebus quibus
fuerunt uiui et mortui ; et sic dissaisiati sumus per
iudicium curie post multos labores et multas expensas
factas, saluis tamen antiquis firmis annuatim reddendis.

Uidebatur dominus abbas decepi quadam specie
recti,[2] quia scilicet scriptura dicit, ' honorem meum alteri
non dabo.' [3] Abbati Cluniacensi uenienti ad nos, et a
nobis sicut decuit suscepto, cedere noluit abbas noster,
nec in capitulo, nec ad processionem factam die dominico,
quin sederet et staret medius inter abbatem / Cluniacen-
sem [4] et abbatem Certesiensem ; unde diuersi diuersa
sentiebant et multi multa locuti, sunt.

Languescente Roberto priore et adhuc uiuente, dicte
sunt multe sententie de substituendo priore. Narrauit
ergo aliquis, quod dominus abbas, sedens in choro et
omnes fratres intuens, a primo usque ad ultimum, non
inuenit aliquem, super quem requiesceret spiritus eius ad
faciendum priorem, nisi Herebertum capellanum eius.
His et consimilibus uoluntas domini abbatis pluribus
claruit. Audiens hec aliquis respondit, hoc esse in-
credibile ; asserens quod abbas, homo industrius et

F.158v

---

[1] Cp. the settlement made with Adam (p. 58), when he was given
a charter confirming all his lands to him ; no mention was made of Cockfield ; Semer and Groton were to be his for life. T. de Burgh won his
claim on behalf of his ward at an assize Utrum held at Tewkesbury in the
King's presence (Easter term of 1201) ; see *Curia Regis Rolls*, I. p. 430,
where the child is sometimes called Margaret, sometimes Margery ; in
later life she was known as Nesta. For the later history of these lands,
see Rokewode, p. 141.

to come to Tewkesbury and take their oath before the King. Our charter was read in public, but in vain, since the whole court was against us. The knights having been sworn said that they knew nothing about our charter or our private agreements, but that they believed that Adam, his father and his grandfather had for a hundred years back held the manors in fee farm, one after the other, on the days on which they were alive and dead ; and thus by judgment of the court after much labour and much expense we were disseized, save for the payment of the annual rents as of old.

The Abbot seemed to have been deceived by a certain semblance of the right, for the Scripture says, ' I will not give mine honour to another.' When the Abbot of Cluny came to us and was received by us as was fitting, our Abbot refused to yield precedence to him either in the chapterhouse or in the procession on Sunday, but sat and stood between the Abbot of Cluny and the Abbot of Chertsey ; whereof divers persons held divers opinions and many men said many things.

When Robert the Prior fell sick and was still alive, many opinions were expressed about the appointment of his successor. Thus, there was one who told us that the Lord Abbot, as he sat in the choir and surveyed all the brethren from the first to the last, could find none on whom his spirit might rest for the appointment of a Prior save only Herbert his chaplain. By such things and the like the Abbot's will was made clear to many of us. And one, when he heard it, said that it was not

---

[2] Horace, *Ars Poetica* 25
[3] Isa. xlii. 8 ; xlviii. 11
[4] Hugh, fifth Abbot of Cluny, visited England in 1200 ; Diceto, II. 173.

sapiens, nunquam tali homini, et iuueni et fere inberbi
nouicio xii. annorum, qui non nisi iiii^{or} annis claustralis
fuit, nec probatus in regimine animarum, nec in scientie
doctrina,—' tali,' inquit, ' nunquam dabit prioratum.'
Mortuo autem priore, morabatur abbas apud Londonias ;
et dixit quidam : ' Nondum transiit mensis quod abbas
fecit Herebertum capellanum subsacristam, et quando
bailiam illam ei commisit in capella sancti Nigasii,[1]
promittendo quod, si posset aliquo modo eum priorem
facere, curam omnimodam ad hoc adhiberet.' Audiens
hoc aliquis, uolens placere abbati et priori futuro, plures
sollicitauit in precibus, senes cum iunioribus, ut data
oportunitate Herebertum nominarent, saltem cum aliquibus aliis, ad prioratum ; et iurauit quod per hoc
possent placere abbati, quia talis fuit uoluntas eius.
Erant autem multi, tam de senioribus quam de iunioribus, qui eundem Herebertum hominem amabilem et
affabilem asserebant, et dignum magno honore. Erant
et alii, pauci quidem numero, set consilio laudabiliores
et de saniore parte conuentus, qui magistrum Hermerum
suppriorem, hominem maturum, literatum et eloquentem, in animarum regimine peritum et expertum, qui
tunc temporis xiiii. annis claustrum disciplinate rexerat,
supprior probatus, et notus,—hunc, inquam, uolebant
preferre ad prioratum, iuxta illud sapientis, ' experto
crede magistro ; '[2] set latenter grunniebat multitudo in
contrarium, dicens illum esse hominem iracundum, im-
F.159 patientem, inquietum, turbulentum / et anxium, litigiosum
et turbatorem pacis, illudentes ei et dicentes quia ' sapientia uiri in eius patiencia dinoscitur.'[3] Item dixit

---

[1] The position of the chapel of St. Nicais is not known ; possibly it was
in the triforium ; see MRJ p. 161.
[2] Cp. Virgil, *Aeneid*, xi. 283
[3] Prov. xix. 11

to be believed ; for he said that the Abbot, being a man
of energy and wisdom, would never give the office of
Prior to such a man, who had been an almost beardless
novice for twelve years and a cloister monk of no more
than four years' standing, proved neither in the cure of
souls nor in doctrine. Now when the Prior died, the
Abbot was in London ; and one said, ' Not a month
has passed since the Abbot made Herbert his chaplain
sub-sacrist ; and when he gave him that office in the
Chapel of St. Nicasius, he promised him that, if he could
by any means make him Prior, he would use all his
efforts to that end.' But, hearing this, another, desiring
to please the Abbot and the Prior that was to be, solicited
many, both young and old, with entreaties that, when
the occasion arose, they should nominate Herbert for the
office of Prior, if not alone, at least with certain others :
and he swore that thus they would please the Abbot,
since such was his wish. Now there were many, both
of the old and of the young, who said that Herbert was
a man both amiable and affable, and worthy of great
honour. There were others, few, it is true, in numbers,
but more praiseworthy in counsel and among the more
prudent members of the Convent, who desired to promote to the office of Prior Master Hermer the sub-prior,
a man of mature years, literate and eloquent, skilled and
experienced in the cure of souls, who had proved himself and become known to us as sub-prior, and had kept
good discipline in the cloister for fourteen years. This
man, I say, they desired to promote, following the saying
of one wiser than most, ' Trust the experienced master ' :
but in secret the majority grumbled against them, saying
that Hermer was hot-tempered, impatient, restless, tur-
bulent, anxious-minded, quarrelsome, and a disturber of
the peace ; and they mocked at him, saying, ' A man's

aliquis : ' Hoc unum, tanquam scandalum, ualde timendum est, ne supprior remoueatur, clerici literati habitum relligionis de cetero dedignentur suscipere penes nos, si forte contingat aliquam statuam mutam erigi, et truncum ligneum [1] preferri in tali conuentu ; ' et adiecit idem frater, dicens quod talis deberet esse prior nostri conuentus, ut, si quid maioris oriretur questionis de ecclesiasticis uel secularibus negociis, abbate absente, ad priorem quasi ad maiorem et discretiorem posset referri. Hec et consimilia audiens, quidam fratrum ait : ' Quid est quod uerba tot et talia multiplicatis ? Cum abbas domum uenerit, uoluntatem suam inde faciet : forte queret consilium singulorum et sigillatim et cum magna sollemnitate ; set in fine operis sui, per allegaciones et per rationes uerisimiles et circumlocuciones uerborum, tandem descendet ad uoluntatem suam implendam ; et sicut ipse precogitauit, facturus est negocium.'

Reuerso ergo abbate, in capitulo sedente, multa proposuit et satis eloquenter, qualis deberet esse prior substituendus ; et respondit Iohannes tercius prior coram omnibus, suppriorem dignum esse et idoneum. Set statim reclamauit multitudo, dicens : ' Homo pacis, homo pacis detur nobis.' Responderunt duo ex nobis tante multitudini, dicentes talem esse substituendum, qui nouit regere animas, et discernere ' inter lepram et lepram,' [2] quod uerbum ualde displicebat, quia uidebatur fouere partem subprioris. Abbas autem tumultum audiens, dixit se uelle post capitulum consilium singulorum audire, ut sic consulte procederet in negocio, et

---

[1] See p. 12
[2] Deut. xvii. 8

wisdom is learned from his patience.' Again another said, ' This is the scandal that we have most to fear, that the sub-prior should be kept out and that literate clerks should for the future disdain to take the religious habit among us, if it should so fall out that a dumb image were set up in our midst and a log of wood given preferment in such a Convent as ours.' And the same brother added that the Prior of our Convent should be such a man that if some great question, whether secular or ecclesiastical, should arise among us, when the Abbot was away, the matter might be referred to the Prior, as having greater power and wisdom than the rest of us. And when he heard these sayings and the like, a certain brother said, ' Why multiply such words as these ? When the Abbot returns, he will do what he will in this matter. Perhaps he will seek counsel of each of us, one by one, and with great solemnity ; but in the end, by allegations and plausible argument and circumlocution, he will at length come down to fulfil his own desire ; and he will settle the matter just as he has already preordained.'

So, when the Abbot was returned and took his seat in the Chapter, he set forth at great length and with some eloquence, the character which the new Prior ought to possess. And John the third prior said before us all that the sub-prior was a worthy and suitable person. But the great majority forthwith protested, crying, ' A man of peace ! Give us a man of peace ! ' Then two of us replied to the many, saying that the man to be appointed should be such an one as understood the cure of souls and could distinguish ' between leprosy and leprosy,' a saying that was very unpalatable to the majority, since it seemed to favour the sub-prior. But the Abbot, on hearing the uproar, said that he wished after Chapter to hear the counsel of individuals, that so

in crastino secundum sese esse operaturum. Interim
dixit aliquis, quod abbas talem sollemnitatem faceret, ut
supprior remoueretur caute a prioratu ; tanquam hoc
fieret per consilium conuentus, et non per uoluntatem
abbatis, et ipse abbas haberetur excusatus, et hac arte
obstrueretur os loquentium iniqua.[1]

In crastino, sedente abbate in capitulo, lacrimatus est
ualde, dicens se totam noctem duxisse insomnem pre
anxietate et timore, si aliquem nominaret qui Deo non
placeret ; iurauitque in periculo anime sue, se nomina-
turum quatuor ex nobis, qui secundum opinionem suam
F.159v magis essent utiles et idonei, ut unum / ex illis iiii^{or}
eligeremus. Nominauit ergo abbas in primis sacristam,
de quo constabat ei quod inpotens et insufficiens erat,
sicut ipse sacrista testatus est cum iuramento statim coram
omnibus. Nominauit etiam Iohannem tercium priorem,
suum consanguineum, et Mauricium capellanum suum
et Herebertum prenominatum, omnes quidem iuuenes,
quasi xl. annorum uel infra, et omnes mediocris scientie,
et ad regimen animarum pocius docendi quam docti,
dociles tamen. Hos tres abbas nominauit et pretulit,
postposito suppriore, et postpositis aliis pluribus senioribus, prioribus, maturioribus, literatis, et antiquitus
magistris scolarum, et omnibus aliis. Morabatur autem
abbas in loquendo, et commendando personam Iohannis
in multis, set tamen allegando in contrarium, dicens,
quod parentum multitudo huius provincie collo eius
incumberet, si prior esset. Et etiam [2] cum uellet abbas

---

[1] Ps. lxii. 12 (Vulg.) ; lxiii. 11 (AV)
[2] The MS reads *eum* ; there may be some corruption here

he might proceed wisely in the matter, and that on the morrow he would act as he thought best. And in the meantime someone said that the Abbot contrived all this solemnity, just in order that the sub-prior might cautiously be ousted from all hope of obtaining the office of Prior, yet in such a way that it might seem to be done by the counsel of the Convent and not by the will of the Abbot, so that the Abbot himself might be excused and ' the mouth of them that speak evil might be stopped.'

On the morrow, as the Abbot sat in Chapter, he wept much, saying that he had passed the whole night without sleep because of his anxiety and dread that he might nominate one who would be unpleasing to God ; and he swore on the peril of his soul, that he would nominate four of us, who in his opinion would be useful and suitable persons, that we might choose one of the four. The Abbot therefore named, first the Sacrist, concerning whom it was known that he was weak and unequal to the task, as the Sacrist himself testified forthwith with an oath before us all. He next named John, the third prior and his own kinsman, and after him Maurice his chaplain and the aforesaid Herbert, all of them young men, of forty years or less, all of them possessed of but a modicum of learning, and as regards the cure of souls needing instruction rather than already instructed, yet still all capable of being taught. These then the Abbot named, putting them above the sub-prior and many others who were older, superior, and more mature, men, too, who were literate and had of old been masters of the Schools, to say nothing of all the rest of us. But the Abbot spoke at great length, commending the character of John in many respects, but alleging against him that the multitude of kinsmen he possessed in these parts would be a weight about his neck if he were Prior. The

possetque idem allegare de Mauricio, ut sic artificiose
perueniret ad faciendam mencionem de Hereberto,
interim interruptus est sermo eius, dicente uno ex prioribus conuentus : ' Domine cantor, tuum est habere
primam uocem : nomina dominum Herebertum.' At
ille, ' Bonus homo est,' inquit. Audito nomine Hereberti,
abbas loquenda suppressit et conuersus ad cantorem,
dixit : ' Herebertum recipiam libenter, si uultis.' His
dictis, clamauit totus conuentus, ' Bonus homo est :
bonus homo est et amabilis ; ' et hoc idem attestati sunt
plures ex prioribus ; statimque cantor et socius quidam
cum eo, et alii duo ex alia parte, cum omni festinacione
surrexerunt, et Herebertum statuerunt in medio. Here-
bertus uero in primis humiliter ueniam cepit, dicens se
insufficientem esse ad tantam dignitatem, et maxime,
sicut dixit, quod non esset tam perfecte scientie, quod
sciret facere sermonem in capitulo, sicut deceret priorem.
Opstupuerunt plures qui talia uiderunt, et pre confu-
sione obmutuerunt. Abbas uero in consolacium eius et
quasi in preiudicium literatorum multa respondit, dicens
quod bene posset recordari et ruminare alienos sermones,
sicut et alii faciebant ; et colores rethoricos et phaleras
uerborum et exquisitas sentencias in sermone dampnabat,
dicens quod in multis ecclesiis fit sermo in conuentu
Gallice uel pocius Anglice, ut morum fieret edificacio,
non literature ostensio. Quibus dictis, iuit prior iam
receptus ad pedes abbatis, et deosculatus est eos. Abbas
autem cum lacrimis suscepit eum, et propria manu posuit /
F.160 eum in sede prioris, et precepit omnibus ut debitam
reuerentiam et obedientiam ei deferrent sicut priori.

Abbot was proceeding to make the same allegations about Maurice (as he might well have done), in order that thus he might be able artfully to bring in the name of Herbert, when he was interrupted by one of the leading brethren, who cried, ' My lord Precentor, you have first voice ; name Dom Herbert.' And the Precentor said, ' He is a good man.' On hearing the name of Herbert, the Abbot suppressed what he was about to say, and turning to the Precentor said, ' I will gladly accept Herbert if you desire it.' At this the whole Convent cried out, ' He is a good man and worthy of our love,' and a number of the seniors testified in like manner. And the Precentor and a supporter with him, and two others from another quarter rose in all haste and set Herbert in our midst. And he at first humbly excused himself, saying that he was unequal to so great a dignity, and above all, as he said, because he was not possessed of such perfect knowledge that he would know how to preach a sermon in Chapter, such as would become the Prior. Many who heard him say this were astounded, and for very confusion kept silence. But the Abbot, for his consolation and (as it would seem) to the prejudice of the literate, replied at length, saying that he could easily commit to memory the sermons of others and inwardly digest them as others did ; and he condemned rhetorical ornament and verbal embellishments and elaborate general reflections in a sermon, saying that in many churches sermons are preached before the Convent in French or better still in English, for the edification of morals and not for the display of literary learning. This said, the now accepted Prior went to the Abbot's feet and kissed them. And the Abbot received him with tears, and with his own hand placed him in the Prior's seat, and bade all to show him due reverence and obedience as to their Prior.

Facto capitulo, sedebam ego hospitiarius in porticu
aule hospitum, stupidus et reuoluens in animo que
uideram et audieram ; et subtiliter cogitare cepi, ob
quam causam et propter quas meritorum gratias, homo
talis ad tantam dignitatem deberet promoueri. Et
animaduertere incepi, quod homo est stature decentis, et
personalis apparentie ; homo pulcher facie et amabilis
aspectu ; semper hilaris, uultu risibilis tam mane quam
sero, benignus omnibus ; homo compositus in gestu, in
incessu grauis, uerbo facetus, dulcem uocem habens in
cantando et facundam in legendo ; iuuenis, fortis, et
sanus in corpore, et expeditus ad laborandum pro
necessitate ecclesie ; pro loco, pro tempore, nunc laicis,
nunc clericis, nunc ecclesiasticis, nunc secularibus uiris
sciens se conformare ; liberalis et socialis et facilis, ad
castigandum non inuidus, non suspiciosus, non auarus,
non studiosus,[1] non desidiosus ; sobrius et uolubilis
lingue in Gallico idiomate, utpote Normannus nacione ;
homo mediocris intelligentie, quem si littere facerent
insanire,[2] homo perfecte probitatis dici posset. Cum hec
aduerterem, dixi in animo meo,[3] talem hominem esse
graciosum, set ' nichil omni parte beatum,' [4] et lacrimatus sum pre gaudio, dicens ' quia uisitauit nos Dominus : [5] sicut Domino placuit, ita factum est.' [6] Set subito
dixit mihi alia cogitacio mea, ' parcius lauda nouum
hominem, quia honores mutant mores, uel pocius
monstrant. Attende prius quos et quales consiliarios
habebit, et quibus credet, quia quidlibet ad suum
naturaliter trahit consimile. Exitus acta probabit,[7] et
ideo lauda parcius.'

[1] So the MS ; altered to *tediosus* in a fifteenth century hand
[2] Acts xxvi. 24 ; cp. p. 13
[3] Judges xvi. 20
[4] Horace, *Odes* II. xvi. 28
[5] Luke vii. 16

The Chapter over, I the Guest-master sat in the porch of the guest-house and, pondering in my heart what I had seen and heard, I began minutely to consider for what reason and for what merits such a man deserved to be promoted to such dignity. And I began to take note that the man was of comely presence and personable appearance ; a handsome man and of friendly aspect ; always cheerful with a smile upon his face from morn till eve, and kindly to all ; composed in gesture, dignified in gait and elegant of speech, a sweet-voiced singer and an eloquent reader ; a young man, strong and healthy in body, and nimble to labour for the needs of our Church, knowing well how to suit himself, as time and place might demand, now to laymen, now to clerks, at one time to ecclesiastics, at another to men of the world ; generous, sociable and kindly, not jealous to chastise, not given to suspicion or to avarice, not a drudge nor a sluggard ; a sober man and fluent in the French tongue, being a Norman by race ; a man of ordinary under-standing whom letters made not mad, and of perfect honesty as well ; all these things he might be called. And when I considered this, I said in my heart that such a man was full of grace, but that ' nothing is wholly blest,' and I wept for joy, saying, ' The Lord hath visited us ; as it pleased the Lord, so hath it been done.' But suddenly my heart within me said to me, ' Be sparing in your praise of a new man ; for honours change men's character or rather show it forth. Note first what coun-sellors he has and of what like they be, and in whom he puts his trust ; for like naturally draws to itself its like. " What's done the end shall prove," and therefore be sparing of your praise.'

---

⁶ Job i. 21
⁷ Ovid, *Heroides* ii. 85

Eodem die conuenerunt quidam illiterati fratres, tam
officiales quam claustrales, et exacuerunt linguas suas,
ut sagittarent in occultis [1] literatos, et repetentes dicta
abbatis que eodem die dixerat, quasi in preiudicium
literatorum, dixerunt ad inuicem : ' Accipiant modo
philosophi nostri philosophias suas ; modo patet quid
prodest philosophia eorum ! Tantum declinauerunt boni
clerici nostri in claustro, quod omnes declinati sunt.
Tantum sermocinauerunt in capitulo, quod omnes
repulsi sunt. Tantum locuti sunt de discrecione inter
lepram et lepram, quod tanquam leprosi deiecti sunt.

F.160v Tantum declinauerunt *musa, muse,* / quod omnes musardi
reputati sunt.' Hec et consimilia protulerunt quidam
in derisionem et opprobrium aliorum, sueque imperitie
consulentes scienciam literarum reprobauerunt, et literatis detraxerunt, multum letantes et magna sperantes que
forte nunquam euenient, quia

fallitur augurio spes bona sepe suo. [2]

Sapiens dixit, ' nemo ex omni parte beatus ; ' nec ergo
abbas Samson. Hoc icirco dixerim, quia, iudicio meo,
non est commendandus abbas in facto quod fecit, quando
cartam fieri et dari iussit cuidam seruienti suo, de sergancia
Iohannis Ruffi habenda post mortem eiusdem Iohannis :
decem marce, ut dicebatur, oculos sapientis excecaue-
runt. [3] Unde et magistro Dionisio monacho dicenti, tale
factum inauditum esse, respondit abbas : ' Non desinam
facere uoluntatem meam magis pro te, quam pro iuuen-
cello illo.' Consimile fecit abbas de sergencia Ade de
infirmario, acceptis c. solidis. De tali facto dici potest,
' modicum fermenti totam massam corrumpit.' [4]

---

[1] Ps. lxiii. 4–5 (Vulg.) ; lxiv. 3–4 (A.V.)
[2] Ovid, *Heroides* xvii. 234
[3] Deut. xvi. 19
[4] 1 Cor. v. 6

On the same day certain illiterate brothers, both officers and cloister monks, gathered together and sharpened their tongues, that they might shoot their arrows at the literate ; and repeating the words which the Abbot had spoken that same day, as it might seem, to the prejudice of the literate, they spoke thus one to the other : ' Let our philosophers keep their philosophies ! for now it is clear what profit is brought them by their philosophy. Our good clerks have declined so often in the cloister, that now they themselves have all been declined. They have prated so much of distinguishing " between leprosy and leprosy," that they have been cast out as though they were lepers themselves. They have declined " Musa, Musae " so often, that they are all accounted bemused.' These words and the like were uttered by certain folk for the derision and reproach of others, and to flatter their own ignorance they condemned the knowledge of letters and disparaged the literate, rejoicing much and full of high hopes, which perchance will never be fulfilled ; for

fair hopes are cheated oft by their own dreams.

A wise man has said that ' No-one is in all things blest ' ; nor was Abbot Samson. I venture to say this, because in my opinion the Abbot is not to be commended for what he did, when he caused a charter to be made out and given to one of his servants, granting him the sergeanty of John Ruff after the death of the said John : ten marks, it is said, blinded the eyes of the wise. And when Master Denys, one of our monks, spoke to him on this matter, saying that such a thing was unheard of, the Abbot replied, ' I will not cease to do what I will, for you any more than I would for that stripling there.' The Abbot did the like also with the sergeanty of Adam of the infirmary, receiving a hundred shillings for it. Of

Item est et alie male operacionis macula quam lacrimis penitentie abluet, Domino uolente, ne tantam summam
bonorum unus deturpet excessus. Stagnum uiuarii de
Babbewella, ad nouum molendinum, in tantum leuauit,
quod ex retentione aquarum non est homo, diues uel
pauper, habens terram iuxta aquam a porta uille usque
ad portam orientis, quin amiserit ortum suum et pomeria
sua. Pastura celerarii, ex alia parte ripe, perdita est,
terre etiam arrabiles uicinorum deteriores facte sunt.
Pratum celerarii periit, pomerium infirmarii submersum
est ex habundantia aque, et omnes uicini inde conque-
runtur. Conuenit eum quandoque celerarius in pleno
capitulo super damno tanto, qui cito commotus respondit,
uiuarium suum non esse perdendum propter pratum
nostrum.

Decanus Londoniensis [1] ita scribit in cronicis suis :
' Rex Henricus secundus, habito tractatu de uacantibus
abbaciis cum archiepiscopo et cum episcopis, sic in
abbatibus substituendis canonum obseruauit censuram,
ut emendicatis aliunde suffragiis [2] uteretur ; arbitrans
forsitan, 'quod si de corpore proprio locis in singulis
F.161 crearentur / pastores,' contracta prius familiaritas uiciis re-
promitteret impunitatem ; conuersatio par indulgentiis
crimina sulleuaret ; remissio nimia uagaretur in claustris.
Dixit quidam alius : ' Non uidetur pastor eligendus de
propria domo, set potius de aliena ; quia si aliunde
sumatur, semper credet, secundum quantitatem con-

---

[1] Ralph de Diceto (*Imag. Hist.*, R.S. I. 401–2). After *crearentur pastores*
the words *regie dignitatis auctoritas vacillaret* are omitted by Jocelin. The
words which follow *contracta prius . . . in claustris* are not found in RS
text. But they are found in MS B, and are given in a footnote to the text.
The meeting took place at Woodstock, July 8, 1175, when a number of
abbacies were vacant.

such a deed it may be said, ' A little leaven leavens the whole lump.'

There is also another stain of evil-doing which, God willing, the Abbot will wash out with tears of penitence, that one transgression should not blacken such a multitude of good deeds. He raised the level of the fish-pond of Babwell by the new mill to such a height, that owing to the holding up of the waters, there is no man rich or poor, having lands by the waterside, from the Towngate to Eastgate, but has lost his garden and orchards. The Cellarer's pasture on the other side of the bank is destroyed, the arable land of neighbours is spoilt. The Cellarer's meadow is ruined, the Infirmarer's orchard is drowned owing to the overflow of water, and all the neighbours complain of it. Once the Cellarer spoke to him in full Chapter concerning the greatness of the loss, but the Abbot at once angrily replied that he was not going to lose his fish-pond for the sake of our meadow.

The Dean of London writes in his Chronicles : ' King Henry II, after discussing vacant abbacies with the Archbishop and Bishops, observed the rule laid down by the canons for the appointment of Abbots in such a manner that he availed himself of assistance begged from other houses, thinking perhaps that, if shepherds were in every case chosen from their own body, friendships formed before election might in return promise impunity to vice, and that former equality might beget indulgence toward offences, and extreme remissness pervade the cloister.' Another has said, ' It seems that a shepherd should not be chosen from his own house, but rather from another. For, if he be taken from elsewhere, he will always believe,

---

² Not 'votes,' but assistance, *i.e.* in the shape of supplying suitable candidates to fill the vacancies.

uentus quem regendum suscepit, plures esse industrios,
quorum consilum appetat, si bonus est ; quorum probitatem timebit, si malus est. Domesticus uero singulorum
imperitiam, impotentiam, insufficientiam, plenius cog-
noscens, securius seuiet, mutans quadrata rotundis.' [1]
Monachi Ramesie, hac ratione ducti, cum libere possent
aliquem eligere de seipsis si uellent, bis abbatem elegerunt
de alienis domibus, diebus istis.

Anno gratie M⁰.cc⁰.i⁰, uenit abbas de Flauiaco [2] apud
nos, qui per assensum abbatis et per predicacionem suam,
fecit mutari publicas empciones et uendiciones, que
fiebant in foro dominicis diebus, et statutum est illas fieri
secunda feria. Consimiliter operatus abbas ille in multis
ciuitatibus et burgis Anglie.

Eodem anno leuauerunt monachi de Heli [3] forum
uenale apud Lachinghehe, habentes inde assensum et
cartam regis. Nos uero inprimis cum amicis et uicinis
nostris pacifice agentes, nuntios misimus ad capitulum
de Eli, et prius domino Heliensi literas quoque precatorias, ut ab incepto desisterent, adiicientes quod xv.
marcas datas pro carta regis impetrata amicabiliter
solueremus pro bono pacis, et occasione mutue dilectionis
obseruande. Quid multa ? Noluerunt desistere ; et
erant uerba hinc et inde comminatoria, ' et pila minantia
pilis.' [4] Nos uero adquisiuimus breue de recognicione,
utrum mercatum illud leuatum fuerit in preiudicium
nostrum, et in detrimentum mercati uille Sancti

---

[1] Horace, *Epistles*, I. i. 100
[2] Eustace, Abbot of Flaix, came to England to preach the word of the
Lord, insisting above all on Sabbatical observance and alms-giving. He
made converts, but aroused much opposition, and soon returned to France ;
his preaching had no lasting effect. See Hoveden, IV. pp. 123 and 172.
[3] For the whole of this complicated story of the quarrel with Ely see
Appendix T.
[4] Lucan, I. 7

according to the size of the Convent whose government he has undertaken, that it contains a number of industrious monks, whose advice he may seek, if he be good, or whose virtue he will fear, if he be bad. But a shepherd taken from his own house, being more fully acquainted with the ignorance, weakness, and insufficiency of each member of his flock, will raven among them with all the greater security, " changing square for round." ' The monks of Ramsey for this reason, though they were free to choose one of themselves, have in our own times twice chosen their Abbot from other houses.

In the year of grace 1201 the Abbot of Flaix came to us, and with the assent of the Abbot and by his own preaching, caused the public buying and selling, which took place in the market on Sundays, to be changed, and it was ordered that it should take place on the second day of the week. This same Abbot did the like in many cities and boroughs of England.

In the same year the monks of Ely set up a market at Lakenheath, having the King's assent and a charter to that effect. At first we dealt peaceably with our friends and neighbours, and after first sending letters to the Lord Bishop of Ely, we sent messengers to the Chapter of Ely, asking them to desist from their enterprise, and adding that, for the sake of peace and for the preservation of our mutual love, we would, in all friendship, pay them fifteen marks, which was the sum given by them to secure the King's charter. I will say no more than this ; they refused to desist, and threatening words were bandied to and fro,

and Roman spears menaced the spears of Rome.

But we secured a writ of recognition to decide whether that market had been set up to our prejudice and to the detriment of the market of St. Edmund. And oath being

Ædmundi. Et factum est iuramentum, et protestatum est, hoc factum fuisse in detrimentum nostrum. Quod cum mandatum esset regi, rex fecit inquiri per registrum suum cuiusmodi cartam dedisset monachis de Eli, et compertum est quod dederat eis predictum mercatum
Fol.161 v sub tali condicione, si non foret / ad detrimentum uicinorum mercatorum. Rex uero, promissis xl. marculis, fecit nobis cartam suam, ut nullum mercatum de cetero fieret infra libertatem Sancti Ædmundi, nisi per assensum abbatis. Et scripsit G. filio Petri, iusticiario, ut mercatum de Lachenheth tolleretur. Iusticiarius hoc idem scripsit uicecomiti de Sutfolchia. Uicecomes, sciens quod non potuit intrare libertates Sancti Ædmundi nec aliquam potestatem ibi exercere, mandauit hoc abbati per breue suum, ut hoc ipsum exequeretur iuxta formam regii mandati. Propositus ergo hundredi, ueniens illuc ad diem mercati cum testimonio liberorum hominum, ex parte regis prohibuit publice mercatum illud, ostendens literas regis et uicecomitis ; set affectus contumeliis et iniuriis, infecto negocio recessit. Abbas uero negocium differens ad tempus, Lundoniis existens, et sapientes inde consulens, mandauit bailiuis suis ut, acceptis hominibus Sancti Ædmundi cum equis et armis, mercatum tollerent, et ementes et uendentes, si quos inuenirent, uinctos secum ducerent. Media autem nocte exierunt fere secenti homines bene armati, tendentes uersus Lachinheth. Cum autem exploratores nuntiarent eos uenire, discurrerunt omnes huc et illuc qui in foro erant, nec inuentus est unus. Prior autem Heliensis cum bailiuis suis uenerat nocte eadem illuc, suspicans aduentum hominum nostrorum, ut pro posse suo uendentes et ementes defenderet ; set domum suam exire noluit : et cum bailiui nostri quesis-

taken, it was declared that it was done to our detriment. This being reported to the King, he caused inquiry to be made by his registrar as to the nature of the charter that he had granted to the monks of Ely ; and it was found that he had granted this charter on condition that it was not to the detriment of neighbouring markets. The King then, on the promise of forty paltry marks, gave us his charter to the effect that no market should henceforth be held within the liberty of St. Edmund without the Abbot's assent : and he wrote to Geoffrey FitzPeter the Justiciar that the market of Lakenheath should be abolished, and the Justiciar wrote to the Sheriff of Suffolk to the same effect. But he, knowing that he could not enter the liberties of St. Edmund nor exercise any power therein, charged the Abbot by his writ that he should carry out the business according to the form of the King's command. The Provost of the Hundred therefore, coming thither on the market day with freemen to bear him witness, publicly on the King's behalf forbade the market, showing the letters both of the King and the Sheriff ; but being received with insult and injury, he retired, having accomplished nothing. The Abbot postponed the matter for a time, being then in London ; but after consulting wise men on the matter, he ordered his bailiffs to take men of St. Edmund with horses and arms and to remove the market and carry off in chains such buyers and sellers as they could find. Now about midnight some six hundred well-armed men set out for Lakenheath. But since scouts gave warning of their approach, all those who were at the market ran this way and that, so that not one of them was to be found. Now the Prior of Ely, suspecting the coming of our men, had come that same night with his bailiffs to defend the buyers and sellers to the best of his power ; but he refused to leave

sent ab eo uadium et plegium standi ad rectum in curia
Sancti Ædmundi de iniuria illata, et dare noluisset, inito
consilio, furcas macelli et tabulas stallorum in foro euerte-
runt et secum asportauerunt, et omnia aueria, oues et
boues uniuersas, insuper et pecora campi,[1] secum duxerunt, tendentes uersus Ikilingheham. Bailliui prioris
sequentes pecierunt aueria sua per plegia usque in xv.
dies, et factum est sicut pecierunt. Infra xv. dies uenit
breue, quo abbas summonitus est, ut ueniret ad scaccarium responsurus de tali facto, et quod aueria capta
interim dimitterentur quieta. Episcopus enim Heliensis,
homo eloquens et facundus, in propria persona conquestus est inde iustitiario et magnatibus Anglie, dicens
inauditam superbiam factam fuisse in terra Sancte
Ætheldrethe tempore pacis, unde et multi commoti
fuerunt aduersus abbatem. /

F.162   Interim est et alia causa discordie orta inter episcopum Eliensem et abbatem. Cum quidam iuuenis de
Glemesford [2] calumpniatus esset in curia Sancti Ædmundi
de pace regis fracta, et quesitus esset diu, et hic in [3] comitatu, tandem senescaldus episcopi produxit iuuenem
illum, petens curiam Sancte Ætheldrethe, cartas et
libertates domini sui ostendens. Nostri uero bailliui,
petentes loquelam et saisinam talis libertatis, audiri non
potuerunt. Comitatus uero posuit loquelam in respectum
usque coram iusticiariis errantibus, unde Sanctus Æd-

---

[1] Ps. viii. 8 (Vulg.) ; viii. 7 (AV)
[2] See Appendix U
[3] *et hic et in* seems necessary

his house, and when our bailiffs demanded gage and pledge from him that he would stand to right in the court of St. Edmund in respect of the injury that he had done, and the Prior had refused this demand, then after taking counsel they overthrew the forked poles of the meat-market and the planks of the stalls in the market, and carried them off, and leading with them all the cattle, ' all sheep and oxen, yea, and the beasts of the field,' they proceeded towards Icklingham. The Prior's bailiffs followed them and demanded back their cattle, offering pledges for fifteen days ; and it was done as they asked. Within fifteen days there came a writ summoning the Abbot to appear before the Exchequer to answer for what had been done, and ordering in the meantime that the captured beasts should be sent away in freedom. For the Bishop of Ely, an eloquent and fluent speaker, com-plained in person concerning this affair to the Justiciar and magnates of England, saying that an act of un-precedented arrogance had been committed on the land of St. Ethelreda in time of peace ; and many others were stirred to indignation against the Abbot by his words.

Meanwhile another cause of discord arose between the Abbot and the Bishop of Ely. A certain young man of Glemsford, having been accused in the court of St. Edmund of breaking the King's peace, and having been for a long time demanded both here and in the County Court, at length the Steward of the Bishop pro-duced him, claiming the jurisdiction of the Court of St. Ethelreda and showing in support the charters and liberties of his lord. Our bailiffs, who claimed both the suit and seizin of such liberty, were unable to make themselves heard. But the County Court placed the suit in respite until the coming of the Justices in eyre ;

mundus supersaisitus fuerat. Abbas uero hoc audiens
proposuit transfretare ; set, quia infirmabatur, rem
uoluit differre usque ad Purificacionem. Et ecce die
sancte Agnetis uenit nuncius regis, breue domini pape [1]
portans, quo continebatur, quod dominus Eliensis et
abbas Sancti Ædmundi scrutinium facerent de G. filio
Petri, et de W. de Stuteuilla, et quibusdam aliis magnatibus Anglie qui crucem acceperant, pro quibus dominus
rex absolucionem petierat, allegans infirmitatem cor-
porum et consilium eorum ad conseruationem regni sui.
Portauit idem nuntius literas domini regis, precipiens,
ut, uisis literis, ueniret ad eum de mandato domini pape
locuturus. Turbatus est abbas, et dixit : ' Angustie sunt
michi undique,[2] uel Deum uel regem offendam ; per
Deum uerum quicquid postea acciderit, sciens non
mentiar.' Ueniens ergo domum cum omni festinacione,
aliquantulum castigatus infirmitate corporis, et humi-
liatus et magis solito timidus, mediante priore quesiuit a
nobis consilium, quod rarissime ante fecerat, quomodo
agendum esset de libertatibus ecclesie periclitantibus, et
unde expense prouenirent, si ipse hoc iter arriperet, et
cui abbatiam committeret custodiendam, et quid faceret
de pauperibus seruientibus suis qui diu seruierant. Et
responsum fuit, ut ipsemet iret, et pecuniam sufficienter
appruntaret, soluendam de nostra sacristia et de pitanciis
nostris, et de aliis redditibus nostris ad uoluntatem
suam ; et quod commendaret abbatiam priori custodien-

---

[1] See Appendix V
[2] Dan. xiii. 22

and St. Edmund was ousted from his honour. The Abbot, on hearing this, proposed to cross the sea, but being in ill-health he decided to put off his departure until the Feast of the Purification. And behold ! on the day of St. Agnes, there came a messenger from the King, carrying a letter from the Lord Pope, commanding that the Lord Bishop of Ely and the Abbot of St. Edmund should hold an inquiry concerning Geoffrey FitzPeter, William de Stutville and certain other magnates of England, who had taken the Cross, and for whom the King has sought absolution from their vow, alleging their bodily infirmity and the need of their counsel for the preservation of his realm. The same messenger also brought letters from the Lord King, ordering him that, on sight of these letters, he should come to speak with him concerning the commands of the Lord Pope. The Abbot was dismayed and said, ' I am beset with trouble on every side, and I shall offend either God or the King. By the true God, whatever may come of it afterwards, I will not wittingly lie.' So coming home in all haste, since he was somewhat troubled by his bodily weakness and was humble and timid beyond his wont, he sought counsel of us through the Prior—a thing which he had very rarely done before—and asked how he should act in defence of the liberties of his Church which were in peril, and how his expenses could be met, if he went on this journey, and to whom he should commit the custody of the Abbey, and what he should do about his poor servants who had served him for so long. And the answer was given him that he himself should go, and should borrow sufficient money, which should be repaid from our sacristy, our pittances and other revenues according as he should desire ; and that he should entrust the Abbey to the custody of the Prior and some

dam et alicui clerico, quem diuitem fecerat, et qui
interim posset uiuere de suo, ut ita parceretur expensis
abbatis, et cuilibet de seruientibus suis denarios daret
secundum quod seruierat. Illo autem audiente tale
F.162 v consilium / gratum habuit : et factum est ita. Ueniens
ergo abbas in capitulum proxima die, antequam recessit,
fecit portari secum omnes libros suos, et eos ecclesie et
conuentui presentauit, et commendauit consilium nostrum, quod significaueramus ei per priorem.

Interim murmurantes quosdam audiuimus, dicentes
quod abbas diligens est et sollicitus de libertatibus baronie
sue, set de libertatibus conuentus, quas perdidimus tempore suo, scilicet de curia et libertatibus celerarii[1] amissis,?
et de libertatibus sacristie[2] super prefectis uille insti-
tuendis per conuentum, nichil loquitur. Suscitauit itaque
Dominus spiritum[3] in tribus fratribus mediocris intelligentie, qui, accitis pluribus aliis, conuenerunt inde
priorem consulentes, ut inde loqueretur cum abbate, et
rogaret eum ex nostra parte, ut in recessu suo prouideret
indemnitati ecclesie sue de libertatibus illis. Abbas hoc
audiens, plura non dicenda respondit, iurans se fore
dominum quamdiu uiueret. Uespere autem adueniente,
micius inde locutus est cum priore. In crastino uero,
recessurus et licentiam petiturus, in capitulo sedens, dixit
se pacasse omnes seruientes suos, et testamentum suum
fecisse, sicut tunc temporis deberet mori, et incipiens
loqui de libertatibus illis, excusauit se, dicens se mutasse
antiquas consuetudines ne esset defectus regalis iustitie ;

---

[1] See pp. 102ff.
[2] See pp. 74ff.
[3] Dan. xiii. 45 (Vulg.)

clerk whom he had enriched, so that he could live on his own purse for the time being, thereby sparing the Abbot's expenditure, and could also give money to each of the Abbot's servants according to his service. And this counsel pleased the Abbot when he heard it : and thus it was done. Therefore the Abbot, coming into the chapterhouse on the day before his departure, caused all his books to be brought with him and presented them to the Church and Convent ; and he commended our counsel, which we had made known to him through the Prior.

Meanwhile we heard certain persons murmuring and saying that the Abbot was zealous and anxious about the liberties of his barony, but never said a word about the liberties of the Convent which we had lost in his time— to wit, the loss of the court and liberties of the Cellarer —nor about the liberties of the Sacrist as regards the appointing of the town reeves with the assent of the Convent. And so the Lord stirred up the spirit of three brethren of moderate understanding, who, calling in a number of others, spoke to the Prior, counselling him to speak with the Abbot upon the matter and to ask him on our behalf that, on his departure, he would make provision that his Church should suffer no loss in respect of his liberties. When the Abbot heard this, he said things which he ought not to have said, swearing that he would be master as long as he lived. But as evening drew near, he spoke more gently with the Prior, and on the morrow, when he was about to depart and take his leave, he said as he sat in Chapter that he had satisfied all his servants and had made his will, as though he were near his end ; and then beginning to speak of those liberties, he excused himself saying that he had changed ancient customs to prevent default of the King's justice ;

et retorsit culpam in sacristam, et dixit, quod, si Durandus prefectus, tunc infirmus, moreretur, sacrista teneret prefecturam in manu sua, et poneret prefectum coram capitulo, sicut consuetudo antiquitus fuerat, sic tamen ut hoc fieret per consilium abbatis ; set dona et xennia annuatim a prefecto facienda nullo modo remitteret. Cum uero quereremus quid fieret de curia celerarii amissa, et precipue de obolis quos celerarius solebat accipere ad plegios renouandos,[1] commotus inde quesiuit, qua auctoritate exigeremus ius regale, et ea que ad regales consuetudines pertinent : et responsum est, quod illud a fundamentis ecclesie semper habuimus, et eciam iii. annis postquam suscepit abbatiam, et hanc libertatem habemus in omnibus maneriis nostris ad renouacionem plegiorum. Et diximus, quod pro c. solidis, quos priuate accipiebat de prefecto singulis annis, non deberemus

F.163 amittere ius nostrum ; et audacte petiui/mus saisinam qualem habuimus suo etiam tempore. Abbas uero, quasi in arto positus quid responderet, uolens nos in pace relinquere et pacifice recedere, iussit ut oboli illi, et cetera que celerarius exigebat, ponerentur in sequestro usque ad reditum suum ; et promisit quod in reditu suo cum consilio nostro operaretur in singulis, iuste dispositurus, et unicuique redditurus quod suum esse debet. Hiis dictis, facta est tranquillitas, set non magna, quia

pollicitis diues quilibet esse potest.[2]

---

[1] See pp. 102 sqq.
[2] Ovid, *Ars Amatoria*, I. 444

THE CHRONICLE OF JOCELIN OF BRAKELOND   137

and he threw the blame on the Sacrist, and said that if
Durand the town-reeve, who was then ill, should die,
the Sacrist should have the reeveship in his hands and
should propose a name in the presence of the Chapter
according to the ancient custom, yet that this should
none the less be done by the Abbot's counsel. But he said
that he would in no wise remit the gifts and presents
which were due every year from the reeve. But when
we asked what was to be done concerning the loss of the
Cellarer's court and more especially of the halfpence
which he used to receive for the renewal of pledges, he
was moved thereat and asked us by what authority we
demanded a royal right and things pertaining to royal
customs : and the answer was given him that we had
possessed that right ever since the foundation of our
Church, and even during the first three years of his own
abbacy, and that we still possessed this liberty of renew-
ing pledges in all our manors. And we said that we ought
not to lose our right for the sake of a hundred shillings
which he privily received from the reeve every year ;
and we boldly demanded such seizin as we had even in
his own time. But the Abbot finding himself in a strait
how to reply and wishing to leave us in quiet and depart
in peace, gave orders that those halfpence and the other
dues exacted by the Cellarer should be sequestrated until
his return ; and he promised that on his homecoming
he would in all things work with our counsel and would
make just disposition and restore to every man that
which was his own. This done, there was a calm, but
not a great calm, since

in promises there's none but may be rich.

Robertus de Kokefelda recognouit domino abbati S.,
multis presentibus, scilicet, magistro W. de Banham,
fratre W. de Dice, capellanis, Willelmo de Breitona, et
multis aliis, se nullum ius hereditarium habere debere
in uillis de Grotona et Semere, quia tempore regis
Stephani, pace turbata, monachi Sancti Ædmundi, cum
consensu abbatis, concesserunt predictas ii uillas Ade
Cokefeldo patri suo, tenendas omnibus diebus uite sue ;
scilicet, Semere reddendo annuatim c. solidis, et Grotone
faciendo annuatim unam firmam pro ea.   Qui Adam
potuit defendere predictas uillas contra castellanos uicinos
contra W. de Mildinges, contra W. de Ambli, utpote
habens castrum suum uicinum predictis maneriis, scilicet,
castellum de Leleseia.   Post mortem predicti A., concesserunt predicta maneria Roberto de Kokefelda, filio
ipsius A., dupplicata censa de Semere, reddendo scilicet
annuatim pro ea x. libras, quamdiu dominus abbas et
conuentus uellent ; set nunquam cartam inde habuit,
nec etiam ad terminum uite sue.   Cartas bonas habuit
de omnibus tenementis que iure hereditario tenuit de
Sancto Ædmundo, quas ego Willelmus, dictus de Dicia,
tunc temporis capellanus, legi, multis audientibus, in
presentia abbatis predicti ; scilicet, de terris Leleseia,
quas Wlfricus de Leleseia tenuit in eadem uilla de Sancto
Ædmundo ; cartam abbatis et conuentus de socagiis de
Rutham, quas domina Rohais de Kokefelda, uxor quondam Ade iunioris, habet in dotem ; de terris etiam quas
Lemmerus progenitor suus habuit in uilla de Kokefelda
iure hereditario, que, tempore regis Stephani, per consensum A. abbatis Sancti Ædmundi, attornate fuerunt in

[Appendix on the lands of Robert of Cockfield, by William of Diss]

Robert of Cockfield acknowledged to the Lord Abbot
Samson, in the presence of many persons, to wit, Master
W. of Banham, brother William of Diss, chaplains,
William of Breiton and many others, that he could not
claim to have any hereditary right in the townships of
Groton and Semer, in virtue of the fact that, when
peace was disturbed in the time of King Stephen, the
monks of St. Edmund, with the consent of the Abbot,
granted the two townships aforesaid to Adam of Cockfield, his father, to be held for all the days of his life ;
to wit, Semer, for an annual payment of a hundred
shillings and Groton for a fixed annual rent. This
same Adam was able to defend the two townships aforesaid against the neighbouring castellans, against W. of
Milden, against W. of Ambli, since he had a castle of
his own close to the aforesaid manors, to wit the castle
of Lindsey. After the death of the said Adam, they
granted the manors aforesaid to Robert of Cockfield,
Adam's son, the rent of Semer being doubled, to an
annual payment of ten pounds, as long as this should
be the will of the Abbot and Convent ; but he never,
even to the end of his life, had any charter for it. He
had good charters for all the tenements which he held
of St. Edmund by hereditary right, which charters, I,
William of Diss, at that time chaplain, read aloud in
the hearing of many and in the presence of the aforesaid
Abbot ; to wit for the lands of Lindsey, which Wulfric
of Lindsey held in the same township of St. Edmund ;
a charter of the Abbot and convent for the socages of
Rougham, which the Lady Rohais of Cockfield, formerly
the wife of Adam the younger, now holds in dower ;
for the lands also which Lemmer his grandfather held
in the township of Cockfield by hereditary right, which

feodum dimidii militis, cum primo essent socagia Sancti
Ædmundi. Cartas etiam habuit abbatis et conuentus
sancti Ædmundi de terris, que sunt in uilla Sancti
F.163v Ædmundi ; de terra, scilicet,/Hemfridi Criketot, ubi
domus domine Adelitie site quondam fuerunt, habent
cartam et hereditariam per seruitium xii. denariorum ;
magnum mesuagium, ubi aula Ade de Kokefelda primi
quondam sita fuit, cum berefrido ligneo septies xx. pedum
in altitudine, eis confirmatum fuit hereditarie per cartam
abbatis et conuentus, in qua carta distinguitur longitudo
et latitudo ipsius platie et mesuagii, tenendum per
seruicium ii. solidorum. Cartam etiam habent hereditariam de terris, quas Robertus de Kokefelda, filius
Odonis de Kokefelda, modo tenet in Bertona ; set cartam
nullam habent de uilla de Kokefelda, illa scilicet porcione
que ad uictum pertinet monachorum Sancti Ædmundi,
nisi breue unum Regis Henrici primi, per quod mandat
abbati Anselmo ut permittat Ade de Kokefelda primo,
tenere in pace firmam de Kokefeld et alias, quamdiu
plene firmas reddiderit : breue autem illud sigillatum
est tantum ex una parte, formam regiam representans,
contra formam omnium breuium regalium. Robertus
tamen de Kokefelda recognouit, in presencia domini
abbatis et predictorum, se credere Kokefelda esse ius
suum hereditarium propter longam tenuram ; quia auus
suus Lemmerus tenuit illud manerium diu ante mortem
suam, et Adam primus, filius ipsius, tempore uite sue,
et ipse Robertus tota uita sua, fere lx. annis ; set nunquam cartam abbatis seu conuentus Sancti Ædmundi
de predicta terra habuerunt.

lands in the time of King Stephen, were, with the assent of Anselm, Abbot of St. Edmund, assigned to a half knight's fee, having previously been socages of St. Edmund. He also had charters of the Abbot and Convent of St. Edmund for lands which are in the township of St. Edmund ; for the land, to wit, of Hemfrid Criketot, where the houses of Lady Adelisia were once situated they hold a charter of hereditary right, by service of twelve pence. The great messuage, where the hall of Adam the first of Cockfield was once situated, together with a wooden belfry, seven score feet high, was confirmed to them with hereditary right by a charter of the Abbot and Convent, in which charter the length and breadth of the place and messuage are set down, to be held by service of two shillings. They also have a hereditary charter for the lands which Robert of Cockfield, the son of Odo of Cockfield, now holds in Barton ; but they have no charter for the township of Cockfield, that portion of it, to wit, which is assigned for the livelihood of the monks of St. Edmund, but only a writ of King Henry the First, whereby he charges Abbot Anselm to suffer Adam the first of Cockfield to hold the lease of Cockfield and others, as long as he pays his rent in full. Now that writ is sealed only with one side of the seal, namely that which represents the person of the King, in which respect it runs counter to the form observed in all royal writs. But Robert of Cockfield acknowledged in the presence of the Lord Abbot and the aforesaid, that he believed Cockfield to be his by hereditary right owing the length of time for which it had been held ; for his grandfather Lemmer held that manor long before his death, and Adam the first, his son, held it all the days of his life, and he, Robert, had held it for almost sixty years ; but they never had any charter of the Abbot or Convent of St. Edmund for the aforesaid land.

APPENDIX

A (page 17)

domi. It was fortunate that this proposal was not accepted, as is shown by what happened after Samson's death in 1212. When letters were received from King John (July 1213) bidding the Convent send representatives fully empowered to elect an Abbot according to the custom of the realm, the monks, presuming perhaps on the quarrel between Rome and the Crown, nominated seven of their number to choose an Abbot ; these seven unanimously chose Hugh de Northwold and presented that name alone. The King, having expected them to submit several names, according to the custom which had been brought into existence after the concordat between Anselm and Henry I, was very angry and refused to accept their choice till 1215. See De electione Hugonis Abbatis, *Mem.* II.

B (page 24)

Martiri. The words run : *Martiri adhuc palpitanti, sed Christum confitenti iussit Hinguar caput auferri, sicque Eadmundus martyrium consummauit et ad Deum exultans uadit.* 'This response occurs with the musical notes in the office for the Feast of St Edmund in a MS Life and Miracles of the Saint of the time of Abbot Anselm . . . the response follows the sixth lesson in the Mattins.' Rokewode p. 115. It may have been composed by Warnerius, Abbot of Rebais, see Herman (*Mem.* I, p. 70). The MS was originally in the Towneley Library, and is described by Rokewode as having been bought by Mr. Booth, bookseller, London. It was purchased by Robert Holford in 1841, and remained in possession of his family till 1927, when it was bought for the Pierpont Morgan Library, in which it is now MS 736. It has been fully described in *New Palaeographical Society, First Series* (Plates 113–15). I am indebted to Mr. F. Wormald for its history after sale by Mr. Booth.

C (page 28)

liberorum hominum. In Samson's Kalendarium the free tenants are divided into *liberi homines* and *sochemanni*, as in the Feudal Book of Baldwin (FD p. clxviii). The distinction had been real but was now blurred (cp. Vinogradoff, *Growth of Manor*, pp. 341–3). In the Kalendarium they fall into different classes, some owing suit to the Hundred Court, others to the *aula* or 'hall' (*i.e.* Manorial Court), cp. FD p. clx *n*). There is also a reference to *altum socagium* : see Gage (Rokewode), *History of Suffolk, Hundred of Thingoe*, where the portion of the Kalendarium describing that hundred is printed in full.

D (page 29)

letis. The hundred is divided into leets and the leets into vills. Cp. the opening of the description of the Hundred of Thingoe (Gage, *op. cit.* p. xii). *In Hundredo de Tingehowe sunt uiginti uille ex quibus constituuntur nouem lete.* A leet might however contain no more than one vill, *e.g. Fwepstede per se est una leta.* This division into leets is peculiar to E. Anglia ; its relation to the hundred is obscure. It is found in E. Anglian Domesday ' composed of a group of vills which contribute so much geld to each pound paid by the hundred.' It is also ' a unit of jurisdiction which owes suit to the hundred and has a separate suit of its own.' 'It was, at any rate in some cases, an economic unit as well ' : D. C. Douglas, *Social Structure of E. Anglia*, pp. 193ff ; FD clxi sqq.

E (page 29)

Suthreia. Southery in the hundred of Clackclose, Norfolk, S. of Downham Market and not far from the Suffolk border. The manor belonged to the Convent, not to the Abbot, and Jocelin accuses the Abbots from the time of ' Edmund the golden monk ' of having unjustly received sixty shillings from Southery, which should have gone to the Convent. A document printed by Douglas (FD p. 139) throws some light upon the matter ; it is addressed by Abbot Hugh ' to all to whom these letters may come,' and states that in the time of Abbot Ording the sum of sixty shillings, which should have been paid to the Convent, had been appropriated by Radulphus de Hastinges, presumably identical with the person of that name who was Steward of the Abbey (see FD p. 97) ; at the end of his life, however, he repented of his sins and restored the sixty shillings to the Convent. Abbot Hugh then proceeds to say that he now orders that from thenceforth the Convent shall possess this manor ' with the augmentation of sixty shillings ' ; but he admits that in the interim since the death of Radulphus he has ' at times converted the sixty shillings to his own use, but never as of his right or due, but always by permission of his brethren.' Of ' the golden monk ' nothing appears to be known.

F (page 33)

glebe ascripto. The phrase is applied (1) to serfs or born bondsmen performing villeins' services ; (2) ' Freemen holding tenements by free services or free customs at the time of the Conquest who, when ejected by the mighty, came back and received the same tenements to hold in villeinage by doing servile works ; and they are called *glebe ascripticii* and none

the less free men ; for albeit they do servile works, they do
these not by personal status, but by reason of their tenure ;
their tenement is villeinage, though privileged villeinage, and
they are called *glebe ascripticii*, because they enjoy the privilege of
of not being removed from the soil so long as they do their right
services.' Bracton ; see PM. I. p. 389. It is to this latter class
that the man here mentioned clearly belongs.

G (pages 45, 46)

Mildenhala. Mildenhall, in Breckland (Hundred of Lackford),
given to the Abbey by Edward the Confessor ; see App. K.
Stigand, while Bishop of Elmham, asked the monks to lend it to
him, which they did, fearing to offend their diocesan. When
at a later date, being then Archbishop of Canterbury, he fell
into disgrace and was deposed, William the Conqueror appropriated it. It remained a crown land until its repurchase by
Samson ; see Dugdale, *Mon.* III, pp. 154-5. Valued in
Edward's reign at £40, its value had risen to £70 in Domesday (f. 288*b*). Samson offered five hundred marks for it on
the basis of that assessment, the Great Roll of Winchester
being but another name for Domesday Book. The King's
demand of a thousand marks (£666 13s. 4d.) was based on the
reasonable assumption that the annual value of the manor
had increased to at least £100. The purchase money was
paid in 1190 (PR. Norf. Suff. 2 Rich. I). The Manor belonged
to the Convent.

H (page 46)

Ellienor. As Queen Mother she was entitled to the ' Queen's
gold,' the King being still unmarried (Sept. 1189). She
accepted the gold cup, which Henry II had given to the Abbey,

as the equivalent of the sum which was her due. Later in 1193, when the church plate of England was requisitioned as a contribution to the King's ransom (Hoveden, III. 209) the cup was sent to London, the Queen bought the cup for 100 silver marks which she paid into the fund collected for the ransom ; the cup itself was sent back to the Abbey on condition that it should never be alienated. The ratio assumed between the gold and the silver mark is here 10:1 a little above the ratio 9:1, given by Lane Poole as normal at this time. The Queen's charter is preserved in Sacr. Reg. p. 27 (Camb. pp. ii, 33).

I (pages 48, 63)

Ecclesia de Wlpit. Woolpit lies eight miles E. of Bury in the hundred of Thedwestrey. The Church had belonged to the Abbot and continued to belong to him (cp. 63), but from its revenues an annual payment of ten marks was due to the Convent for the benefit of sick monks. Of this sum the monks had been deprived for more than sixty years (see 49), *i.e.* from before 1123, possibly because it had become the practice of the reigning King to demand it in frankalmoin for one of his clerks. The living became vacant in 1159 or 1160, and it was hoped that the monks would now recover their due. Fearing that Abbot Hugh desired to continue the abuse, they sent their representatives to Rome to secure their rights. Of these Samson, though not yet a monk, was one. He succeeded in securing a letter from the Pope granting the monks their desire. Two papal documents exist in which reference is made to this matter. (1) A letter dated Jan. 10, 1161, in which Alexander III lays it down that when vacant the church should return *in usus fratrum* (see *Mem.* III, p. 79, Pensio de Woolpit). This, however, is a long document addressed to Abbot Hugh and his monks, wherein the sentence dealing with Woolpit occupies little more than one line, while most of it deals

with other matters such as the appropriation of certain manors
to certain uses ; and it is to be noted that these appropria-
tions do not specially concern the monks.   Indeed the only
other matter that does closely concern them is the grant of the
privilege to be ordained by any Bishop they may choose.   Moreover the tone of the whole letter is markedly kind and courteous ;
he actually praises the Abbot for the reforms he has made in the
interest of the monks (sc. *ea uero que ab aliis abbatibus in denariis
cibariis et potu cum multo grauamine fratrum a cellerario monasterii
quondam solebant exigere, sicut a te rationabiliter remissa sunt et
statuta, ita nos apostolica auctoritate confirmamus*).   (2) A very short
letter addressed to Abbot Hugh alone, dated May 23, but
without indication of the year.   After the formal opening it
continues :   *Unde quia ecclesia de Wolpet monasterii uestri usibus
est, sicut accepimus, deputata et apostolica auctoritate confirmata,
uobis . . . indulgemus ut episcopo Norwicensi uel eius ministris ad
eandem ecclesiam idoneos clericos presentare possitis, qui de ipsa ecclesia
competenter uite necessaria percipiant et episcopo et ministris suis
rationabiles consuetudines persoluant et reliquum cedat in usus conuentus*
(*Mem.* III, p. 85).   This letter was clearly written when the
church of Woolpit was vacant, *i.e.* about 1161 or 1173.   The
letter is short and deals only with the theme of Woolpit ;   it
would have been easy for Samson to conceal, as he actually
states that he concealed it.   The words *sicut accepimus* well fit
the circumstances.   Finally the course recommended or permitted is that which was actually followed by Samson on the
present occasion (see on 36).   It may be urged that it is a very
mild document (cp. *indulgemus*) and can have given Samson
no assurance of success.   None the less, of these two documents it
is more likely that this is the one which Samson carried home
with him.   At any rate when Samson returned he found that the
church had been given to Geoffrey Ridell, presumably in frankalmoin.   Geoffrey probably vacated it in 1173 (on his appointment as Bishop of Ely) or in 1174 (after his consecration).   In

his place Walter of Coutances received it in frankalmoin at the request of the King (FD p. 102). But it is laid down in the Charter that, after the death or resignation of Walter, the church shall return to the use of the monks. Walter had now been made Bishop of Lincoln and had resigned the living, which now at last was free.

J (page 48)

Alexandrum et Octauianum. On Oct. 7, 1159 there were two candidates, the Cardinal Octavian supported by the party of the Emperor Barbarossa, and Cardinal Roland supported by the anti-imperialists. The latter was elected by a large majority ; but the party of the Emperor, refusing to accept this defeat, proclaimed Octavian Pope under the name of Victor IV, while his adversary was proclaimed under the name of Alexander III. Hostilities broke out and Alexander was forced to take refuge in France in 1162, only returning to Rome three years later.

K (pages 51, 65, 76)

A Charter closely resembling, if not identical with, that put forward by the Archbishop is preserved in the Library of Canterbury Cathedral (*Chartae antiquae*, C. 3). In it Edward the Confessor grants (*c.* 1052) to Archbishop Stigand, sac and soc, toll and team, grithbrece, hamsocne, forstal, infangthef and flaemene fioringe ('harbouring of outlaws') over all his land. As regards St. Edmunds, of the numerous charters given by Edward, which are printed by Kemble (*Cod. Dipl. Anglo-Sax.*), three are of outstanding importance : 883, 1346 (Latin version, 915) and 1342. All are undated ; but 883 certainly and 1342 probably, both date from 1044, the year of the original grant of the $8\frac{1}{2}$ hundreds. For 883 is addressed to Bishop Grimketel (intermittently Bishop of Elmham between 1038 and 1044), who held the see, when his rival Stigand was in disgrace (Nov. 1043–44), while 1346 reads like the original grant itself. (i) In 883 the King grants sac and soke over the 8½ hundreds held by his mother Emma. (ii) 1346 is of wider scope ; the 8½ hundreds are granted ' with all their town sokes in respect of their land which they now possess or may yet obtain,' a phrase which the Latin version (915) para- phrases *et omnium uillarum suarum iura regalia*. (iii) 1342, addressed to Stigand's brother, Bishop of Elmham (1047–70), and Earl Aelfgar (reinstated in Suffolk in 1053 and transferred to Mercia in 1057) grants or confirms possession of the 8½ hundreds ' as fully as her mother had them and Aelfric the son of Wihtgar held it on my behalf with hamsocne, grithbrece, forstal, fichtewite and ebberethef.' While all of these docu- ments may have been produced to counter the claims of Canterbury, the last (1342) perhaps ' fills the bill ' best, as it gives more detail, is on the same lines as the Canterbury charter and would be most likely to have called forth Henry's comment *carte adinuicem repugnant*. It may be added that 1346 grants also the manor of Mildenhall and freedom from geld, while it further forbids the establishment of any other monastic order in the town of St. Edmund ; it may also be noted that in the Pinchbeck register (14th cent.), f. 130, the Latin trans- lation of this charter is headed *optima carta de libertatibus*. For a discussion of these charters cp. H. W. C. Davis (E.H.R. xxiv, 417ff.). The marginal note in Jocelin (see text) carries no weight, though it is right in claiming that St. Edmund held an older charter.

L (page 61)

Hopetuna. Hopton (Blackburne) belonged to the Abbot. The story of the dispute is inadequately told by Jocelin, and must be supplemented by the version given in Camb. MS Mm. 4. 19, ff. 122–3, which runs : 'A dispute arose between Samson, Abbot of St. Edmund and Robert de Holmia concerning the advowson of half the church of Hopton, on the death of Nicholas the chaplain, parson of the said half. They therefore met on a certain day in the said church, and with them were Gilbert FitzRalph, who was, after the Abbot, the chief lord of the fee, and Robert de Cockfield, who held it of him ; and from the latter Robert de Holmia held the fee to which that advowson was said to belong. By common consent they chose seventeen law-worthy men and placed themselves upon their verdict concerning the right of the advowson. After taking counsel together they said that Abbot Anselm had given that half to Nicholas and that this was the right of the Abbot. But Jordan de Ros proclaimed that he was the parson of that half of the church, and on being cited to the Exchequer, because he seemed to deprive the Abbot of the advowson, he showed a charter of Abbot Hugh, with the seal of the Convent, giving the whole church of Hopton to himself, in the presence of Ranulph de Glanvill, Hubert Walter and others, including Robert de Cockfield and Gilbert FitzRalph.' To this Jocelin adds the detail that Abbot Hugh and Robert de Ulmo had both given him the Church and that Nicholas was his vicar in respect of half the church and received a stipend from him. From this we may conclude that the Abbey owed one half and Robert de Ulmo (or de Holmia) owed the other. The Abbot lost his case, but saved his face by the compromise which follows. The date is 1191.

M (page 62)

Herlaua. Harlow in Essex (Half-hundred of Harlow). Here again the story given by Jocelin must be supplemented by the ampler version in the same MS. (f. 123). 'A controversy arose between Abbot Samson and Master Jordan de Ros, parson of the church, about the land which Erardus held in the township of Harlow, on the ground that this land was a free fief of the church. The Abbot demanded a writ of recognition to settle the matter. Twelve recognitors were therefore nominated. At length they received permission from the King's Justiciar that the recognition should be held in the court of Harlow by the same recognitors. It was so done in the presence of the Hundred in the churchyard of Harlow ; and the oath was made and verdict given, and a writing was made out in triplicate, the Abbot receiving one copy, Master Jordan a second, and Michael the provost of the Hundred a third, in this form of words : ' This is the verdict of the recognitors concerning the land which Herardus held, concerning which a dispute arose between the Abbot of St. Edmund and Jordan de Ros. They say that that land and the church of Harlow have never been separate in the days of their lifetime, but that the parson always held that same land in return for such service, as the land of Maurice and Eustace is held of the King and of the Abbot for forty acres of lands in all kinds of services.' The names of the *iuratores* follow, and the passage concludes : ' Master Jordan de Ros afterwards recognised in full court at St. Edmund's that the land was a lay fief, and the land was granted to him to be held during his life by service of twelve pence.' Jocelin says nothing of the presence of the Hundred ; and the holding of the recognition before the Hundred Court would seem to be an abnormal proceeding. It may be noted that the Half-Hundred of Harlow like the Hundred of Stowe (Suffolk) had been granted to the Abbey by Stephen (see FD p. 90). But these grants seem to have been revoked after the death of Stephen. It would appear that Jocelin has confused the proceedings at Harlow with the final appearance of Jordan in the Abbot's Court at St. Edmunds.

N (page 64)

staffacres et foracres. Etymologically the most natural meaning of
' staffacres ' would be acres enclosed by a wooden fence of
staves. There is no authority for supposing that they were
dues payable to the Abbot's staff or crozier. ' Foracres ' are
headlands ; cp. Orwin, *The Open Fields*, pp. 34–5. Lands
cannot be ploughed right up to the edge of the fields if the
boundary be a fence or stream. The plough-team and plough
must have room to turn, leaving a margin of 15 to 20 feet.
This margin at top and bottom is called ' headland ' in most
parts of the country. In E. Kent it is still known as ' foraker,'
and the same name is found in Medieval German, *sc.* ' voracker.'
The headland itself was ploughed lengthwise, when the rest
of the field was finished. That these staffacres brought in
revenue is clear (cp. FD 141) for a charter of Abbot Hugh
granting ' Henry, son of Henry, the Clerk ' *stafacre* from places
scattered over the lands of St. Edmund, reaching from Stapleford Abbots in Essex to Rungcton Holme in Norfolk. It would
seem possible that staffacres and foracres were small pieces of
land separated from the open field, for which a small rent was
paid, the difference between them being that the staffacre was
enclosed, while the foracre was a headland necessarily left
unenclosed. We may perhaps compare the ' forlands ' mentioned in P. Vinogradoff, *Growth of the Manor*, pp. 330–1.
He states that farmers, settlers and squatters were accom-
modated in this way with small plots on the demesne. A for-
land would be out of the ordinary course of cultivation of the
open field community, and was managed in severalty by the
tenant who got a lease for a term of years or for life. The
reclaiming of the waste under the leadership and licence of
the manorial administration mostly took this course. In the
charter printed by Douglas (*loc. cit.*) it is associated with
decimationes and *decimae*.

O (page 65)

Abbas Samson iniit certamen. While the general sense of this long
sentence is fairly clear, it is (1) ungrammatical, and (2) rendered
unnecessarily obscure in Rokewode's text which brackets
proposuit . . . tenebant as a parenthesis. The difficulty lies in
the fact that *quare . . . militum* requires a verb of asking. The
simplest solution is to place a colon after *omnes contra eum,*
delete the brackets, and assume that a participle or gerund
has dropped out after *tenebant, e.g. interrogans* or *interrogando.*
The error may however go back to Jocelin himself.

The quarrel had first arisen immediately after Samson's election
(see page 27). He had then sworn to have his revenge, and
now fourteen years later (1196) the time was come. The actual
position requires some explanation. When William the Conqueror fixed the military service to the Crown, he left his tenants
free to furnish their contingents as they chose. Many enfeoffed
more than the number of knights demanded by the king, and
derived considerable profit by these extra feoffments. Henry II,
wishing to secure these profits himself, in 1166 issued a writ
ordering his tenants-in-chief to inform him how many of their
knights were enfeoffed before the death of Henry I, and how
many since. Having secured this information, at the next
levy—an *auxilium* in connection with his daughter Matilda
(1168)—he demanded from his tenants-in-chief payment in
respect of all their knights, whether enfeoffed before or after
1135. On this basis the Abbot should have paid in full for
fifty-two and a half knights (see H. M. Chew, *English Ecclesiastical Tenants-in-Chief*, pp. 15ff.). The extra sum in respect
of the twelve and a half knights was actually demanded in
1168, and again in connection with the ' Scutage of Ireland ' ;
but in neither case was it ever paid, as the Pipe Rolls testify from
1168–96. The practice of the knights of St. Edmund was to
provide the sum demanded in respect of the service of forty
knights by the contribution of an equal quota from each of the

fifty-two and a half. Samson now demanded full service from
each one of them, and won his case, first in his own Court, and
then in the King's Court, thereby increasing his revenues by
the full contributions of the extra twelve and a half knights.

P (page 67)

ad wardam castelli. This service had at an earlier date been
either challenged or neglected by the Abbey (see FD p. 160).
The situation was now as follows : the castle of Norwich had
now, like other royal castles, a permanent guard, the personal
service of the knights having been commuted to a money payment ; the forty knights of St. Edmund owing this service had
to pay a total of 120 shillings ; but this total was actually
provided by equal contributions from 50 knights. The first
four constabularies each, at intervals of 20 weeks, produce
30 shillings, at the rate of 3 shillings per knight ; each 3 shillings
is made up of 28 pence plus a penny for the ' marshall ' plus
7 pence from a knight of the fifth constabulary. The total of
120 shillings is thus collected over a period of 80 weeks. After
Samson's victory (recorded above) each of the 50 knights pays
3 shillings, thus making a total of 150 shillings. The Abbot
therefore pockets 30 shillings for each period of 80 weeks, less
the amount which he has to pay owing to the default of Roger
Bigot's three knights. To make good this default he had previously paid 7 shillings (*i.e.* 28 pence per knight), the penny
due to the marshall being ignored : under the new system
on this basis he would pay 8 shillings and 9 pence. Jocelin
does not say whether the interval of 20 weeks was reduced to
16. But as he clearly regards 16 as the correct interval, we may
perhaps assume that the reduction was made, and that each
of the five constabularies paid its due at the end of 16 weeks,
the total period of 80 weeks being retained. How this
period of 80 weeks came to be adopted is not clear. For a

writ of Stephen (see FD p. 84) enjoins that each turn of service should be for three months, and this is further supported by the fact that the ' waite-fe ' was paid four times in the year. One can only assume that while personal service was required, the turn of three months was normal, but that when the payment of castle guard took its place the turn was lengthened. A short period would be in the interest of those called upon to serve in person, a longer period more acceptable for the collection of money. It may further be noted that whereas the total number of knight's fees was $52\frac{1}{2}$ or $52\frac{3}{4}$ (see Appendix O, p. 152), Jocelin once more gives the number as 50. That there were ten knights in each of the first four Constabularies is clear from the list given by Douglas (FD p. lxxxvi). Concerning the organisation of the fifth constabulary we have no information.

Q (pages 85, 28)

Precepit rex Ricardus. In 1197. Hoveden (IV. 40) gives an account which differs considerably from that which is here given by Jocelin, for he states that Richard demanded from all his tenants-in-chief that they should ' find him three hundred knights to remain with him in service for one year or that they should give him so much money as would suffice him to keep three hundred knights in service for a year at the rate of three shillings per day ; and whereas all the rest were ready to do so, Hugh, Bishop of Lincoln, a true servant of God, replied for himself that he would in no wise obey the King in this respect.' The statement that lay tenants-in-chief were also involved does not contradict Jocelin ; for the latter is only concerned with ecclesiastical tenants. But the assertions that the King offered to accept a money alternative and that he demanded a year's service are in absolute contradiction with Jocelin's account. The King did, it is true, eventually, after a blank refusal, allow Samson to compound for a sum of £100 ; but that is far less than the total required for a year's service of four knights at three shillings a day. Jocelin's relation is contemporary, and in itself more probable ; since forty days' service was a normal, if not a universal, condition. On the other hand Jocelin's statement that the Bishop of London got into trouble receives no support in other quarters ; and as a matter of fact the Bishop of London, Richard FitzNigel, actually obeyed the King's demand. The only Bishops who absolutely refused seem to have been Hugh of Lincoln, who stood firm and eventually emerged victorious from the struggle ; and Herbert of Salisbury, whose lands were, at any rate for the time being, seized by the King (cp. Gervase of Canterbury I. 549) ; *Magna uita S. Hugonis* (pp. 240–50). It is conceivable that Jocelin's *Londiniensi* is a slip for *Lincolniensi*. For a discussion of the whole matter, see Round, *Feudal England*, pp. 528ff. ; Chew, *Eccl. Tenants-in-chief*, pp. 42 and 57.

R (page 94)

commissio domini pape. This was granted by Celestine III, whose letter is given *in extenso* by Hoveden (IV. 357). The re-investiture of the monks by the Archbishop took place on Jan. 18, 1198. R. Wendover (II. 275 ; cp. M. Paris, *Chr. Maj.*, II. 380 and 443–4) states that the Pope in question was Innocent III ; and it is true that Innocent III did order the complete restoration of the monks of Coventry (June 3, 1198) : see *Letters* of Innocent III (ed. Migne,) I. p. 208. This letter is almost identical with that of Celestine, save that the persons appointed to carry out his commands are the Archbishop of Canterbury, the Bishops of Worcester and Lincoln, and the Abbot of Tewkesbury, and that there are a few verbal diver-gences of no importance ; like Celestine he assumes that Hugh Nonant, the Bishop of Coventry, who had ejected the monks in 1190 and substituted secular canons, was still alive. He had actually died on March 27, 1198, at Bec, repenting of the wrong that he had done (Matt. Paris, *Chr. Maj.* II. 380). Why Innocent III should have thought it necessary to repeat the letter of his predecessor is uncertain. We must assume that he was ignorant of the fact that the re-investiture of the monks had taken place, or that there were some doubts as to the validity of the earlier commission, or that delays had arisen as to the restitution of some of the possessions of the monastery. The story that he took action because of the importunity of an exiled monk of Coventry (cp. Wendover and M. Paris, 11. cc.) need not be taken too seriously, though the incident may possibly have occurred. It may be noted that he appointed a further commission in Feb. 1199 (*Cal. Pap. Lett.* I. p. 5), by which the Bishops of Winchester and Lincoln and the Abbot of St. Edmund's are ordered to settle matters in dispute between the monks and the new Bishop Geoffrey Muschamp. But the reinvestiture described by Jocelin was in any case the first step towards the settlement of a long and bitter quarrel. The story of the original dispute may be summarised as follows. In 1188 Hugh Nonant claimed that Pope Clement III had conferred the Priory and its domain upon him (Wendover and M. Paris, 11. cc.). After violent altercations, in the course of which the Bishop was hit on the head with a processional cross, the monastery was surrendered into his hands in 1190, and secular canons were subsequently introduced (*Red Book of the Exchequer*, I. 74). The monks appealed to Rome, and after eight years were restored. See also Gervase I. 550, Richard of Devizes, pp. 64–7.

S (page 120)

descripcio de militibus. The total is 52¾. Douglas (FD p. lxxxvi) gives a list dealing with the forty knights owing service to the Crown, who are grouped in their four constabularies ; he dates it ' about 1200.' It is, however, almost certainly a little later, since in one case a knight of Jocelin's list (Walter de Saxham) is replaced by his son, and in three other cases Hugo de Illega, Gilbertus de Manetuna, Normannus de Manetuna, Normannus de Risebi are replaced by minors of the same family. In Douglas' list each constabulary is headed by its constable (I. Thomas de Mendham ; II. Gilbertus filius Radulphi ; III. Reginaldus de Brockleye ; IV. Gerebertus de S. Claro). Of these T. de Mendham does not appear in Jocelin's list, but is probably concealed among the 5½ knights whose service was owed by Alberic de Ver ; for T. de Mendham owes service of 4 knights in Douglas' list, and Alberic de Ver owes 1½ ; while among the localities associated with Alberic's 5½ knights in Jocelin are found Mendham and Livermere, in both of which places T. de Mendham owed a knight's fee.

T (pages 132, 103)

Monachi de Hely. Jocelin's chronology is obscure, and he has at times lost himself in the narration of a series of events covering a considerable period. It is difficult to dovetail his account into the facts as we know them from the records. These are as follows :

(A) On March 25, 1201, the prior and monks of Ely secured a new charter from the King, allowing them to hold a weekly market at Lakingheath on Thursdays, *ita tamen quod non sit ad nocumentum uicinorum mercatorum* (*Rotuli Chartarum.* Record Commission, 91). Then must have followed the Abbey of St. Edmund's offer of compromise as described by Jocelin. When this was rejected, Samson in return for 40 marks and two palfreys obtained from King John a charter (dated 17 August 1201) forbidding the holding of any market or fair within the liberties of St. Edmund, *ubi esse non debet nec solet ad nocumentum uille et mercati illarum libertatum nec ubi mercatum uel feria possit esse ad nocumentum illarum libertatum* (Rotulus de oblatis. Record Commission, p. 177, A.D. 1201). Cp. L. 172.

(B) The Abbot's next step is recorded in the Rotulus de oblatis (p. 186, May 22, 1202, the last day of John's third regnal year). The Abbot gives fifty marks for an Inquisition *secundum con-suetudinem Anglorum* to decide whether the new market of the monks of Ely is to the detriment of the town and market of St. Edmund or no ; if it is to their detriment, it is to cease, and Geoffrey FitzPeter is ordered to see to it.

The inquiry took place in the Michaelmas term of 1202 (Curia Regis Rolls, II. 135–6). After a preliminary meeting the 16 knights acting as recognitors found, on their second meeting, that the market was to the detriment of St. Edmund, since flesh both living and dead, fish corn and other merchandise were sold there, which used to be carried to St. Edmund's market or to be sold therein ; and that the Abbot's *consuetudines* were thereby lost. On being asked how great the damage was, they replied that they did not know, nor did anyone know save only God. It may be noted that Jocelin seems to have con-fused the first documents cited in A and B, since he states the sum offered by the Abbey on the second occasion to have been forty marks, not fifty.

(C) But this was not all, for a wider issue had been raised by one or other of the parties (more probably by Ely) ; see Curia Regis Rolls, p. 136, the entry immediately preceding the above. It runs : *Assisa uenit recognitura si ecclesia Sancti Eadmundi saisita fuerit de assisa et de more consuetudinario de sectis et de uisu franci plegii et de placitis corone domini regis de tenentibus Sancte Athelrede infra uiii hundreda et dimidium abbatis Sancti Eadmundi.*

Both inquiries (B and C) were adjourned to the Octave of St. Hilary, 1203 ; the case of the market (B) for hearing judgement, the wider inquiry (C) for further consideration. Nothing was done on that date. C was adjourned owing to default of recognitors to three weeks after Easter. C.R.R. II. p. 140, while on pp. 141 and 163 we hear that the Abbot sent an attorney to hear judgement concerning Lakenheath ; on

p. 167 comes the entry : *dies datus est Episcopo Eliensi et Abbati Sancti Eadmundi de placito mercati de Lakenheath in octabis Medie Quadragesime* ; on p. 211 (Easter term) the Abbot once more sends an attorney. Finally on p. 266 we find this mutilated entry : *A die Sancte Trinitatis in xv dies. Loquela inter dominum Eliensem et Abbatem Scti Eadmundi de placito libertatum et inter eundem abbatem et priorem de Ely de mercato.* There the entry breaks off. The dispute over the market is not mentioned again. It is possible that the judgement was heard then. The dispute over the wider issues (*de placito libertatum*) was adjourned a number of times in 1203, 1204, 1205, 1206, 1207, until in 1208 (Hilary term) there occurs an entry describing a fresh dispute. The Abbot complains through his representative that the bailiffs of the Bishop of Ely have entered his liberties and buried a murdered man there *sine uisu seruientium abbatis.* The Bishop replies *quod aliquando questus fuit Abbas quod episcopus deforciabat ei uisum francorum plegiorum et sectam hominum suorum et alias libertates quas habere deberet infra hundreda sua,* and he goes on to remind the Abbot that it was agreed between them in the presence of the Archbishop Hubert Walter and the Justiciar Geoffrey FitzPeter that they would place themselves on a jury of 18 knights, 6 to be chosen by the Abbot, 6 by the Bishop, and 6 by the Archbishop and Justiciar, to recognise what seizin the Abbot had in the liberties he demanded ; and that the Bishop was then in seizin. See C.R.R. V. 132–3. The hearing of the case of the murdered man was put off to mid-Lent and then adjourned *sine die,* and we hear of it no more.

Such being the evidence of the records, it remains to be considered at what date the Abbot made the great raid on the market of Lakenheath—a violent procedure which led to his receiving a summons to appear *ad scaccarium.* It is at first sight attractive to suppose that it was in the autumn of 1202, immediately after the recognitors decided that the market at Lakenheath was detrimental to the market of St. Edmund. But the inquiry, apparently, was not ended then, but continues to recur till the summer of 1203 ; and it seems most unlikely that the King would have given orders for the removal of the market at this stage. Alternatively if we assume the final judgement to have been given on the last occasion on which the Market of Lakenheath appears in the records (a fortnight after Trinity Sunday, 1203), and that the judgement was in favour of the Abbey, we might place the raid somewhere near Midsummer 1203.

Whatever the end of this quarrel, analogous to that which had arisen with Canterbury over the erection of a weigh-beam at Monks Eleigh (see on f.135), and again over a case of homicide (see on p. 99), it was natural that feeling should run high on both sides. St. Edmund's claimed jurisdiction over the whole of the West Suffolk, which constituted its soke, while Canterbury and Ely claimed a large autonomy. The latter's claim may be judged from the statements attached to the description of all its manors lying within the soke of St. Edmund (see B. Mus. Cotton. Claud, C. xi). The claim for Rattlesden is typical (see FD clvii n). *Istud manerium est in comitatu Suffolchie et in hundredo de Thedwardestre quod est libertatis Sancti Eadmundi . . . sed istud manerium habet libertatem per se, sc. tol et them infongenthef hutfongenethef furchas tumberellum et uisum franci plegii lagenarum et aliarum mensurarum placitum namii uetiti et omnia placita quod potest placitare per breue domini regis et sine breui.*

The problem was obviously very hard to solve. It would be interesting to know whether the agreement between Abbot Samson and the Bishop of Ely to submit the question to 18 Recognitors was ever tried. Was it the body who met in the Michaelmas term of 1202 to decide whether ' the Church of St. E. was by assize and custom seized ' of the divers important rights mentioned in C (above), and if so was the agreement made when the Abbot was *summonitus ad scaccarium* ?

U (page 134)

Glemsford. A young man of Glemsford, another *enclave* of Ely
within the soke of St. Edmund, had been charged in the Abbot's
court with a breach of the King's peace. But he had escaped
arrest, and was for a long time demanded both by that court
and by the county court as well ; the county court had presumably intervened because the offence had been committed
outside the soke of St. Edmund, or because the accused was
believed to have escaped from the soke. He was at last produced
by the Seneschal of the Bishop of Ely in the county court, presumably that the claim of Ely might be established against that
of St. Edmund. The claims both of the Bishop and the Abbot
were disregarded and the matter was referred to the justices in
eyre. In so doing the sheriff was following the spirit, if not the
letter, of the principle laid down by Henry I (see W. Stubbs,
Select Charters, ed. 9, p. 122). But it was, none the less, galling
in the extreme to Samson, since the Abbey claimed *iura regalia*
within the soke of St. Edmund. It is not clear whether at this
time the justices in eyre functioned within the soke, though at
later date they did, though not within the bannaleuca of the town
of St. Edmund ; for it was privileged in this respect by an injunction of Henry I (see Douglas, FD p. 62), and the privilege
still existed in the time of Edward I. The practice in the rest of
the soke during the abbacy of Ording is thus described in Cambridge Univ. Lib., MS. ff. 2, 29 (*The Pinchbeck Register,* ed.
Lord F. Hervey, II. p. 298) : *Quocienscumque aliqua loquela de
aliquo homine de viii hundredis et dimidio cuiuscunque homo esset in
comitatibus exorta fuisset, Abbas sancti Edmundi siue dapifer eius
et ministri illius deracionando loquelam tulerunt secum ad curiam sancti
Edmundi ibique deducebatur qualiscunque loquela siue calumnia
fuisset excepto thesauro et murdro.* It is to be noted as regards the
claims of Ely that the claims of jurisdiction made by Ely for its

manors within the soke of St. Edmund are omitted in the case of Glemsford (Cotton, Claud, C. xi). This may be an oversight ; if it is not, the claims of Ely on this occasion must have been all the more exasperating. It is clear that this dispute took place in 1201 about the same time that the trouble over the market at Lakenheath arose. It may well have intensified Samson's anger and dismay. There is no evidence of any sequel. The mischief was done, and as far as we know the matter dropped. *et hic et in comitatu* would have been clearer ; but there is no doubt about the meaning.

V (page 135)

mandato domini Pape. The statement is somewhat misleading. For the affair did not arise on the initiative of the Pope. A letter of Innocent III is preserved (Epp. Inn. III : Migne, no. 214, p. 1088) addressed to the Bishop of Ely and the Abbot of St. Edmund, stating that King John had asked that Geoffrey FitzPeter and others should for reasons of state be absolved from their Crusader's vows, and ordering the Bishop and the Abbot to investigate the cases and report to him. William de Stuteville was Sheriff of York ; the other *magnates* were Hugh Bardolf, Justice of the Curia Regis, William Brewer, Robert of Berkely, Alan and Thomas Bassat (for all of whom see D.N.B.). Both W. de Stuteville and Hugh Bardolf died in 1203. The problem remained unsettled, as in 1204 King John wrote again to the Pope asking that G. FitzPeter should be absolved from his vow (Rymer, *Foedera*, I. p. 91). John on the present occasion summoned the Archbishop of Canterbury, the Bishops of Salisbury, London and Norwich, and the Abbots of Tewkesbury and Westminster as well as the Bishop of Ely and Abbot Samson (cp. Diceto, R.S. III. 173).

INDEX

*The name of the hundred is given in square brackets for place names in Suffolk;
in other cases the county is given as well.*

Tivetshall [Diss, Norfolk], 60, 63, 68
Topcroft [Loddon, Norfolk], 120
Tostock [Thedwestrey], 120
Troston [Blackbourne], 121
Turstan, 17 ; Turstan the little, 114

Valognes, Robert of, 61
Vere, Alberic de. *See* Oxford

Ulmo, Robert de, 61

Walchelin, Archdeacon, 61–62
Wallingford [Oxon], 22
Waltham [Hants], 21
Waltham, Little [Essex], 121
Wangford [Lackford], 121
Warin, a monk, 9
Warkton [Brixworth, Northants], 31, 64
Wattisfield [Blackbourne], 121
Wattisham [Cosford], 120
Weald, 121

Wendling [Launditch, Norfolk], 60, 64
Westley [Thingoe], 60, 64
Wetherden [Stowe], 64, 95
Whatfield [Blackbourne], 121
Whelnetham, Geoffrey of [Thedwestrey], 121, 122
Whepstead [Thingoe], 6, 64
Wickhambrook [Risbridge], 57
William the Sacrist, 2, 9, 10, 16, 30, 31
Wimer the Sheriff, 25
Winchester, Bishop of, Richard (1174–88), 21, 22, 23
Windsor, 55
Woolpit [Thedwestrey], 48, 49, 64
Wordwell [Blackbourne], 122
Worlingworth [Hoxne], 63
Wortham [Hartismere], 63, 120
Wrabness [Tendring, Essex], 64

York, Geoffrey, Archbishop of York, (1191–1212), 21, 85

Printed in Great Britain at the Press of the Publishers